The Beat Fatigue Workbook

How to identify the causes of your
unnatural tiredness, and how to set
about designing a self-help programme
to revive your energy without the use
of drugs.

By the same author
A WORLD WITHOUT AIDS (with Simon Martin)
ABOUT LAETRILE
ACUPUNCTURE TREATMENT OF PAIN
AMINO ACIDS IN THERAPY
ARTHRITIS
ASTHMA AND HAY FEVER
CANDIDA ALBICANS
HEADACHES AND MIGRAINE
HEALING POWER OF AMINO ACIDS
HIGH BLOOD PRESSURE
INSTANT PAIN CONTROL
NEW SLIMMING AND HEALTH WORKBOOK
PROSTATE TROUBLES
SKIN TROUBLES
SOFT TISSUE MANIPULATION
VARICOSE VEINS
YOUR COMPLETE STRESS-PROOFING PROGRAMME

The
Beat Fatigue
Workbook

How to identify the causes and discover
new vitality

by

Leon Chaitow
N.D., D.O.

THORSONS PUBLISHING GROUP

First published 1988

© Leon Chaitow 1988

British Library Cataloguing in Publication Data

Chaitow, Leon
The beat fatigue workbook: how to
identify the causes and discover new
vitality.
1. Man. Health. Improvement — Manuals
I. Title
613

ISBN 0-7225-1979-6

*Published by Thorsons Publishers Limited,
Wellingborough, Northamptonshire,
NN8 2RQ, England*

Printed in Great Britain by
The Bath Press, Bath, Avon

3 5 7 9 10 8 6 4 2

Contents

Introduction   7

Chapter

1   Keeping track on your fatigue   15
2   Lifestyle, exercise and fatigue   20
3   Environment and fatigue   26
4   Energy cycles: how the body makes energy   30
5   Carbohydrates and energy   36
6   Fats and energy   42
7   Protein and energy   47
8   Deficiency and fatigue   52
9   Toxicity, detoxification and fatigue   68
10 Stress and fatigue (including breathing, relaxation, meditation
    and visualization methods)   78
11 Adaptogens and stress   94
12 Glandular extracts   96
13 Strategies   98
14 Adrenal insufficiency and fatigue   100
15 Allergies and fatigue   104
16 Anaemia and fatigue   108
17 Candida albicans and fatigue   110
18 Cardiovascular disease and fatigue   117
19 Chronic ill-health, old age and fatigue   119
20 Depression and fatigue   122
21 Diabetes and fatigue   133
22 Headaches and fatigue   135
23 Hyperventilation and fatigue   138
24 Hypoglycaemia and fatigue   144
25 Infections and fatigue   149
26 Myalgic encephalomyelitis/Post-viral Fatigue Syndrome   153

27   Obesity and fatigue   161
28   Pain and fatigue   164
29   Posture, musculoskeletal tension and fatigue   167
30   Premenstrual Syndrome and fatigue   170
31   Thyroid problems and fatigue   174
32   Young people and fatigue   179

Further reading   183
Index   185

This book is affectionately dedicated to Dr Emanuel Cheraskin M.D., D.M.D., not just a great scientist but a truly good human being, who first suggested to me that 'fatigue' was an area of human suffering which had received insufficient attention.

Introduction

Of all the problems patients complain about to their medical advisers, fatigue is amongst the most common; second only to pain, the primary symptom suffered by mankind. On an average day a general practitioner will be confronted by at least one patient whose main problem is one of tiredness, lethargy, and exhaustion. In the USA the Department of Health and Human Services estimate that some 15 million people a year report for medical assistance with a primary complaint of tiredness.

How many complain of this as a secondary factor, and how many people feel just plain 'washed out' and do not bother their medical adviser, is anyone's guess, but experience tells us that it is probably an enormous number.

The problem of fatigue is a major one, and one which severely reduces people's ability to function, let alone to enjoy life. As with pain, fatigue is a non-specific symptom. It can have many different causes, and in order to be able to remove or alleviate it, these causes must be uncovered and dealt with.

There is no specific medical treatment for fatigue since it cannot in itself be successfully treated, and it must be recognized and not forgotten that in order to remove fatigue the cause, or more accurately causes, have to be found and corrected. Only then will fatigue diminish and hopefully vanish. Any attempt to overcome the symptom of fatigue by stimulating the body into producing more energy is doomed to fail, especially in the long term, for this approach often makes matters worse. Such an approach might be likened to whipping a tired horse. There might be a spurt of extra energy, but this would literally be being borrowed from almost exhausted reserves. The end result would be even greater exhaustion.

Fatigue can take many forms. There may be a disinclination for any muscular effort. There may equally be an inability to concentrate so that the day's tasks become difficult to achieve. Alongside these feelings of tiredness and exhaustion may be noted many other symptoms, and these may assist you in uncovering the underlying causative elements of the condition.

● **Headaches, joint aches, backache, as well as bloating of the stomach and other digestive complaints such as diarrhoea or constipation, may all be part of the picture, leading to suspicion of Candida albicans involvement.**

• Frequent colds and other infections, indicating either reduced immune (body defence) function or allergic reactions.

• Negative emotional feelings such as irritability and depression, which might result from psychosocial elements or quite often be part of a possible allergic condition.

• Depression may also be the result of Candida.

• There may be a washed-out physical appearance, often accompanying anaemia. This in itself may be related to menstrual irregularities or other reasons for excessive blood loss such as haemorrhoids. Or anaemia may relate to nutritional deficits.

• There may, along with fatigue, be an accompanying fever which would point to an infectious nature to the problem.

• Serious health conditions such as heart disease, liver disorders and kidney problems may all have fatigue as an accompanying symptom, and most would have individual clues and signs to implicate them.

• Chronic digestive problems such as colitis may impede adequate nutrient uptake from food leading to gross deficiencies, and so to fatigue.

• If fatigue is accompanied by loss of weight this may be part of the symptom picture of diabetes mellitus, or an over-active thyroid gland; or it may have more serious implications associated with malignant disease.

• Old age itself, if accompanied by inadequate exercise and diet is often associated with fatigue, although this is by no means an inevitable consequence of ageing.

• Poor nutrition is the major reason for fatigue and this is not necessarily confined to financial need, since the diseases of western industrialized nations often result from what has been termed the 'malnutrition of over-consumption'. Too much food of poor nutritional quality containing abundant calories but little actual food value is a major component of civilized societies' disease burden.

• If there is fatigue and weakness but no loss of weight then we might look to underactive thyroid gland, obesity or other causes, such as excessive alcohol consumption (leading to deficiency diseases), age factors etc.

• The psychological component of fatigue should not be underestimated since it is one of the main symptoms of that most common of all mental problems, depression.

• A total inability to do anything may accompany certain mental problems such as schizophrenia, depression and anxiety states, as well as hysteria. In such cases it will be all too obvious that fatigue is a symptom associated with other symptoms, which make up a complex identifiable as one or other of these conditions.

• Non-disease causes of fatigue, however, should not be forgotten. Just plain boredom, frustration and loneliness can account for such feelings, as can ongoing anxieties regarding job, marriages, children, economic problems and poor interpersonal relationships etc. These are all potent causes of stress and hence of fatigue.

• The presence of chronic tiredness in an elderly person with no obvious physical or mental ailments immediately points to the likelihood of just such social causes, most notably loneliness and lack of purpose.

• In children fatigue often relates to school or domestic anxieties.

In trying to find causes you must look at

some of the major areas listed briefly above, beginning with the non-medical causes, those which relate to your life and lifestyle rather than to physical disease processes or nutritional imbalances.

That there is almost always an overlap of causes is obvious, and the division of causes in the way described is simply a means to an end, to assist you in pinpointing those major factors which can be dealt with, individually or comprehensively, by self-help or with assistance.

As will be seen in Chapter 4 there are a number of interacting nutrients which are essential for the generation of energy in the body, without which fatigue is inevitable. Another process in the body is the detoxification (urea) cycle which can also become impaired, resulting in fatigue. The energy-producing cycles are directly related to the detoxification processes and both require nutritional excellence and adequate exercise for optimum function. There are other less tangible reasons for fatigue, including mood and psychological factors, themselves intertwined with biochemical processes which can be influenced by diet and lifestyle elements.

The purpose of this book is to explain what the causes of fatigue might be; to help in identifying these in any particular case, and to describe methods whereby they may safely be dealt with. The main emphasis will be on self-help, but this should in no way be taken to mean that professional advice should not be sought. Hopefully self-help measures may be used alongside any conventional or alternative medical therapy in an endeavour to correct and remove underlying health problems. Often these self-help methods may be adequate in themselves, where causes are readily identifiable and capable of being dealt with by improved nutrition and a change in lifestyle, habits, attitudes or behaviour.

● **Around 40 per cent of all patients who have fatigue as a major symptom have causes which are based in physical factors.**

● **A further 40 per cent have as the main causes of their fatigue what are known as psychosocial factors.**

● **A further 20 per cent have no obvious cause.**

Many people suffering from fatigue have an interaction of physical and psychosocial causes and these two general areas will be looked at closely, as will more specific causes of fatigue, such as endocrine (hormonal) imbalances, anaemia, hypoglycaemia, allergic conditions, and immune function problems such as occur

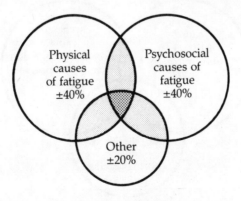

Causes of fatigue

in the condition known as post-viral fatigue syndrome or myalgic encephalomyelitis (see page 153).

In speaking of fatigue it must be borne in mind that the reference is to *unnatural* tiredness. If a great deal of physical and/or mental effort is being expended then tiredness is a normal and natural result and does not need attention. At the end of a game of football or tennis or a long walk, there is bound to be a feeling of fatigue. Similarly a natural tiredness is to be expected at the end of a day's work, whether in factory, office or home. This natural tiredness — justifiable fatigue — should, however, pass with appropriate rest.

On the other hand, if tiredness is regularly apparent at inappropriate times, after rest for example, then attention *is* called for. To simply put up with this because it is so common is a bad idea as there is much more likelihood of remedying the problem in the early stages.

Many interacting elements need to be considered, not least your age and past health history, together with your current situation, lifestyle, emotional relationships, nutritional pattern, job situation, environmental pollution, drug usage (medical and social), exercise patterns, habits and attitudes.

There are many aspects to the achievement of abundant energy and zest which impinge upon the way you feel about your life and what you are doing with it. These are as important as nutrition, exercise, fresh air, clean water, negative ionization and adequate sleep.

There are, therefore, a number of areas that need to be explored in order to uncover the reasons for unnatural fatigue. In many cases just simple alterations to your pattern of existence in relation to one or more of the causes mentioned will be adequate to restore your energetic joy in living. It may be, though, that a more complex task awaits you in establishing the interacting elements which are depriving your body and mind of its vitality.

The modern syndrome, popularly known as 'burn out' has a variety of causes, but there are three interconnecting components which are seen to be:

1 Emotional exhaustion (tiredness, irritability, accident proneness, depression and excessive alcohol consumption).
2 Depersonalization (treating others as objects).
3 Low productivity and low achievement.

This affects professional people to a large extent, with doctors and others in the caring professions often affected. It is seen very much to be an interaction between

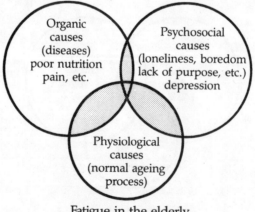

Fatigue in the elderly

personality and the particular characteristics of the work/lifestyle involved.

In most cases of mento-emotional/lifestyle dependent fatigue there is something which *can* be done, even if full recovery is not possible. This book looks into the biochemical elements which influence and govern energy in your body — such as the amino acids, enzymes, vitamins and minerals — and also at some recent research knowledge which has shown the amazing influence of such little known substances as the mineral germanium. It also describes substances which can help your body to adapt and cope with the myriad stresses it is subject to — the adaptogens such as ginseng and Eleutherococcus.

The influence of the mind is critical in achieving the ability to function energetically, and a variety of measures are introduced which will help in developing healthy and harmonious mental functioning. There are many self-help methods and techniques available in this area. The ways in which the hormone producing centres of the body influence energy levels will be explained so that you can see, for example, how the adrenal and thyroid glands function and how they might be involved in your chronic tiredness.

A number of little known but extremely widespread conditions such as the yeast infection, Candida albicans, and the previously mentioned post-viral fatigue syndrome are described, and questionnaires provided in order to help in identifying whether or not these are causes in your case. These are the words of Sue Finlay, in her late thirties, happily married with a family and living in the unpolluted Pentland Hills, as she described the symptoms of post-viral fatigue in *The Observer* (1 June 1986): 'I could hardly wheel a barrow any more, and after walking on the hills for only a short time I returned home exhausted. My legs began to ache when I did the ironing. I started to feel constantly exhausted, irritable, weepy and depressed.' Along with this her joints began to ache, she had palpitations, her eyesight deteriorated and her appetite waned, and she suffered digestive disturbances.

Medical examination revealed 'everything normal', and so began two years of deteriorating health, being shuttled from specialist to specialist without success, and with the suggestion that the problem was a psychological one. Recovery began when Sue Finlay began to tackle the problem herself, using nutritional methods which are described in this book. Now she can walk several miles, when at one time walking across the room took all her strength. She is regaining her zest for life, and is involved in supplying information to other sufferers of this devastating complaint.

'It is criminal to tell people that it must be your nerves,' she says, 'when it is obviously not the "nerves" which cause the exhaustion, but the helplessness and exhaustion which plays on the mind and "nerves".'

Here are the words of a woman of 32 living in Belfast and suffering from previously undiagnosed Candida albicans infection: 'My symptoms are tiredness all the time, no energy, severe abdominal bloating, fingers, legs and feet swollen, premenstrual tension, acne, pains in my joints, shivering in my back even when I am warm. My eyes feel glazed and are puffy above and below. I never want to bother with anyone. I come home from work and feel so tired and sick that I go and lie down. I feel my life is passing me by and I can do nothing about it.'

This helplessness is not an uncommon feeling associated with fatigue, and such feelings of helplessness and exhaustion are what this book aims to alleviate, for you can help yourself as others have done.

These are the words of Mrs J.H. describing her feelings after months of being told she was suffering from psychological problems and finally having Candida overgrowth diagnosed: 'I tried to keep working but had so little energy I felt as though I was working on willpower alone. I try to go out, but lack of energy keeps me indoors. I'm dizzy in the mornings and panicky. I've never been so tired in my life. My whole body aches; I shake badly and experience a deep depression. I am so afraid of these symptoms especially when I'm alone. My GP refuses to speak to me on this subject [Candida] having said the idea was "rubbish" and I have had to consult another doctor privately.'

The sheer volumes of such cases is amazing and the amount of private grief and misery suffered immeasurable. The tiredness experienced is not just a pleasant fatigue; it is incapacitating and devastating in terms of its ability to disrupt normal life. One of the major symptoms which medical science ascribes to the all too common condition of depression is fatigue, and yet it may well be that the view that depression results in fatigue is in many cases a reversal of the truth. The words of Mrs V.G. highlight just this possibility.

'I'd like to suggest that in some cases depression is caused by exhaustion. There can be few things more depressing than chronic exhaustion. All those wasted hours lying down when there are so many fascinating things that you are just longing to do. I now do very little and do not get exhausted. I am therefore not depressed just very frustrated and miserable.'

Whether the causes of such fatigue involve allergies, as is often the case, or whether there are deficiencies of essential nutrients such as iron or iodine; or whether there are excesses of toxic metals,

such as lead and mercury, or whether, as in most serious cases of fatigue, there is an interaction between a number of these and other factors, it is often possible to provide methods to identify such causes, and then show how something constructive can be done about them.

There are over 60 symptoms associated with post-viral fatigue syndrome and these vary greatly from person to person. However, there are three which are almost always present:

1 Extreme weakness and/or profound fatigue.
2 Extreme malaise with or without accompanying depression.
3 A pattern of relapse and recovery.

Also dealt with in this book are the many ways in which drugs commonly used to treat certain diseases and ailments can have, as major side-effects, the symptom of chronic fatigue. Ways will be described to establish whether this is in fact a contributory factor to your fatigue. Replenishing and re-invigorating the body and mind is the major emphasis throughout.

Weakness: not the same as fatigue

The terms fatigue, loss of energy and weakness are, in most people's minds, interchangeable, although medically they tend to have more precise individual meanings:

Fatigue: Usually means loss of power or strength associated with effort or exertion of some kind.
Loss of Energy: Usually is taken to refer to a generalized sense of not being able to even begin activities, even ones which involve no exertion.
Weakness: Is used to describe a loss of

strength in one or more groups of muscles, which may be shown to be accurate by testing of the muscles involved.

Once measurable weakness is established medical interest usually heightens since this is at least a symptom which can be shown to have real objective elements, unlike 'feelings' which the patient describes but which are hard to measure, such as 'I just feel so tired'.

It should be understood that muscle weakness is not the same condition as generalized tiredness and fatigue which are the major concern of this book. Self-help, without expert guidance is not indicated for many of the conditions connected with muscle weakness.

CHAPTER I

Keeping track of your fatigue

To better understanding your fatigue it is a good idea to keep a 'fatigue diary' in which you regularly record a written picture of its nature and changes. This can be a major help to you and your physician in identifying and understanding the features of your individual and unique fatigue pattern. These may be familiar to you, but you may have failed to see aspects of it as part of a pattern. Remember that I am talking about unnatural fatigue, not the normal healthy fatigue resulting from strenuous activity or hard work.

What should you write in your fatigue diary? First of all, answer these questions. Use this book, if you wish:

1 Note down when you first became noticeably fatigued and, if you can recall, how it began (under what circumstances; was it sudden or slow in onset etc.)?
2 Do you recall any illness which preceded the onset of your fatigue by six to twelve months?
3 If so what was it?
4 What treatment did you have (medications such as antibiotics)?
5 How long have you been feeling fatigued, tired, exhausted?
6 Is this an unchanging factor or does it vary very much?

7 If it varies what seems to influence this (time of day, weather, meals, activity, company you are with etc.)?

8 If it varies, how often is it apparent (daily, weekly etc.)?

9 What sort of fatigue is it (does it affect your whole body or just your mind or your legs etc. In other words what does it feel like)?

10 What effect does your fatigue have on your everyday life?

11 Is there a situation or place in which you know you will feel fatigued?

12 Are there any particular people who make you feel fatigued?

13 Are there any particular activities which make you feel fatigued?

14 What makes the fatigue better?

15 What makes the fatigue worse?

16 Do you normally associate your fatigue with any other signs or symptoms of ill health or dysfunction (for example headache, pain of any other sort, feelings of hunger, digestive upsets, edginess etc.)?

Note these signs and symptoms, and whether they occur before, during or after fatigue.

17 What do YOU think caused or causes your fatigue?

18 What does your fatigue prevent you from doing that you actually don't want to do anyway?

19 What would you be able to do that you want to do if your fatigue left you?

20 Is there any food or drink which you associate with your fatigue?

When you have completed the questionnaire, read through your answers once or twice and see whether they give you a clearer picture of your condition. After you have been following self-help or professional treatment for your fatigue for a month or so, refer to the questionnaire again and see if any of your answers have changed.

Remember that there is unlikely to be only one causative factor behind your fatigue. What you should be able to see from your comparisons is which elements are contributing to your fatigue; be they nutritional deficiencies, toxic build-up, emotional problems or lifestyle factors (inadequate exercise, smoking etc.). This will enable you to evolve a suitable long-term self-help strategy.

Keep a record in your fatigue diary, or in this book, of your answers to the other questionnaires which will be found in subsequent sections. As you progress through these various chapters you will find question lists relating to most of the major possible causes of your fatigue, and the answers you give will indicate the likelihood of their involvement in your case.

Fatigue is a difficult problem to sort out as it is a subjective symptom. It is not measurable or palpable. Therefore, the more you can localize it through answering questions and making specific links with other factors, the closer you will come to understanding its unique presence in your life and body.

The chapters which follow cover a range of health problems which are often associated with fatigue. One, some, or none of these may apply to your fatigue problem.

Before looking at the major health problems associated with fatigue I want you to consider the possibility of either nutritional deficiencies or toxicity (or both) being involved.

NUTRITIONAL CHECKLIST

These questions are to focus your attention on your eating habits. All the questions should ideally be answered 'NO', or at worst 'SOMETIMES'. The more 'YES' answers you give the more you can assume that poor choice of food is affecting your health and energy levels.

	YES	SOMETIMES	NO
1 Do you eat white flour products?			
2 Do you add sugar to cereals/drinks?			
3 Do you eat sweets, cakes, biscuits, sugary snacks?			
4 Do you drink more than the equivalent of 1½ glasses of wine or one pint of beer daily?			
5 Do you eat foods containing chemical additives, colouring, flavouring etc.?			
6 Do you skip breakfast, lunch or supper?			
7 Do you eat snacks between meals?			
8 Do you add salt to food at table?			
9 Do you eat fried or highly seasoned foods?			
10 Do you eat fatty meats, smoked or preserved foods?			
11 Do you eat cereals which already contain sugar?			
12 Do you drink more than one cup of coffee or two cups of tea daily?			
13 Do you drink bottled soft drinks (cola etc.)?			

Now let's turn it around and look for 'YES' answers. The more of these in response to the following questions the better. All 'NO' answers indicate room for improvement.

	YES	SOMETIMES	NO
1 Do you eat fresh fruit?			
2 Do you eat salad?			
3 Do you ensure adequate fibre in your diet?			
4 Do you eat wholewheat bread, wholegrain cereals?			
5 Do you use herb teas instead of tea and coffee?			
6 Do you choose fish or poultry instead of red meat?			
7 Do you eat main meals based on pulses (lentils, beans etc.) at least once a week?			
8 Do you eat natural 'live' yogurt?			
9 Do you believe that what you eat is a major influence on your health?			

	YES	SOMETIMES	NO
10 Do you use/drink skimmed milk instead of full fat milk?			
11 Do you drink bottled or filtered water rather than tap water?			
12 Do you make a point of not overeating?			
13 Do you chew your food well and not rush meals?			
14 Do you eat garlic (cooked or raw)?			

Your answers to these two sets of questions will give you an idea of just where you are in the spectrum of health/nutrition awareness. I am not suggesting that you become fanatical, but it should be easy for you to try to deal with one or two of the 'wrong' answers at a time and to slowly reform those things which your answers indicate are in need of attention.

CHAPTER 2

Lifestyle, exercise and fatigue

Do you get enough exercise? Is your lifestyle conducive to optimum health? Are you really taking care of yourself adequately?

Answers the questions below with a 'YES', 'SOMETIMES' or 'NO'. 'YES' means regularly; 'SOMETIMES' means infrequently, say less than weekly; 'NO' means never.

1	Do you work more than 5½ days weekly?
2	Do you work more than 10 hours on a workday?
3	Do you take less than half an hour for each main meal?
4	Do you eat quickly and not chew thoroughly?
5	Do you smoke?
6	Do you get less than 7 hours' sleep daily?
7	Do you listen to relaxing music?
8	Do you practise daily relaxation or meditation exercises?
9	Do you take at least thirty minutes' exercise, three times weekly?
10	Do you have a creative hobby, gardening, painting, needlework etc?
11	Do you play any non-competitive sport, walking, cycling, swimming or attend a yoga or exercise class?
12	Do you try to have a siesta or short rest period during the day?
13	Do you have regular massage or osteopathic attention?
14	Do you spend at least half an hour outside in daylight each day?

The answers to the first six questions should be 'NO', all 'YES' answers in these show a need for modification of your lifestyle. The answers to questions 7 to 14 shuld be 'YES' and all 'NO' answers call for a modification of lifestyle. All 'SOMETIMES' answers should be modified to the appropriate 'YES' or 'NO'.

Let us focus a little more strongly on exercise. Answer the following questions which apply to your weekly level of exercise with a 'YES' or 'NO'.

Do you get:
1 A period of twenty to thirty minutes of aerobic exercise (see below for description) daily?
2 A session of group or organized fitness training at least three times weekly?
3 A self-devised fitness programme at least three times weekly?
4 Exercise or participation in sport, at least once weekly?
5 A walk several times a week?
6 Little or no exercise at all?

The number of the question is the number of points you score and the lower the better. Re-check your rating after a month of adopting the programme suggested below and try ultimately to reach a score of no more than 3.

Exercise and energy

The paradox of exercise is that while using energy it seems to generate more. This may not be the view of the fatigued individual, for whom every little thing is a major effort. Nevertheless, for anyone suffering from fatigue exercise is not only desirable but an essential part of getting better. The exception, though is anyone suffering from post-viral fatigue syndrome (myalgic encephalomyelitis) for whom physical exercise is not advised until a great improvement is seen.

Dr Holly Atkinson summarizes the effects of exercise clearly when she says: 'Remember the five processes that lead to fatigue? They are:

1 Depletion of substances vital to energy production.
2 Accumulation of waste products.
3 Changes in the body's energy producing machinery.
4 Disruption of the body's ability to regulate itself.

5 Failures in the body's communication system.

The very act of exercising fights all of these fatigue processes.'

But the exercise cannot be just any exercise. Stretching, yoga-type exercise is excellent for general mobility, relaxation and suppleness. However, it does absolutely nothing for the body in terms of fatigue. Weight-training is a great way to build muscles, but it doesn't help fatigue. A gentle stroll can assist in unwinding the mind, and in obtaining fresh air and sunlight, but it does nothing for fatigue.

Aerobic exercise fights fatigue. Aerobic exercise does not have to mean leaping about and torturing yourself. Aerobic exercise can be tailored precisely, by you, to meet the needs of your body. Indeed, unless you are ready to go off and seek professional advice as to how much and what type of exercise you need, it will have to be self-designed and self-monitored. So read the next short section very carefully a number of times.

Aerobic principles

Unless there are medical reasons why not, everyone should have at least twenty, and ideally thirty, minutes of active exercise three or four times a week. (Be sure to take advice about exercise if you are currently under medical care for any condition.)

It is necessary to monitor the results of exercise by taking the pulse regularly during exercise performance. This is the method used to establish when you are doing enough, when you are doing too much or, more often, when you are not doing enough. It requires a little arithmetic.

From the number 220 deduct your age. Let us say you are 40. So 220 minus 40 = 180. This is the top limit of pulse rate beyond which, at age 40 you must not go in order to avoid strain on the cardiovascular system.

You then find three quarters of the result. 180 divided by four = 45; and multiplied by three = 135. This is the pulse-rate level you need to reach before you are achieving a training (aerobic) effect. Your aerobic exercise pulse rate may be easily attained at first when you begin exercise vigorously, but as you become fitter it will take more and more effort to reach that level.

This is the aerobic principle in action. You are using your body, in its present state of (un)fitness to monitor how much exercise you need in order to get fit. Not only must you make sure that you are reaching the desired pulse rate (and not exceeding the top level allowed for your age) but that this desired level needs to be maintained for at least 20, and ideally 30, minutes, not less than three times weekly, with never more than a day in between sessions.

There is a more accurate and much more mathematically complicated formula for finding out precisely your required level of exercise, also using the pulse rate as a monitor, which provides a range in which you should maintain the pulse rate during the whole of the 20/30 minute session. These target zones are outlined below.

In his classic book *Aerobics* (Bantam), Kenneth Cooper MD outlines a variety of ways in which it is possible to create an

Age	Pulse rate range	Never above
35	130-175	185
40	126-153	180
45	122-149	175
50	119-145	170
55	115-140	165
60	112-136	160
65	108-131	155
70	105-127	150
75	101-123	145
80	98-119	140

individual pattern of exercise which will achieve aerobic results.

For someone thoroughly out of condition you will need to start with what may appear only light exercise — walking, cycling, swimming, skipping etc. — to produce the desired pulse rate. As time passes the effort required increases; the body gets fitter; the heart function improves; fatigue diminishes and it becomes easier to make the greater effort demanded. Cooper spells out examples of different form of exercise and gives targets in terms of time for different age groups.

Thus males between ages of 20 and 49 score a 'good' for covering a distance of one and a half miles in 12 minutes of running. If they run 1.65 miles in those 12 minutes they would score an 'excellent'. Walking 4 to 5 miles at between 15 and 20 minutes per mile is equivalent to the running described above. So is swimming 950 yards in 25 to 32 minutes, or cycling 9 miles at between 3 and 3½ minutes per mile.

Thus you have choices as to type of exercise, and guidelines as to whether you are doing enough, or whether you need to try harder. The results are worth the effort. Aerobics can lift depression, improve self-imate, diminish hypochondriacal behaviour, reduce muscle tension and anxiety, and ease fatigue, replacing this with a healthy tiredness.

Before you join an exercise class it is a good idea to have a check-up. Finding the right exercise is important as it is vital that you enjoy the process. It should not be hard labour. Avoid competitive exercise as this can only increase stress. Make sure you have adequate time for the regular exercising called for. Motivation should come from the feelings of renewed energy which follow.

Sleep

A common symptom of depression and anxiety, along with fatigue, is the apparently contradictory one of insomnia. Feeling tired all the time and yet being unable to sleep creates greater tiredness.

The point about fatigue of this sort is that it is unnatural and therefore often associated with biochemical aberrations affecting, not least, the brain. It is in the brain that sleep patterns are determined. Sleeping pills should never be used except for the odd night when for crisis reasons sleep seems essential. The habitual use of sleeping tablets has a negative impact on health and sleep since they soon become ineffective and they can also create a range of side-effects including indigestion, respiratory ailments, loss of appetite, skin rashes, increased blood pressure, kidney and liver dysfunction, lowered resistance to infection, mental confusion and memory lapses and circulatory problems. Most sleeping tablets are also addictive. Even when they do work they do not produce refreshing sleep. Being unconscious is not the same thing as being asleep. Sleep has a natural sequence of biological rhythms relating to brain-wave patterns. Unnatural (drugged) sleep does not have these patterns.

The major negative influences on sleep involve:

- **Irregular hours (a regular pattern is important).**

- **Use of stimulants such as coffee, tobacco etc.**

- **Nutritional deficiency.**

- **Disturbance of pre-sleep rituals (we get used to certain patterns, when these change sleep may be disturbed. Go back to old habits such as bath before bed, or reading, or whatever else has changed.)**

- **Sex or lack of it may be involved in sleep disturbance. Take advice from a professional if this is so. Counselling can help.**

- **Anxiety. This can be corrected by use of relaxation and meditation.**

- **Allergies can disturb sleep patterns.**

- **Pain can disturb sleep.**

The amino acid tryptophan is found to be an excellent natural sleep enhancer. A one gram dose combined with calcium and vitamin B_6 with water is suggested twenty minutes before bed.

An afternoon siesta is highly recommended for anyone with sleep problems. The taking of an hour or less to completely relax, not reading or watching TV, is an excellent method of retraining for sleep. Whether sleep comes or not at this time is not important. If it does it will not detract from the night's sleep but will enable the remainder of the day to be faced with renewed energy. At first there may be a heavy feeling after midday sleep periods. A short walk will clear this.

General lifestyle changes

1 Avoid working for unduly long hours or too many days each week. Ensure at least 1½ days away from work routines weekly when other activities and interests can be enjoyed.

2 Introduce daily relaxation/meditation periods.

3 Introduce regular exercise patterns. Apart from aerobic exercises try to take part in yoga or other stretching type movements. Either at a class or at home using tapes, videos or books for guidance.

4 Balance your diet and eliminate stress-inducing stimulant drinks.

5 Slow down if you are habitually in a rush. Work, walk, speak and behave in a relaxed manner until it becomes natural to you.

6 Seek advice if there are any emotional or sexual problems that are causing you anxiety.

7 If there are changes which you see as necessary stop putting them off, make decisions and move forward in life.

8 Cultivate creative hobbies whether these are painting, music, gardening or knitting.

9 Try to bring yourself into present time. Avoid dwelling on past events or future possibilities. Be here now, is the command to give yourself.

10 Apply attention to whatever you are currently doing. This is the way to do it well, to gain satisfaction and to avoid only half doing one thing before starting another.

11 Avoid deadlines wherever possible. Only take on what you can happily cope with. Learn to say 'no' to excessive demands (made by yourself or others).

12 Learn to express what it is you want to say in an open, non-aggressive but firm manner. Do not be apologetic for having an opinion or a desire to have things a certain way. Equally, learn to listen to what others are saying to you, without feeling threatened.

13 Accept personal responsibility for your life and health. Look inside yourself for causes and for help. Take advice, but learn that it is you who will heal you.

14 Greet and respond to people as you would want them to deal with you.

15 Apply the advice regarding health enhancement relating to ionizers, humidifiers, exercise, diet etc. in the knowledge that these are positive and helpful to your desire to achieve higher levels of health.

16 Learn to love yourself, not in a selfish way but in a manner which allows you to treat yourself with kindness and respect.

17 Do not judge yourself or others.

18 Act according to your deeper intuitive feelings and needs. Be healthy and happy.

ALCOHOL CHECKLIST

The following questions will help you to assess whether or not alcohol is a major factor in your life. Answer honestly 'YES' or 'NO'.

1 Do you have a drink at night to help you unwind or go to sleep?
2 Has your work ever been affected (or have you actually missed work) because of your drinking the night before or that day?
3 Have you ever not remembered what happened when you were drinking?
4 If anyone talks to you about your drinking level are you defensive, angry, evasive?
5 Do you ever need a drink to give you a lift in the morning?
6 Are there moments when you are actually craving an alcoholic drink?
7 Before attending a party at which drinks will be available, do you have a drink at home or on the way?

8	When on your own, do you tend to want to have more than one drink?
9	Do you have secret feelings of anger, despair at your drinking habits?
10	Can you envisage life without having an alcoholic drink?
11	Do you lie to others about how much you drink?
12	Do you drink more than you did five years ago?
13	Do you use alcohol as a prop, to give you courage, settle your nerves etc., before an important date, meeting etc.?
14	Do you use alcohol as a medicine?
15	If alcohol is not offered or served on a visit do you get edgy?

If any of these are answered with a 'YES' then chances are that alcohol is more important in your life than it should be. The words marijuana, cocaine etc. could be used instead of 'alcohol' in all these questions. There is help available and self-help can be useful.

CHAPTER 3

Environment and fatigue

Our state of health has long been associated with the weather, and changes ranging from atmospheric pressure and humidity to temperature and the degree or otherwise of positive ionization, and more usually a combination of these, can greatly influence how we feel. The time of day influences body processes. A science now known as chronobiology has shown that the same medication given at different times of day has different effects. Even the time of year has a strong influence on our health status and our body processes, as, not as surprisingly perhaps, does the phase of the moon.

There is also the pretty obvious link between the amount of daylight/sunshine we are exposed to and our vitamin D status. Just how strong these influences are can be judged from the fact that there is a higher mortality rate from all causes (that is more people die) between the months of December and February in Western Europe, with the lowest mortality rate between July and August. People with mental illness show the highest degree of unrest in the spring months. Most schizophrenics are born in January to March. Most suicides take place in spring, and the fewest in winter.

Diabetic coma is seen most in winter months. Rheumatic conditions are more commonly complained of to doctors in cold, humid, windy seasons. General metabolism of the body is at its highest level in the summer months and lowest in the winter.

Most legitimate children are conceived in June. Most illegitimate children are conceived in May. Most stillborn babies are conceived in January. Duodenal ulcers, in males, are more commonly diagnosed in May and November. Peptic ulcers, in all sexes, are more commonly diagnosed between December and February, with the lowest incidence in June. Bronchial asthma is at its worst between August and November. Arteriosclerotic heart disease is at its worst between January and February and at its best between July and August, but cardiovascular distress as measured by myocardial infarction (heart attack) is at its worst in hot climates in the summer months. (Tromp, S., *Medical Biometeorology*, Elsevier, 1963 and Gauquelin, M., *How Atmospheric Conditions Affect Your Health*, ASI Publishers, New York.)

Temperature
Physical work in a temperature of 75°F/24°C is 15 per cent less efficient than physical work performed in a temperature

of 68°F/20°C. School children function best at temperatures of 61°F/16°C according to Canadian research, which seems about the optimum for mental work.

Atmospheric pressure
When this falls or rises we note changed 'feelings' of well-being. A fall of atmospheric pressure, as in an approaching storm, leads to feelings of lethargy, headaches and increased rheumatic discomfort. A rise in atmospheric pressure, if it is very rapid, causes feelings of sluggishness, with measurable slowing of reaction times. On high pressure days traffic accidents increase by between 40 and 70 per cent.

Humidity
General lethargy is noted most when relative humidity rises above 55 per cent, the most comfortable levels being between 45 and 55 per cent. The opposite is also seen to have a negative effect. A centrally heated room can have relative humidity of as little as 3 per cent (desert humidity seldom drops below 20 per cent) in winter, which dries the skin and mucous membranes of the nose, eyes and throat much increasing risks of infection of the upper respiratory tract.

In offices and buildings where relative humidity is very low, due to central heating, complaints of tiredness, restlessness, insomnia and other vague symptoms often associated with fatigue are noted. Simply placing the odd bowl of water in front of radiators will have little effect in modern offices where there is little air movement. The answer lies in greater use of humidifiers. This, together with the use of negative ionization of the air, can bring energy and well-being back to those sapped by what has been dubbed 'sick-building syndrome'.

Air movement
With many houses and buildings now double and triple glazed, with efficient draught excluders, there is very little movement of air. This leads to stagnation and feelings of lethargy and heavy-headedness. If windows cannot be opened, then movement of air should be sought by use of a form of air-conditioning which brings outside air into the building. If this is not possible then a brisk walk outside is called for at regular intervals.

Ionization
We live in air which is alive with electrically charged particles called ions. These derive from a variety of natural phenomena ranging from cosmic rays to friction of wind and water, to radioactive elements in the soil. These enter our body through the air we breathe and our skin and they are taken up by the bloodstream.

Negative ions have a stimulating effect on our cells' oxygenation processes. The opposite is true of positive ions which slow oxygenation of cells and make us feel lethargic and heavy. Modern buildings containing machinery, artificial materials and stagnant air are particularly rich in positive ions. The ideal ratio between negative and positive ions is thought to be 12 to 10. At this level we feel energetic and perform tasks untiringly. When levels of negative ions drop, or positive ions rise, and the ratio is altered to favour the positive ions, we feel fatigued and heavy, and perform our work with less attention and a greater degree of perceived effort.

In such conditions the productivity of factory or office workers drops alarmingly; there are more days off for illness; there are more accidents; there are more industrial stoppages and generally there is a far less happy workforce.

These are the conditions we note before a storm and when a warm prevailing wind is blowing (sirocco, mistral etc.). At such times the incidence of patients complaining to doctors of lethargy, tension, headaches, irritability etc. increases dramatically. Reversing this by the use of ionizing machines, now so inexpensive that they are within everyone's reach, produces the opposite effect, that of mental well-being energy and even euphoria.

Where the use of such machines has been introduced to the workplace there has been noted an increase in productivity of up to 40 per cent, as compared with the period before the use of ionizers. Time off work drops; stoppages are reduced; accidents decline. This is not surprising since a happy, healthy workforce is bound to produce better results than a tired and edgy one.

Athletes exposed to high negative ionization for some weeks have increased their performances before tiring by almost 60 per cent in Russian studies. You may not have this ambition. Yours may be confined to merely wanting to feel less tired, to a regaining of the zest that comes with high energy levels. This is the feeling we may recall having been aware of after a storm or when on a high mountain, where the air feels crisp and clean and we feel energized. This is largely a matter of negative ions.

Ensuring clean air in the home/office/ workplace together with attention to the factors of optimum temperature and humidity as well as air movement and ionization can do much to restore energy and remove fatigue.

Full spectrum light

The work of John Ott in the USA (*Light, Radiation and You*, Adair, 1980) has demonstrated that the light we derive from electric bulbs and fluorescent tubes is deficient in some of the wavelengths found in normal daylight.

When we spend a great deal of time in environments thus lit we suffer adversely. We become deficient in these light stimuli just as we may become nutritionally deficient when ill-fed.

The habitual use of sunglasses adds to this by cutting our access to full spectrum light. Days spent indoors, inside cars and hidden from daylight by spectacles or contact lenses add together to compound this 'deficiency', all of which is further compounded by atmospheric pollution cutting out the rays of the sun from reaching us.

The results are quite alarming. Nervous fatigue, hyperactivity in children, lowered immune function, irritability, lapses of attention, increased incidence of dental cavities, and many other negative effects have been found to occur when full spectrum light is deficient, and most importantly to be rapidly reversed when it is restored.

A period sitting by an open window, not necessarily in direct sunlight, is all that is needed for anyone housebound. Half an hour a day of this is sufficient to produce measurable benefits. If going outside is possible, again this does not need to be in direct sunlight, but merely in daylight, without wearing spectacles or contact lenses for a similar period daily.

If either of these options is not available, and as a desirable change anyway, the introduction of full spectrum lighting is suggested. Strip lighting which approximates the full spectrum is now available. This is highly recommended if you spend a good deal of time indoors, whether at work or at home, especially if fatigue is a factor in your life.

The allergic house syndrome

For many people the sensitivities they have developed to many materials and inhaled elements has led to their being literally allergic to the homes they live in.

Anyone who notices symptoms as outlined in the section on allergy and fatigue (see page 104) relating to sensitivites or allergies, disappearing or easing markedly when they are away from home, and returning when they go back should consider this possibility, which could also relate to local air pollution. Fatigue is frequently one of the major symptoms noticed. Of course the symptoms could just as easily relate to emotional stress associated with being at home, and this too should be considered. Many materials used in modern construction can be to blame, not least chemicals used in insulation of house cavities which gradually releases fumes into the house.

Similarly fumes related to central heating, most notably gas and oil-fired boilers, can produce reactions in those sensitive to petrochemical fumes. There is also the element of allergy to house dust, which can be largely overcome by the laborious but effective method of sealing all curtains, furniture, carpets etc. with a special sealant which reduces markedly the amount of dust in the home.

Those people who have yeast sensitivities and are affected by Candida albicans overgrowth may find that any parts of their homes which are damp, or in which mould or mildew exists, upset them. This too can be remedied by drastic action involving, unfortunately, contractors and a good deal of money. In all instances touched on above the advice in this book relating to nutrition and allergies and stress reduction will greatly assist in easing reactivity to fumes, allergens etc. Sometimes, though, moving house is the only answer.

CHAPTER 4

Energy cycles: how the body makes energy

In order to understand the many ways in which the body supplies itself with energy it is necessary to get to know several apparently complex cycles. The citric acid cycle, also known as the Krebs cycle or the tricarboxylic acid cycle, is that complex process in which the body takes raw materials and turns them into energy with a major by-product waste material, ammonia, which in turn is removed and detoxified in another complex procedure, called the urea cycle.

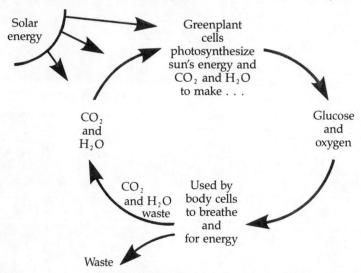

Scheme of energy cycle in nature

The energy generating sequence involves processes of chemical respiration, and a process called oxidative phosphorylation which results in a reaction producing a most important substance called adenosine triphosphate, better known by its initials as ATP. Another major product of the citric acid cycle is alpha-ketoglurate. You need to know a little about these two substances which are products of, and participants in, the energy chain, if you are to fathom the complexities of energy.

ATP (adenosine triphosphate)

ATP is called the 'energy carrier'. The most efficient form of energy production within the body is the metabolism of food. This process in the citric acid cycle requires not only the fuel (fat, proteins, carbohydrate etc.) but oxygen, and various essential enzymes and co-factors. The high-energy phosphate bonds of ATP are used to store and carry the resulting product. Fully 90 per cent of the energy used in and by the body derives from energy released by food processed in the citric acid cycle.

A less efficient energy production method, also used by the body at times, involves what is called glycolysis, which occurs without oxygen. This, however, produces unwanted lactic acid.breakdown products and is of use for only short periods of time (quick energy), unlike the energy produced by the citric acid cycle which is a longlasting 'stamina' form of energy.

Alpha-ketoglurate

Alpha-ketoglurate acting with the B-vitamin pyridoxine (B_6) in its form as a coenzyme called pyridoxal phosphate, detaches molecules of nitrogen from the protein we eat in order to counteract excessive acidity. As mentioned, a major by-product of the whole process of food combustion into energy is ammonia, and an excess of this depletes alpha-ketoglurate, leading to toxicity, the main symptomatic features of which are: irritability, tiredness, headache and allergic food reactions, with nausea and diarrhoea also occurring at times.

Confusion in the mind may also result from such lack of alpha-ketoglurate, because it is eventually transformed into glutamic acid which is the main precursor (a substance which goes on to become something else) of brain energy.

If there is deficiency in the body, for whatever reason, of the mineral zinc or vitamin B_6, then there will be a severe limit in the ability of the body to produce pyridoxal phosphate from B_6, and therefore inadequate alpha-ketoglurate.

Other nutrients required in large amounts by the body for energy production in its citric acid cycle include pantothenic acid (available supplementally in the form of calcium pantothenate from Health Food Stores). This is also known as vitamin B_5 and has been shown to increase stamina enormously when supplemented to highly stressed animals or humans.

Apart from being an essential aspect of the citric acid cycle vitamin B_5 has a further role to play in the transmission of messages from muscles to nerves. This is because it is needed to convert lecithin and/or choline into the neurotransmitter acetylcholine. This allows nerves and muscles to communicate, and nerves to communicate with each other. These processes are essential for normal function, for if deficient all efforts become very laboured indeed. Lack of acetylcholine could well be part of a pattern of general lassitude and fatigue.

A further B vitamin, B_3 or nicotinamide, is a contributor to efficient ATP activity via processes of hydrogen transfer. Another nutrient, manganese, is important to the maintenance of alpha-ketoglurate levels within the body.

Many researchers maintain that one of the features of all mental and physical degenerative diseases is a severe lack of alpha-ketoglurate. Inefficiency of detoxification processes leading to excessive amounts of nitrogen waste, in the form of ammonia, is a prominent reason for the problems outlined above, and this is therefore of important in our attempt to understand the mechanism by which the body manufactures and uses energy. It is possible to actually supplement alpha-ketogluteric acid where excess ammonia is a factor in a condition of ill health. Amounts of between 500mg and 2,500mg are prescribed as appropriate. Or citric acid may be supplemented to enhance the Krebs cycle's energy production. The amino acid arginine can also be sometimes used to assist in some of the complex waste disposal processes. Researchers such as Dr William Philpott have pointed out that the link between the energy generating citric acid cycle and the waste disposal urea cycle, is a substance called aspartic acid. Its supplementation is also sometimes suggested to enhance urea cycle efficiency.

It is interesting to note the effect of stress on some of these processes. Californian research has shown that when the body is functioning normally there are 38 molecules of ATP (the energy carrier) produced for every single molecule of glucose burned by the body. When someone is in a state of shock or severe stress a process of oxygen deficiency occurs with acidity building up. In such a situation only two molecules of ATP are produced to store and transport the energy being produced.

Stress reduction can, therefore, be seen to be a major strategy in correcting such imbalances, and thereby enhancing energy production. When there is a very low presence of ATP, protein synthesis decreases, with a resulting disruption of many vital processes. At the same time certain acidic amino acids tend to be retained whilst neutral ones are excreted, increasing the degree of acidity present in the tissues. There are many complex interacting possibilities as to the relationships between these and other biochemical changes, and a variety of symptoms may result, including extreme exhaustion.

No attempt should be made at self-treatment of such processes without professional advice, although it is perfectly safe to supplement the body with the essential nutrients mentioned, in doses which will be outlined later. Such a tactic can often enhance general function of the energy producing system as well as improving detoxification of acidic wastes which are impairing normal ATP and alpha-ketoglutaric acid function.

It is in your best interests to consult a doctor or a naturopathic practitioner familiar with clinical nutrition, so that advice can be obtained as to the best course of action in normalizing the cycles of the body described above. Of course, normalization may take place spontaneously through your body's own recuperative and self-healing (homoeostatic) mechanisms, if underlying causes are corrected. This is the aim of this book.

You must realize, though, that understanding the minutiae of the processes already briefly touched on is not a guarantee of being able to manipulate or correct them when they go wrong. A far more likely method of doing so is that which returns the body to a correct balance of nutrients and other vital needs, to allow its innate self-healing abilities to correct imbalances where these exist. The provision of basic sound nutrition with additional vitamin B_3, B_5, B_6, lecithin, choline, zinc and manganese, as appropriate, can be seen to offer a great opportunity for this to occur.

You should by now have a general picture of the energy producing cycles of the body. Much of these processes and the actual use of the energy produced takes place in the cells of the body.

Energy production at the cellular level

The minute mitochondria in the cells are miniature power houses which oxidize food particles into water, carbon dioxide and energy. In this process they transform low energy particles called ADP (adenosine diphosphate) into high energy adenosine triphosphate (ATP) the major energy carrier in the body. Sugar, fat and protein molecules are taken through the cell membrane where they are processed by the mitochondria into energy. Carried by ATP, the energy is used by the cells according to their needs. The byproducts of the process have to be disposed of (detoxified) efficiently for the process to continue.

Coenzyme Q_{10}

Recent research has highlighted another key element in the energy production process. This is a substance known as ubiquinone or Coenzyme Q_{10} (CoQ_{10}). This is similar in structure to vitamin K (see section on deficiency and fatigue page 52). It is an important element in the chain (biochemical pathway) of cellular respiration from which ATP is derived. It is thus vital for all human tissues which require energy, and this means practically all of them.

Japanese research has shown the potential for CoQ_{10} in therapeutic terms, with major beneficial effects noted in cardiovascular disease, where it is frequently seen to be deficient. Supplementation of CoQ_{10} has in trials been effective in improving exercise tolerance in angina pectoris patients. Other cardiac conditions which have been shown to improve are congestive heart failure, where CoQ_{10} is seen to be a treatment of choice, and cardiomyopathy where cardiac function improved dramatically with its use. Hyperthyroid heart failure has also been improved, as has hypertension and diabetes mellitus, where it has been found to enhance control of sugar levels; and periodontal disease, where the increased healing noted has been described by researchers as 'extraordinary'. Also, an immune system boost has been recorded with CoQ_{10} supplementation, and both physical performance and obesity have

been beneficially influenced.

Because CoQ_{10} is involved in the biological energy production at cellular level it has the ability to improve physical performance, especially if you are in a sedentary occupation and indulge in very little aerobic exercise, it is known to be effective in relieving some cases of chronic fatigue. (Reference Coenzyme Q_{10} by Alan Gaby MD in *Textbook of Natural Medicine*, JBCNM, Seattle, 1986.)

Clearly, if there is any deficiency, perhaps from inadequate raw materials, lack of ATP, lack of oxygen, increase of toxic debris and waste materials from metabolism, and free radical activity, energy will be slow to be produced and the cells will function poorly as a result. If this occurs on a large enough scale then overall energy will be poor and fatigue or lack of stamina will result.

CoQ_{10} may be supplemented at a rate of 30mg to 50mg daily, with larger doses in cases of cardiac disease (up to 100mg daily). Clinical results are slow and supplementation may need to be carried on for eight or more weeks before results are apparent. This is because of the slow process of synthesis in the body of the enzymes dependent on CoQ_{10}

Oxidation and free radicals

The actual process of energy production involves the simple transfer of electrons from one molecule to another. Technically this is called oxidation-reduction (or redox for short). The molecule which is losing an electron becomes oxidized and the molecule which is gaining an electron is being reduced. The best known oxidizing atom is oxygen (O_2), although other atoms or molecules may be involved.

A fire is a perfect example of this process. We cannot, however, contemplate an uncontrolled reaction such as a fire being allowed to take place in the body, or at least not without damage. In order that the constant process of oxidation-reduction may continue efficiently, substances called enzymes are essential. These allow the process to occur in a controlled manner without themselves being involved in the final chemical interchange. They are, therefore, known as catalysts.

The complexities of the whole process need not be of concern, but it is important to realize that there is a fine dividing line between the essential life-supporting nature of oxygen in this process, and its potential to do untold damage if in excess. For in this whole process of oxidation there are often produced a group of substances called free radicals (or more accurately free oxidizing radicals (FORs)). These are essentially unstable molecules which are highly reactive. The body produces these naturally as part of its defence mechanisms, but deactivates them as soon as they have been used. Where many are present due to toxicity (heavy metals such as lead or mercury, for example) or excessive presence of certain types of cells (e.g. fat cells) a process can be triggered where a chain reaction, causing immense tissue damage, may result from these unstable oxidizers.

Atherosclerosis, arthritis, cancers and many other degenerative processes including the whole sequence of ageing have been directly linked by research to FOR activity.

The reason for the success of many natural therapies, which use natural elements such as vitamins, relates directly to their ability to neutralize the processes of oxidation damage. Vitamins A, C and E are all anti-oxidants offering protection from the tissue mayhem which free radicals can cause.

The current vogue for the use of hydrogen peroxide (H_2O_2) in treating human ailments runs counter to all physiological sense since it encourages production in the body of additional free radicals. The body itself produces extremely minute amounts of hydrogen peroxide in its dealing with invading micro-organisms, which it literally kills by free radical action. This is, however, no reason to ingest the stuff, a method being touted as a cure for a wide variety of ailments, not least Candida infestation (see page 110).

Nutritional experts such as Professor Jeffrey Bland, formerly director of research at the Linus Pauling Institute for Science and Medicine, have labelled this as a crackpot and totally unproven method, fraught with risks.

Antioxidant protection

In a free radical reaction the antioxidant protects the sensitive tissues in the region of the reaction (blood vessel, brain etc.) as well as neutralizing the free radical and preventing the chain reaction from occurring, which uncontrolled FOR activity would result in. In a very real sense such ongoing free radical processes are like a forest fire, where one reaction (fire) leads to another. The quenching of this by antioxidants protects the body but also exhausts the antioxidant. The most powerful of these antioxidants is vitamin E, one molecule of which is capable of neutralizing free radical activity in 1,000 lipid (fat) molecules.

The body has its own powerful antioxidants such as super oxide dismutase (SOD) and glutathione peroxidase, and when these are deficient or inefficient or exhausted, many disease processes become evident, with fatigue as a common symptom. It is SOD which protects the mitochondria in cells from free radical damage, SOD is itself dependent upon manganese and zinc for its efficiency just as glutathione peroxidase is dependent upon certain amino acids such as cysteine and the mineral selenium. Thus, links between inadequate energy production and free radical activity can be seen, and both of these can be shown to be directly linked to a person's nutrient status.

Normalizing the innate defensive capabilities of the body to boost SOD and glutathione peroxidase activity is possible nutritionally, and strategies to help achieve this will be outlined later.

You have to keep in mind the balance which exists between energy production via oxygen dependent processes and the damage which excessive oxygen can cause. The whole process of energy production and use in the body can be compared with the working of a motor car engine. Both require a good mixture of fuel and air (oxygen) for metabolism, or in the case of the car the 'burn', to be clean and efficient in order to produce maximum power (energy). If the diet is unbalanced and there is inadequate aerobic activity (exercise) then we achieve a situation in which the fuel is too rich with too little oxygen. Toxicity ensues, with poor energy production a further result. This itself leads to free radical activity and tissue damage.

Conversely there may be excess oxygen and too poor a fuel source. This would lead to free radical activity compounded by deficiency of antioxidants which can only be found if there is a good supply of fresh food.

Both of these alternatives result in inadequate energy and toxicity. It is essential for general body energy production as well as that occurring in the mitochondria of the cells for there to be not only a good mix of fuel and oxygen, for optimum energy production and antioxidant presence, but that there should be a flushing of the tissues of acidic wastes (such as lactic acid which builds up after muscular effort leading to cramping or aching). A great deal of benefit can be derived from an approach which includes:

● **Optimum dietary supply of fresh essential food factors.**

● **Additional detoxifying elements and antioxidants such as vitamins A, C, and E, minerals zinc, manganese and selenium and other nutrient aids such as amino acids glutathione and cysteine; as well as specific safe procedures such as short term fasting or detoxification diets.**

● **Aerobic exercise to flush the tissues, and to supply adequate oxygen.**

● **Specific aids to energy producing cycles such as the B vitamins, manganese etc., as outlined above.**

● **Additional substances such as the mineral germanium which is now known to have remarkable abilities in enhancing energy production in the body.**

● **Assistance to the health of the bowel flora which can influence absorption of essential nutrients as well as the manufacture of specific substances vital to health and energy production.**

To feel energetic and not exhausted and fatigued it is necessary for the body to be able to produce energy, and to do so in such a manner that it does not increase its tasks or defence against free radical activity and toxicity.

Whatever the health problem associated with fatigue the ground rules established in the description of energy production and free radical danger should give strong direction as to the best strategy for you. We will now consider the raw materials from which the body derives energy, the foods which yield up energy in their metabolism by the body: fats, carbohydrates and proteins.

CHAPTER 5

Carbohydrates and energy

There is a beautiful energy transfer cycle between ourselves and the world of plants, and a knowledge of it helps a great deal in understanding the ways in which energy is produced.

Plants absorb carbon dioxide from the air and moisture from the soil in which they grow, and they combine these elements with the aid of the sun's energy to produce chains of molecules called carbohydrates (hydrated carbon chains).

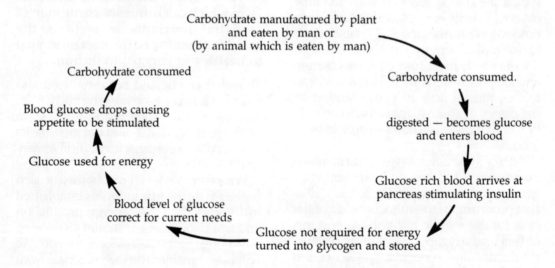

Carbohydrate manufactured by plant
and eaten by man or
(by animal which is eaten by man)

Carbohydrate consumed

Blood glucose drops causing
appetite to be stimulated

Glucose used for energy

Blood level of glucose
correct for current needs

Carbohydrate consumed.

digested — becomes glucose
and enters blood

Glucose rich blood arrives at
pancreas stimulating insulin

Glucose not required for energy
turned into glycogen and stored

Body's carbohydrate energy cycle (normal)

In eating the plants, we consume these carbohydrates, and we metabolize (burn) them with the assistance of the oxygen which is our respiratory medium, in order to release the locked-in energy for our own use. We eliminate the excess water from this process of energy release through our breathing (and urinary systems) along with the carbon dioxide, which is then once again available for plants to use. In producing carbohydrate, plants release oxygen into the air for us to use, thus completing a harmonious cycle of energy production.

If an animal eats the plants, and is subsequently eaten by man, the energy transfer is a little more complex. However, the end result is the same for us, in that energy is received via this chain of production.

There are different types of carbohydrate, and the types depend upon the various arrangements of their constituent elements — carbon, hydrogen and oxygen — in their molecular structures. The simplest of all is sugar, which itself comes in several forms, the commonest being fructose (fruit sugar). Another form is glucose, which is found in our blood, and a combination of these two sugars makes up sucrose which is the common sugar used so abundantly in food manufacture and as a sweetening accompaniment to so many foods and drinks. Sucrose intake at today's level of consumption is identified by the enlightened as a major threat to the overall economy of the body.

It is generally accepted that prehistoric man was almost vegetarian, eating the fruits and young green plants of his early jungle existence. But man, by virtue of either a fortuitous or designed quirk of his digestive ability, was able to adapt to a quite different source of food when climatic conditions forced him to become a hunter-gatherer, deriving much of his sustenance from meat.

It is surely logical to suppose that when fruits and vegetables were the major element in our eating pattern, we were attuned to eating sweet fruits, for their very sweetness of taste was an indication of ripeness and therefore suitability for eating. Whether true or not, our desire for sweetness has remained, despite a marked change in the type of foods we eat.

The level of sugar present in your blood acts as a signal for your hunger mechanism. Thus, when blood sugar is low you will feel hungry and seek food which will replenish your body's energy source.

In nature, when a carbohydrate-rich (and therefore sugar-rich) food is eaten it comes together with a variety of other nutrients such as fats, proteins and essential elements, including vitamins and minerals. Unfortunately today's proliferation of refined carbohydrate foods means that the elements associated with natural carbohydrates are removed, leaving the simple sugars which act on and in the body in a most unnatural and dramatic manner.

The fact is that our bodies have little need for simple sugars, but we do have great need for the complex unrefined carbohydrates. Refined sugars are absorbed into the bloodstream very quickly indeed, whereas the sugars from complex carbohydrates are absorbed slowly. The difference is important, since with a speedy rise in blood sugar level the body is obliged to restore normality, and it does so by producing the hormonal substance, insulin. This reduces the blood sugar level and, more often than not, takes it to below the level previous to the intake of sugar. Thus a swing occurs from a raised blood sugar level to a relatively low blood sugar (hypoglycaemic) state. At this point you would feel decidedly shaky and would want more sugary food. Thus the cycle repeats itself, as blood sugar rises and insulin is again produced to reduce it.

No great harm would result were it not for the fact that constant repetition of this cycle often impairs the pancreatic function of insulin production, the ultimate effect of which is a diabetic state, i.e. your body is no longer able to control your blood sugar levels by itself. A further complication exists in that insulin in excess can be highly damaging, especially to the blood vessels servicing your heart. Thus the scenario outlined above often leads not just to a diabetic state but also to cardio-vascular disease.

A further twist to this tale is the fact that diets rich in sugar are often also rich in stimulants, such as coffee, tea, cola drinks, alcohol and cigarettes. All of these, in one way or another, and in different degrees, cause your body to release from its own stores even more sugar into the blood, compounding the levels introduced from the food and drink you consume.

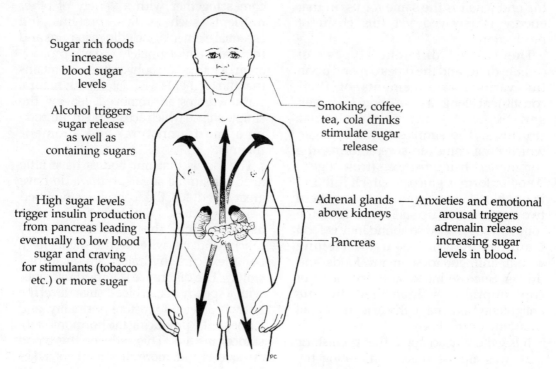

Sugar rich foods increase blood sugar levels

Alcohol triggers sugar release as well as containing sugars

High sugar levels trigger insulin production from pancreas leading eventually to low blood sugar and craving for stimulants (tobacco etc.) or more sugar

Smoking, coffee, tea, cola drinks stimulate sugar release

Adrenal glands above kidneys — Anxieties and emotional arousal triggers adrenalin release increasing sugar levels in blood.

Pancreas

These blood sugar levels are accompanied by a variety of symptoms. Low blood sugar is characterized by a shaky feeling, weakness and a variety of symptoms from headache to allergies. Mood swings are also common, and a good deal of so-called 'neurotic' behaviour is directly linked to these biochemical alterations, which are often self-engineered through relying too heavily on refined sugary foods.

Both high and low blood sugar can result in fatigue and it is essential if you are caught in this cycle to follow the advice given on pages 133/4 for the nutritional treatment of the problems.

A further reason for avoiding the over-use of refined sugar is the effect it has on restricting intake of more nutritious foods. Most heavy sugar eaters become deficient in essential nutrients which are abundantly present in foods requiring greater degrees of chewing and digesting, such as vegetables and complex carbo-hydrates (whole grains, brown rice and pulses.)

Just what is lost in refining can be seen from refined sugar's abysmally low complement of nutrients compared with those found in the substance from which it is extracted, molasses, the first state of the refining of sugar from sugar cane.

	100g Molasses	100g Refined sugar
Calories	220	400
Vitamin B_1	245mcg	nil
Vitamin B_2	240mcg	nil
Vitamin B_3	4mg	nil
Vitamin B_6	270mcg	nil
Vitamin B_5	260mcg	nil
Biotin	16mcg	nil
Calcium	258mg	1mg
Phosphorus	30mg	trace
Iron	7.97mg	0.4mg
Copper	1.93mg	0.2mg
Magnesium	0.4mg	nil
Sodium	90mg	0.3mg
Potassium	1,500mg	0.5mg

The minerals and vitamins, which were present in the molasses and then refined out, are used for animal feed. The 'pure white and deadly' product is for you. Similar degrees of nutrient loss are evident in refined grains, such as wheat and rice.

Obesity is a major end-result of a diet too rich in sugars and refined carbohydrates (white flour products, white rice etc.) and this in itself is a threat to health. A further factor is that complex carbohydrates are almost always accompanied by fibre, whereas refined carbohydrates and sugars are not. The lack of fibre in food leads to a variety of health problems, such as gall bladder disease, high blood cholesterol levels (and therefore heart and circulatory problems), diabetes, digestive problems (constipation, haemorrhoids etc.) as well as certain forms of cancer.

Fibre is automatically present in complex carbohydrates as indicated in the following table.

Very high fibre foods	% fibre by weight
Wheat bran	44
All Bran	26
Dried apricots	24
Dried figs	18.5
Prunes	16.1
Almonds	14.3
Soya bean flour	12
Rye crispbread	11.7
Wholewheat pasta	10.0
Wholemeal flour	9.6
Brazil nuts	9.0
Wholewheat bread	8.5
Redcurrants	8.2
Raspberries & blackberries	7.3
Baked beans	7.3
Oatmeal (raw)	7.0
Raisins	6.8
Hazelnuts	6.8
Spinach (boiled)	6.3
Garden peas	6.3
Sweetcorn	5.7

Very high fibre foods	% fibre by weight
Walnuts	5.2
Chickpeas (cooked)	5.2
Lemons	5.2

Medium fibre foods	% fibre by weight
Broad beans (boiled)	4.9
Broccoli tips (boiled)	4.1
Leeks (boiled)	3.9
Spring greens (boiled)	3.8
Cabbage (raw)	3.4
Watercress	3.3
Carrots (boiled)	2.7
Apples	2.4
Bananas	2.0

These examples indicate the pleasant choices available for reasonable fibre acquisition.

The sugars which we need are those contained in complex carbohydrates and fruits. Fruit sugar when taken as part of the whole fruit is a slow release form of energy. If the fruit is juiced, however, and the fibre removed so that the fructose (fruit sugar) is consumed rapidly as a liquid, then the same problems will exist as with sucrose ingestion. Simple sugars provide quick calories, and not energy of any lasting value. They can lead to health problems, and this is true of all sugars, even honey.

WAYS TO REDUCE SUGAR INTAKE

First, remember that there are many foods which you may not suspect as having had sugars added in their processing. For example: most frozen foods; baked beans; canned fruit.

If labels on cans or packets indicate that the contents include added sugar, corn syrup, liquid glucose etc., then avoid them. Reduce your use of conventional jams, marmalade and honey and replace with 'no-sugar' jams in modest amounts. Reduce your use of conventional sweetened breakfast cereals and replace with unsweetened types, adding dried or fresh fruit to sweeten.

Reduce animal fat intake by using diluted fruit juice on breakfast cereal instead of milk.

Avoid sugary biscuits and chocolates as between-meal snacks, and replace with fresh nuts or seeds, or eat some fresh raw salad, such as carrot or celery, or fruit, such as an apple.

For desserts avoid the usual sugar-packed varieties and have yogurt (unsweetened) or fresh or stewed fruits (no added sugar) instead. If cakes are being made, use far less sugar than the recipe demands (say a third less than listed) and introduce spices for extra flavour. Stop adding sugar to your tea and coffee, etc. Try herb teas, with their subtle aromas and flavours, instead. Avoid artificial sweeteners.

If you want 'fizzy' drinks, try natural carbonated spring water (Perrier, for example) instead of carbonated drinks with sweetening; or instead, drink diluted natural fruit and vegetable juices. If you need alcohol, stick to dry white wine or dry cider.

These simple strategies will modify your sugar intake markedly.

Although, in this book, I have divided the various nutrient families such as fats and carbohydrates into different sections for consideration, you should bear in mind that faulty eating patterns in one almost always lead to imbalances in others. Thus, anyone eating a great deal of sugar-rich food automatically does not obtain enough fibre, and often ingests a high saturated fat load. White bread or rolls eaten together with meat or cheese, or hamburgers, cakes, biscuits and pastries, pizzas etc., are all examples of high fat, high refined carbohydrate and low fibre combinations. These play an ever increasing part in the 'fast food' meals of today.

The end-result of diets rich in these involves the diseases associated with the over-use of refined sugars as well as a high fat intake. This interrelationship is dramatically highlighted in cardiovascular disease, obesity and diabetes (which are often all present in the same person at the same time).

Fatigue is usually part of the picture in all these conditions. A balanced vegetarian diet, or one which avoids most dairy produce and animal fats, and which includes abundant use of vegetables, wholegrains, pulses, nuts, seeds and fruits, and which uses game, poultry or fish for its animal protein sources, is ideal for avoidance of the imbalances described above.

CHAPTER 6

Fats and energy

Oils and fats are a major source of energy for your body. However, some forms are particularly undesirable since they have been shown to be linked to serious chronic disease patterns. Nathan Pritikin has described the essential damage which an excess of fats does to your body in these words (*The Pritikin Program for Diet and Exercise*, Bantam, 1980).

> First of all they suffocate your tissues, depriving them of oxygen. Second, they raise the level of cholesterol and uric acid in your tissues, contributing to atherosclerosis and gout. Third, they impede carbohydrate metabolism and foster diabetes.

The major diseases of diabetes and cardio-vascular degeneration are, therefore, linked to high fat diets, as are obesity, gall bladder disease and gout. Some forms of cancer are also noted to be more prevalent when a diet high in saturated fats is consumed.

From the fatigue point of view high fat intake reduces the efficiency of the circulation, 'sludging up' the blood and adversely affecting the metabolism of energy-rich foods by increasing toxicity levels of metabolic waste products.

A fat comprises a chain of carbon atoms with additional hydrogen, and the various types of fats and oils are defined by the number of hydrogen atoms which attach to the carbon atoms. Each of the carbon atoms is capable of holding on to four additional atoms. In a chain each carbon atom would be linked to two other carbon atoms, thus leaving only two free arms. If these attach to two hydrogen atoms then it is said to be 'saturated', but if some positions in the chain remain vacant then the oil or fat is said to be unsaturated.

When many vacancies occur, the oil is referred to as polyunsaturated, and in this state is more likely to remain a liquid at room temperature than a highly saturated fat, such as butter, which remains solid until heated. This solidity or liquidity is further influenced by the number of carbon atoms present in any given chain. Thus butter, and animal fat such as lard, are different in terms of their carbon chain lengths (from 4 to 14 in the case of butter and around 18 in the case of lard.)

In many cases the fats you eat are arranged in groups attached to another substance called glycerol. The bonds between these are severed on digestion so that the individual fatty molecules (fatty acids) can be absorbed by your body. They are then rearranged so that three fatty acids are grouped together with glycerol (to form a triglyceride) and these are transported

Model of unsaturated fatty acid

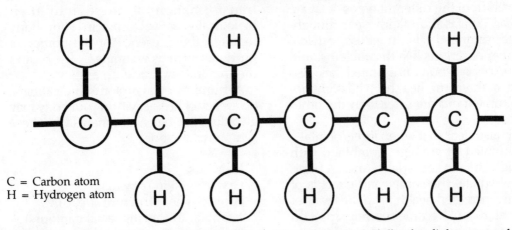

C = Carbon atom
H = Hydrogen atom

This chain has carbon atoms with free links. It is, therefore, *unsaturated*. If all carbon links were used then it would be saturated.

in your blood for energy use, or to be stored in your liver or other areas of your body. When needed for energy the links are again broken so that free fatty acids are available for metabolism.

There are three major groups of fats. The saturated ones as described above; the polyunsaturated ones, which have abundant space left for more hydrogen, and an intermediate group, monounsaturated fats (olive oil, fish oil etc.) which have some, but not many, free carbon 'arms'.

Saturated fats

These provide concentrated energy but excessive intake is associated with cancer, cardiovascular disease, diabetes, obesity, gall bladder disease and gout.

Main sources of saturated fats are dairy produce, meat, processed fats (most margarines and cooking fats, some oils, cakes, biscuits, pies, sausages etc.), coconut oil and palm oil.

Monounsaturated fats

These are not only said to be 'neutral' in health terms, but recent evidence has confirmed that they are protective of heart function. Main sources are olive oil, fish, game.

Polyunsaturated fats

These are a good source of energy. Indeed, fresh polyunsaturated oils are essential for health. Excess is harmful, however, and an overall reduction in saturated fats should not be accomplished by an increase in polyunsaturated fats.

Essential fatty acids

These substances, also known as vitamin F, are essential for health. Two important EFAs are linoleic acid and linolenic acid and these are found in polyunsaturated oils; game meat; fish (especially cold water varieties); grains; many vegetables; seeds, especially linseed and evening primrose.

Cholesterol

This vital substance, required for hormone production, as well as for bile which digests fats, and which is a part of every cell in the body, is manufactured in the body and is also found in animal fats and eggs. Too much is harmful. Dietary cholesterol has a limited impact on blood levels which are thought to be mainly manufactured within the body in response to an unbalanced diet, excessively high in sugars.

From an energy viewpoint, the calories derived from the different types of fat are similar. What is abundantly clear, though, is that saturated fats, in excess, cause a number of serious health problems, and that excessive polyunsaturated fats also pose a threat to health, whilst mono-unsaturated oils are safer than the other forms.

It is also clear that when levels of intake of saturated fat are high, combined with a high intake of sugar and refined carbohydrate, the compound effect is of greatly increased health risk. The levels of cholesterol can become severely upset on a high fat/high sugar diet, causing degeneration of the cardiovascular structures and ultimate heart disease.

Fats when heated alter their structure and become potentially dangerous. Thus, oils and fats should be carefully selected in your diet; frying should be avoided, and freshness should be a major consideration in selecting foods rich in oils and fats (nuts for example).

Your strategy should be to reduce your intake of animal fats, particularly from farm-raised meat and dairy produce, and to increase the unrefined carbohydrate element in your food, since fibre helps reduce excess levels of saturated fats and cholesterol in the system. However, energy production within your body calls for adequate levels of fat intake. Fatty acids, for instance, are of vital importance to the economy of your body, and some of these must be supplied by the food you eat. These are the essential fatty acids (EFAs).

There are two types of EFA, the omega 6 and the omega 3 groups, and they are the building material from which your all important cell membranes are built, as well as the material which binds cells together. They also play a major part in the constant exchange of oxygen and nutritional substances which occurs in your cells. Merely having adequate supplies of the EFAs is not enough since the transformation of these into their biologically active forms in your body requires the presence of a number of nutrients such as vitamins C, B_3, B_6 and the minerals magnesium and zinc.

A number of symptoms indicating a deficiency of EFA activity in your body may give clues as to such a nutrient lack. These symptoms include:

Hair loss.
Dry scaly skin (eczema).
Poor tissue structure (leading, for example, to sagging facial contours).
Lethargy and fatigue.
Poor immune function and therefore prone to infection.
Irritability.
Painful and/or swollen joints.
Premenstrual tension syndrome.

A diet which contains an abundance of raw foods (vegetables and fruits as well as seeds and nuts) together with fish and/or game and/or wholegrains and pulses will provide your body with the EFAs it needs, as well as the nutrients which allow their conversion to the vital substances gamma-linoleic acid (GLA), eicosapentaenoic acid (EPA) and docosahexaenoic acid (DHA). Such a diet would also provide ample fibre and limited saturated fat, thus taking account of the major needs of your body, and allowing ample energy production with minimal toxic stress to your system.

The everyday food of most people today contains as much as 45 per cent fat, and a lot of this in the undesirable saturated form. Leading health authorities world-wide have urged that this should be brought down to no more than 30 per cent of our bodies' energy requirements. The ratio between saturated and polyunsaturated fats should be around 1.4:1, which should be the case if about one and a half times the quantity of polyunsaturated to saturated fat is eaten, but it is plainly impossible for you to sit down with a slide rule and calculator at each meal. So here is a method which is simplicity itself. It calls for the following approach:

HOW TO REDUCE UNDESIRABLE AND INCREASE DESIRABLE FAT INTAKE

● Avoid all canned food in which fats are listed as major ingredients.

● Avoid recipes which include meat or dairy products.

● Try to replace some meat in the diet with pulses and cereals (lentils, soyabeans, chickpeas, etc.).

● When you buy meat choose lean cuts for preference, and ideally avoid beef and pork.

● Choose game whenever possible (average fat content of game is 4 per cent compared with beef which may be as high as 30 per cent. The fat is a better type as well, with more unsaturated fats and EFAs.

● Choose poultry (avoiding skin) or fish instead of meat if game not available.

● Avoid minced meat which is usually very fatty unless you make your own.

● Remove all visible fat before cooking meat and remove the skin from poultry before cooking in a casserole.

● Grill rather than fry; don't baste.

● Don't use meat dripping for gravy.

● If fatty meat is being used (e.g. lamb) cook the previous day and skim solidified fat off, before reheating and serving.

● Use non-stick pans to avoid use of fats if you have to fry. Never use saturated fats for this.

● If oil is used let it be monounsaturated oil, olive or corn oil. Don't ever let oils smoke when heating as this alters their chemistry dangerously.

● Eat jacket or boiled potatoes rather than fried or roast. Don't add butter or margarine to cooked vegetables. Instead use olive oil and lemon juice and/or herbs on vegetables. On jacket potaties use low-fat yogurt or cottage cheese rather than butter.

● Use olive oil and lemon on salads, or yogurt and chopped herbs.

● Avoid milk if possible. If not use skimmed milk.

● Use polyunsaturated spread instead of butter on bread.

● Use low to medium fat cheese instead of full fat ones. (Cottage cheese is only 4 per cent fat, Ricotta 9 to 15 per cent, Camembert 23 per cent, Cheddar around 35 per cent and Stilton 40 per cent.

● Use low-fat yogurt instead of cream wherever this is called for.

● Avoid cakes and pastries as these contain a great deal of saturated fat, as do hamburgers and sausages.

● Wherever lard is called for in recipes use polyunsaturated fats instead. There is hidden fat in the following foods, so avoid them.

Bacon	Fried chips and
Biscuits	potato crisps
Cakes	Ice cream
Cheese	Roasted nuts and
	seeds
Chocolate	Pastries

All processed meats
including meat pies,
sausages and salami

Those foods highest in saturated fats are:

| Brains | Eggs | Kidney | Shellfish |
| Butter | Heart | Liver | |

CHAPTER 7

Protein and energy

Fatigue is one of the major symptoms of protein deficiency. It is well established that in western industrialized nations the average intake of protein is seldom lower than that prescribed as necessary. How then could anyone in such circumstances become protein deficient?

Eating a food does not guarantee that it will be adequately digested, or that if it is it will then be adequately absorbed and transported, or converted into a bio-logically useful form, in your body. Bioavailability requires that all these stages be successfully carried out before your body can use the food you eat to satisfy its needs.

It is often found that people have inade-quate digestive enzymes or acids, and so the protein eaten does not get properly broken down into its constituent amino acids, the only form in which protein is of any use to the body.

Protein digestion/metabolism

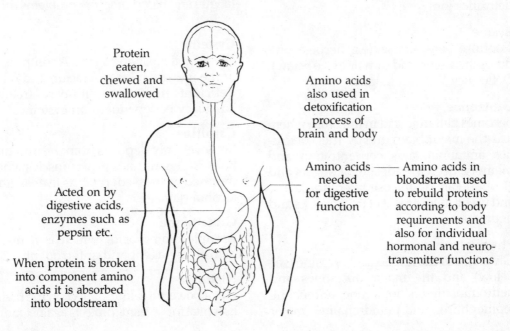

Protein eaten, chewed and swallowed

Amino acids also used in detoxification process of brain and body

Amino acids needed for digestive function

Amino acids in bloodstream used to rebuild proteins according to body requirements and also for individual hormonal and neuro-transmitter functions

Acted on by digestive acids, enzymes such as pepsin etc.

When protein is broken into component amino acids it is absorbed into bloodstream

Free amino acids

There are some 20 amino acids forming the component parts of protein which are used by your body as building blocks, and eight of these are termed essential as your body cannot synthesize them from other materials and it therefore has to rely on the food you eat for its vital supply.

Most of the amino acids have specific functions in your body, ranging from pain killing to sleep enhancement, but unless the bulk protein that you eat (in which the amino acids are strung together in long chains) is suitably broken down into individual free amino acids, none of the processes of restructuring, building and synthesizing of amino acids into new body tissues and elements can take place adequately.

Among the myriad roles played by individual amino acids in the body are the following.

Arginine

Important for sperm motility, wound healing, immune function, glucose tolerance, insulin production, fat metabolism and detoxification.

Lysine

Control of some viruses (e.g. herpes), produces the amino acid carnitine (see below). Deficiency leads to fatigue.

Glutamine

Becomes glutamic acid in the brain where it is the major brain energy fuel, detoxifies ammonia, aids concentration and memory, decreases desire for sugars and alcohol. Part of glucose tolerance factor, and useful in treatment of peptic ulcers and depression.

Phenylalanine

Gives rise to the amino acid tyrosine (see below) and the major hormones and neurotransmitters dopamine, adrenaline (epinephrine) and noradrenaline, major energy producing factors. Useful in some cases of depression. As DLPA is a potent non-toxic pain reliever, and enhances weight reduction naturally.

Methionine

Produces the amino acids cysteine and taurine (see below). Detoxifies heavy metals, is a powerful anti-oxidant, detoxifies the liver, essential for availability of vitamin B_{12} and selenium.

Tryptophan

Essential for synthesis of vitamin B_3 in the body, becomes the neurotransmitter serotonin (essential for sound sleep). Influences choice of foods, therefore aids slimming and weight control. Acts as an antidepressant.

Tyrosine

Essential for the production of thyroid hormones, as well as dopamine, adrenaline and noradrenaline (neurotransmitters and hormones involved in stress management and energy release). A useful antidepressant where tryptophan is ineffective. Useful in the treatment of fatigue and blood pressure problems (high or low).

Cysteine

Powerful detoxifying agent. A component of the glucose tolerance factor, and often deficient in chronic illness. Insulin adequacy is dependent on cysteine.

Carnitine

Removes fatty deposits from the liver and body in general, aids heart muscles when diseased or stressed, protects liver against alcohol damage.

Glutathione

A triple amino acid, which is a major detoxifying agent and anti-oxidant.

Histidine

Has a powerful calming effect on the brain. Essential for orgasm, protects against radiation damage, and detoxifies heavy metal traces in the body.

Taurine
Assists in cholesterol control; reduces chances of gall stones; useful in epilepsy; influences blood sugar levels in the same manner as insulin, and saves potassium in heart muscle.

Ornithine
Releases growth hormone, and is vital in detoxification processes of the body. Experimentally used in weight control, and is a substitute for arginine when this is undesirable (e.g. during viral infections such as herpes) strengthens immune system function.

Leucine, Isoleucine, Valine
Important for muscle growth and repair. Purported use in mental illness and obesity control.

Glycine
Part of glutathione tripeptide; helps in liver detoxification; a component of the glucose tolerance factor; inhibitory neurotransmitter (calming agent).

Fatigue is often associated with an underactive thyroid gland. The hormone thyroxin may be inadequately produced by the body, and in such cases iodine is sometimes prescribed to enhance the thyroid function. This is logical since thyroxin is based on iodine, and yet without the amino acid tyrosine, thyroxin cannot be manufactured by the thyroid gland. Thus it can be seen that proper protein digestion is fundamental to normal body function in general and fatigue prevention or reduction in particular.

If there is any lack of particular protein digesting (proteolytic) enzymes in the digestive tract, or if hydrochloric acid is deficient, then protein digestion may become seriously impaired, and no matter what quantity is being eaten there will be a deficiency of amino acids, with consequences which will almost certainly include fatigue and lack of energy.

Your primary objective, therefore, must be to ensure that your digestive system is working well and that adequate protein of the right type is being eaten.

Proteins derived from plants are often regarded as second class compared with those from animal sources (meat, fish, dairy produce, etc.). The fact is that eating animal protein is a short cut, in that the animal has taken on the task of combining the proteins present in plants in order to manufacture their bodies, which we, in turn, consume.

If we eat a balanced vegetarian diet we can do this synthesizing for ourselves, and the end result is the same in terms of the complement of amino acids which we supply to our bodies.

A combination of cereals (wholegrains such as rice, wheat, etc.) and pulses (such as lentils and beans) contains all the amino acids known to be essential to life. From these the body makes other non-essential amino acids and the whole range of body tissues and substances, just as efficiently as if the protein eaten is derived from meat.

Examples of good combinations of cereals and pulses which will provide all the essential amino acids to the body, at the same time, are:

Any of these with legumes	Any of these grains
Lentils	Barley
Chickpeas	Buckwheat
Butter beans	Millet
Mung beans	Wheat
Lima beans	Rice
Soya beans	Oats
Blackeye beans	Rye
Green peas	
Kidney beans	

Sprouted beans are as useful (some say more useful) nutritionally as dried beans. All grains used should be whole, never refined.

Other combinations of vegetarian foods which provide all the essential amino acids include the use of seeds, and the following are recommended:

Rice (or other whole grain) plus sunflower seeds.
Wholegrain plus peanuts.
Wholegrain plus sesame seeds.
Wholegrain plus pumpkin seeds.
Corn plus any legume (see list above).
Peanuts plus sunflower or sesame seeds.
Sesame seeds with any legume.

To avoid the flatulence often associated with eating beans they should be soaked for at least 12 hours prior to cooking. Fresh water should be used in the cooking and this should be changed during cooking.

Whether we eat animal or vegetable protein, the critical factor is whether enough protein is being digested and absorbed properly. How much is enough? Health authorities suggest we eat something in the order of 70g to 100g of 'first class' protein daily, depending upon our body size and energy output. If vegetarian sources are being relied upon then about 50 per cent more in weight is required.

Stone Age man ate something like ten times as much animal protein — around 700g or 1½ lb daily (Eaton and Konner, 'Paleolithic Diet' N.E.J. of Medicine, Jan 1985, pp 283-9), and his health was superb (as is that of the present day hunter-gatherers who follow a paleolithic way of life). It may seem odd that this much meat could be eaten each day without raising fat levels, but the secret lies in the type of meat consumed. Stone age man ate free-living animals (game) and, as previously mentioned, such animals have barely 4 per cent of their body weight as fat, which compares with upwards of 30 per cent in the case of domesticated beef, much of which is 'hidden', and consequently not easily removed by trimming. The type of fats differs as well, since almost half of game fat is polyunsaturated, and there is also a reasonable quantity of desirable EFAs and monounsaturated oils present, which are absent in domesticated animal fat.

Also paleolithic man ate little or no dairy produce, since domestication of animals began barely 10,000 years ago. Thus, despite a heroic meat intake, the fat content of his diet was low, as it is in people eating a balanced vegetarian diet today.

What we can learn from this is that there is an apparent biological option open to us. We may choose, for whatever reason, to be vegetarian, and be healthier than average, as long as we pay attention to supplying the body with its correct nutrient needs.

Free form amino acid supplementation

A method of bypassing the problem of amino acid acquisition exists for those in chronic need of free amino acids, and this is the supplementation of the diet with free form amino acid capsules. Among those who have been shown to benefit from supplementation with a complete blend of all the amino acids are people with:

Anorexia
Brittle nails
Cancer
Digestive problems
Fatigue
Dizziness
Hair loss
Hypertension (low blood pressure)
Immune incompetence (e.g. frequent infections)

Intolerance to cold

People who are highly stressed

People who are slimming or on a low protein diet

People who are about to undergo, or who have just undergone surgery

Athletes (especially long distance) and bodybuilders

Vegetarians (unless certain of their nutritional status).

It is suggested that for those in great need 15g to 30g daily of complete free form amino acid formula for men, and 10g to 20g daily for women, in three divided doses away from mealtimes with water, should be taken. For lesser needs the recommendation is 6g to 10g for men and 4g to 8g for women in similarly divided doses.

Dosage and individual uses of amino acids are described in more detail in the section on deficiency and fatigue (see page 52). In terms of energy, proteins are vital. A deficiency here will almost always be a factor in cases of chronic fatigue.

CHAPTER 8

Deficiency and fatigue

Almost any nutrient deficiency can produce the symptoms of fatigue, and so that you can identify such deficiencies, the major functions as well as the signs and symptoms of individual nutritional deficiencies, are given below. It is important to remember that there are seldom single deficiencies. More usually, it is an interaction of a number of deficiencies, and research has proved that in most people there exist unique, idiosyncratic requirements for particular nutrients. This is known as biochemical individuality, and it makes it difficult to give more than broad guidelines on what the average needs may be for any given nutrient. In each of us there could be variations from 'average needs' of as much as 500 per cent in our real biochemical requirements for any of the essential nutrients.

The only way to identify such needs is by the use of complex biochemical analyses of body fluids and tissues, or by the identification of tell-tale signs and symptoms such as those outlined below.

The brief examination of the major food groups — protein, carbohydrate and fats — (see pages 36-51) has indicated the types of basic foods which are essential to the activities of the body, especially in relation to energy production and fatigue, and unless the raw materials of life are provided in a steady supply, and in forms which are acceptable to the body, there is little chance for health and energy to be maintained at high levels.

You might think that once your basic food needs are taken care of, the individual nutrients such as vitamins and minerals would be adequately supplied automatically. This is not so, since:

(a) There exists this phenomenon of biochemical individuality, creating particular and unique needs, which diet alone may not be able to meet.

(b) Foods produced under modern industrialized conditions frequently fail to contain the nutrients which they are supposed to carry.

(c) There occur in each of us, from time to time (stress, pregnancy, infection etc.), specific heightened needs for major nutrients (such as vitamin C and A). Supplementation of desirable and necessary nutrients, therefore, becomes a strategy which reasonable people should adopt once specific needs and requirements are identified.

It is, though, important to bear in mind

that some of the essential nutrients are potentially toxic in large doses and should only be supplemented in the amounts recommended. This applies particularly to fat-soluble vitamins such as A, D, E and K. You should also be aware that there are times when supplementation of one nutrient may produce a deficiency of others due to biochemical competition for absorption by the body, or due to complex interactions.

Thus, there are nutrients which may be deficient, and therefore requiring supplementation, which need to be taken with others which are not deficient, simply to avoid imbalances. This is so with many of the B vitamins, and there are also some nutrients which are known to act better when accompanied by others, as in the case of vitamin E and the mineral selenium.

Some nutrients can be supplemented not to replace deficiencies but because the substance has a specific pharmacological action in the body. If this can be shown to be safe, then the use, in this way, of a food as a medicine, is surely a reasonable action. An example of this is the use of vitamin C in megadoses, as described in the section dealing with vitamin C and mercury toxicity (page 68) where tissue saturation of vitamin C is recommended, far in excess of normal biological requirements, in order to assist in the detoxification of mercury.

Just how widespread is vitamin deficiency in the Western world, where more food seems available than ever? The evidence is overwhelming that amongst most groups of the population of Europe and the USA many people are nutritionally deficient. Dr Holly Atkinson, author of *Women and Fatigue* (Macmillan, 1985) states: 'Mineral and vitamin deficiencies can clearly lead to fatigue. And fatigue is a particular problem for women. That might lead one to think that women may suffer more mineral and vitamin deficiencies than men. Some studies now suggest that approximately half of all American women are deficient in some essential mineral or vitamin.'

To answer why this should be, Dr Atkinson comes up with a formula which includes:

1 The major role of women in childbearing, lactating and, of course, in having monthly periods during which iron and other nutrients are lost. Unless nutrition is excellent, she maintains, this leads to a particularly sensitive group in the population.

2 Added to this is the self-inflicted element of 'slimming' and dieting, created by excessive slimness as an ideal. Not all such diets are harmful, but many are less than adequate, if followed for more than a brief period.

3 In addition, use of the contraceptive pill has been shown to interfere with nutritional balance in a number of ways, as has the increasing use of alcohol by women whose biological ability to handle it is less efficient than in males.

Thus unique physiological factors, as well as sociological elements, place women at greater risk of fatigue, but in other areas of society it has also been established that there are major nutritional deficiencies to be found.

For example in a wide ranging survey in the USA, Drs Basu and Schorah (*Vitamin C in Health and Disease*, Croom Helm, 1981) showed that:

3 per cent of young healthy people had a deficiency of vitamin C, as did:
20 per cent of healthy elderly people
68 per cent of elderly outpatients at hospitals
76 per cent of cancer patients
95 per cent of institutionalized elderly
100 per cent of institutionalized young people.

Professor Emanuel Cheraskin, of the University of Alabama, a world authority of nutrition and disease, has shown that the following percentages of men and women received, from their diets, less than two thirds of the recommended daily allowance (RDA) of the nutrients listed. Remember that RDA is the absolute minimum amount we should be obtaining. This relates to what is thought to be an 'adequate' intake under normal conditions. It allows little leeway for increased demand, or idiosyncratic requirements which affect all of us periodically, and some of us constantly (Cheraskin, E., Ringsdorf, W. and Clark, J., *Diet and Disease*, Keats, 1977).

Percentages of women in the USA aged 30 to 60 (cross section of population) who are ingesting less than two-thirds of various nutrients.

Protein 10%   Vitamin B_3 20%
Iron 18%   Vitamin A 45%
Vitamin B_1 20%   Vitamin C 35%
Vitamin B_2 30%   Calcium 60%

Percentage of men in the USA age 30-60 (cross section of population) who are ingesting less than two-thirds of various nutrients.

Protein 5%   Vitamin B_3 9%
Iron 12%   Vitamin A 20%
Vitamin B_1 15%   Vitamin C 35%
Vitamin B_2 10%   Calcium 30%

On this evidence from Drs Cheraskin, Ringsdorf and Clark, Dr Atkinson is seen to be correct in stating that women are more likely to be nutritionally deficient than men, and therefore more prone to fatigue. It hardly seems, though, that men come out of this survey too well, with a third of men, in this active and productive age group, deficient in vitamin C and calcium; two of the major nutrients.

Cheraskin and his associates show equally disturbing deficiencies in children.

He examined nine to eleven year olds in Kansas, and found that 10 per cent of boys and 11 per cent of girls of this age group were obtaining less than two-thirds of their requirements of vitamin B_2, with resultant serious potential for brain damage. He also found that 18 per cent of boys and 14 per cent of girls, aged nine to eleven, were receiving two-thirds or less vitamin B_3 than RDA, with the potential for depression, anxiety, memory impairment and emotional instability. In a general and random survey of 860 people attending Alabama University School of Dentistry clinics for routine care, Cheraskin found that half of them had blood concentrations showing vitamin C deficiency with 6.6 per cent (about 55 people in this survey) showing zero plasma ascorbic acid levels. This means that many people, walking the streets of a major city in the USA, in the latter half of the twentieth century, were in a state where scurvy was imminent.

At another hospital, in Jersey City, Cheraskin assessed 120 randomly selected patients and found 88 per cent had a significant deficiency of at least one vitamin, after blood tests, and 64 per cent had deficiencies in two or more vitamins.

European citizens need feel no sense of complacency, since surveys and studies throughout the Continent indicate very similar levels of nutrient inadequacy, whether these look at housewives in England, or schoolchildren in Vienna. It is clear that RDA levels, which are strongly criticized by many experts as being far too low, are not even being met. Professor Jeffrey Bland, one of the world's leading nutritional experts, states (*Your Personal Health Programme*, Thorsons, 1984): 'The RDA promotes adequate nutritional status; however, many people are asking not about adequate, but optimal states of nutrition.'

He makes it clear that of the 44 nutrients known to be essential for health and good function, only about a third have been ascribed an RDA figure. This does not mean that the others are less important, only that at this time the experts simply do not know what level to establish as adequate, since no acute deficiency disease exists to which reference can be made. He lists the variables which make 'adequate' become inadequate, for most of us, at some stage of life. These include:

Infection
Metabolic disorders
Chronic disease
Body size and sex (see Dr Atkinson's findings above)
Heavy physical activity or work

Extremes of climate, hot or cold
Changes due to illness or rehabilitation
Intestinal parasites
Unique metabolic considerations based upon biochemical individuality.

Dr Bland makes the important observation that the RDA figures only represent a crude approximation of what healthy individuals are consuming with no regard for optimal levels (that is levels which would produce the very best function of the body) or of specific needs.

Just how can we tell what our requirements are? The following notes may be used to guide you as to average requirements (RDA), as well as to your own

Signs of nutrient deficiency

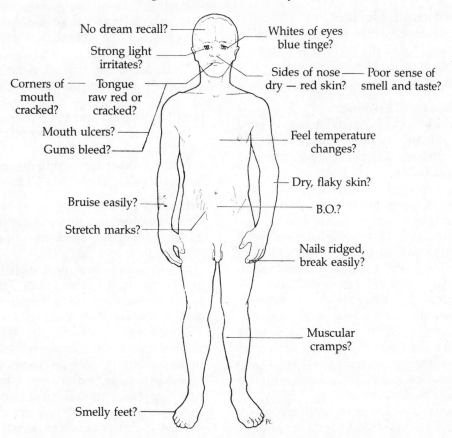

No dream recall?
Strong light irritates?
Corners of mouth cracked?
Tongue raw red or cracked?
Mouth ulcers?
Gums bleed?
Whites of eyes blue tinge?
Sides of nose dry — red skin?
Poor sense of smell and taste?
Feel temperature changes?
Dry, flaky skin?
Bruise easily?
Stretch marks?
B.O.?
Nails ridged, break easily?
Muscular cramps?
Smelly feet?

specific needs, for nutritional factors.

It is clear that if the knowledge currently available about nutrition's relationship to health and disease were applied to the populations of the world there would be a massive decline in ill health and an improvement in well-being such as has never previously been achieved. For all its mastery over so many health problems, modern medicine has failed to project the need for the achievement of positive health. Rather it has projected the need for dealing with disease. The difference is great, and those in industrialized societies who suffer massive degrees of nutritional deficiency, despite the plentiful availability of food, have the potential for such a health gain, not the least of the benefits of which would be a decline in fatigue.

Nutritional Deficiency

Each substance will be named followed by its major uses in the body, major sources and signs of deficiency, as well as any pertinent notes about it.

Vitamin B₁ (Thiamine)

This enables the brain to harness energy from glucose and protein and is involved in the transmission of impulses from and to nerve cells.

Major sources are potatoes; milk; nuts; beans; wholegrain cereals; green vegetables; fish; wheatgerm and yeast.

Signs of deficiency include loss of appetite; emotional instability; fatigue; loss of recent memory; confusion; depression; and loss of muscular co-ordination.

Chronic deficiency results in beri-beri.

A sensation of burning or tingling may be experienced in the hands, feet or mouth when there is deficiency of B₁, and such deficiency is noted most dramatically in alcoholics and in individuals who use antacids habitually.

Vitamin B₁ is lost from food in cooking especially when baking soda is used.

Normal dose for supplementation is 50mg to 100mg (RDA 1.3mg).

Vitamin B₂ (Riboflavin)

This is essential for the making of myelin (the substance which sheathes the nerves) and it assists in making energy available to the brain and body. Vitamin B₂ is also involved in the function of neurotransmitters.

Major sources are liver; milk; eggs; green vegetables; yeast and wholegrain cereals.

Deficiency can cause impaired development of the brain in children and abnormal behaviour in adults.

Signs of deficiency may include cracks at the corners of the mouth; dry cracked lips; enlargement and prominence of the taste buds on the tip of the tongue and/or a bright red smooth and sore tongue; dermatitis around the genitals; red scaly skin at the side of the nose (see also vitamin B₆, zinc and EFA); bloodshot and 'gritty' eyes; and oily skin.

Those at most risk of deficiency of vitamin B₂ include the elderly, alcohol abusers, users of the contraceptive pill, lactating women and vegetarians.

Vitamin B₂ is easily destroyed by ultraviolet light.

Normal dose for supplementation is 50mg to 100mg daily (RDA 1.8mg).

Vitamin B₃ (Niacin)

This is involved in your body's and brain's access to energy via metabolism of protein, carbohydrate and fat.

Major sources are meat; fish; wholegrains; pulses; yeast and nuts. The body also manufactures niacin from the amino acid tryptophan (see page 65).

Deficiency of vitamin B₃ results in depression; anxiety; hyperirritability and hypersensitivity; fatigue; memory loss; headaches; dementia and nerve degeneration; gastrointestinal problems with malabsorption of incompletely digested foods and consequent allergic symptoms.

Chronic deficiency results in pellagra.

Signs of deficiency may include a tongue with deep fissures in it, or one which is bright red and very smooth. There may be a tendency to burn rather than tan when exposed to direct sun.

Those most at risk are lactating mothers, the elderly and young children.

In cooking, up to a quarter of the niacin present in food is lost. Normal dose for supplementation is 100mg to 300mg daily (RDA 21mg).

Vitamin B₅ (Pantothenic acid)

This is involved in growth function and antibody production, as well as the metabolism of fats and carbohydrates. It takes part in the production of neuro-transmitters and the myelin which covers and protects nerves.

Major sources are animal protein of all sorts; yeast; pulses; royal jelly and egg yolk.

Deficiency of vitamin B₅ may result in fatigue; loss of appetite; depression; insomnia; pins and needles in limbs; nausea and adrenal gland insufficiency leading to failure to cope with stress; and possibly allergic symptoms.

Normal dose for supplementation is around 500mg to 1,000mg daily (RDA is 10mg).

Vitamin B₆ (Pyridoxine)

This is arguably the most important of the B vitamins. It helps in the manufacture of neurotransmitters and of haemoglobin for the blood, as well as in the repair of nerve structures. It is necessary for the conversion of protein into energy for use by the brain.

Major sources are liver; wholegrains; bananas; soya; fish and sweet potatoes.

Deficiency results in growth retardation in children; depression; hypersensitivity; brain abnormalities; deficiency in energy production leading to fatigue; premens-

trual tension syndrome.

Signs of deficiency may include cracking at the corner of the mouth (see also iron, folic acid and vitamin B₂); enlarged tastebuds at end of tongue which are red and sore; red greasy skin on face, especially at the side of the nose (see also vitamin B₂, zinc, EFA); dandruff (see also vitamin C, zinc, EFA); insomnia (see also magnesium and tryptophan).

Oral contraceptives often cause deficiency.

An excess can be toxic (over 1,500mg daily) although this is unlikely if taken with the full B-complex.

Normal dose for supplementation is around 100mg to 200mg (RDA is 2mg to 3mg).

Vitamin B₁₂ (cyanocobalamine)

This assists in cell replication, the repair of the myelin sheath covering the nerves, and in folic acid (see below) function.

Major food sources include meat; poultry; fish; eggs; dairy produce; and fermented soya products such as bean curd (tofu).

Deficiency produces pernicious or mega-loblastic anaemia, as well as damage to nerve structures. Symptoms could include confusion, memory loss, apathy and fatigue, paranoia, tremors and hallucinations.

Signs of deficiency may include smooth red sore tongue and recurrent mouth ulcers (see also vitamin B₂, folic acid and iron); pale appearance due to anaemia. Vegans may become deficient easily, as may those who smoke, drink heavily or use the contraceptive pill.

Normal dose for supplementation is around 100mcg (RDA is 3mcg). If it is not well absorbed in the stomach for a variety of reasons, there are forms which dissolve under the tongue. Injections of vitamin B₁₂ are commonly given to boost energy levels in fatigued people.

Folic acid

This is required for much the same purposes as vitamin B_{12}. It is involved in the manufacture of DNA and RNA, the nucleic acids which are vital for normal cell reproduction; also for the manufacture of special enzymes and other proteins. It is used in the manufacture of acetylcholine, a neurotransmitter vital for memory function.

Major food sources are liver; yeast; green leafy vegetables; meat; poultry; fish; wholegrain cereals; bananas and oranges.

Deficiency leads to growth retardation in children, and to memory loss; apathy and fatigue; irritability insomnia and depression in adults. Anaemia and oxygen deprivation to the brain may result. Neural damage results from lengthy deficiency.

Signs of deficiency may include smooth red sore tongue, cracking at the corners of the mouth, recurrent mouth ulcers, and pale appearance due to anaemia (megaloblastic).

A large loss of folic acid results from cooking and canning of food (up to two thirds). Absorption is impaired by anti-epileptic drugs and oral contraceptives. Normal dosage for supplementation is between 10mcg and 400mcg, but doses of up to 15mg are used under medical supervision (RDA is 400mcg).

Biotin

This nutrient helps the body and the brain to metabolize fat and to manufacture special fat-based materials. A healthy bowel flora will manufacture adequate biotin, but when Candida becomes active and spreads (after antibiotic treatment, or use of the contraceptive pill, for example) biotin manufacture in the bowel decreases or stops.

Major food sources include organ meats; egg yolk; wholegrain cereals; fish; fruit; vegetables; yeast and nuts.

Deficiency of biotin leads to depression; extreme fatigue; muscle pain and skin sensitivity.

Biotin is vital for preventing Candida albicans from altering from its relatively benign yeast form to its active, root producing, mycelial form, and is required regularly as part of an anti-Candida programme (see page 110). Egg white contains a substance which destroys biotin, and anyone eating whole raw eggs frequently, could become biotin deficient.

Normal dose for supplementation is 300mcg to 500mcg daily. The higher dosage is suggested for Candida treatment (RDA) is 300mcg.

Vitamin A

This is essential for eye function as well as integrity of skin and all mucous membranes of the body. It is a vital aspect of immune (defence) function; it acts as a potent anti-oxidant, protecting the body against cellular damage of many sorts. It is also involved in the manufacture of DNA and other essential proteins.

Main food sources are dark green and orange/yellow vegetables; fish; liver; and egg yolk. NOTE: the form of vitamin A found in vegetables is beta-carotene (provitamin A) which the body turns into vitamin A. This is non-toxic, whereas those forms of vitamin A derived from animal sources are toxic when taken in excess.

Deficiency leads to retarded brain development and susceptibility to infection in infants and children. In adults deficiency results in depression, apathy and fatigue, night blindness and problems with the mucous membranes.

Signs of deficiency may include gritty, bloodshot eyes, and night blindness.

Normal dose for supplementation is around 5,000IU; above 20,000IU is likely to be toxic (RDA is 4,000IU to 5,000IU). Beta carotene may be taken in doses of 25,000IU to 50,000IU daily.

Vitamin C

This is essential for adequate iron absorption; it assists folic acid function; is involved in manufacture of neurotransmitters; is a major constituent of the body's defence mechanisms (immune function) being also a powerful antioxidant; as well as assisting in maintaining structural integrity since it is a component of the 'cement' which holds us together, collagen. It is also vital to the health and function of the adrenal gland which is the major organ supporting us against the effects of stress.

Major sources in food include blackcurrants; brussels sprouts; cabbage; cauliflower; kale; mustard greens; sweet peppers; citrus fruits; most salad vegetables; and liver.

Deficiency leads to easy bruising; hypersensitivity; depression; fatigue; weakness; headaches; internal bleeding and easy haemorrhage.

Signs of deficiency may include bruising after only light blows; enlargement of veins under the tongue; and dandruff.

Supplementation is usually in doses of 550mg to 1,500mg daily but, as will be seen in the section dealing with heavy metal toxicity (page 68), it can be used pharmacologically in very high doses as well (RDA is 60mg).

Toxicity has been alleged, but the evidence for this is so poor and the degree of supplementation so high, that this can be discounted. Those people with very high uric acid levels (suffering from gout, for example) could supplement an additional 300mg of magnesium and 100mg of vitamin B_6, to ensure against the unlikely chance of kidney stone development whilst they are supplementing vitamin C.

Vitamin D
The function of this fat-soluble vitamin includes the absorption and metabolism of calcium, which in brain function is a factor of neurotransmission.

Major sources of vitamin D are in fatty fish, eggs and exposure to sunlight.

Deficiency leads to rickets in children and bone softening in adults, as well as muscular twitching and cramps. Those most at risk are the elderly, children, and people who utilize laxatives frequently, as well as pregnant and lactating women.

Supplementation is usually around 400IU (RDA is 400IU). It is toxic in high doses.

Vitamin E
The function of this fat-soluble vitamin is to act as a powerful antioxidant, increasing the life of cell tissues by slowing the degenerative processes produced by free radicals, resulting from toxicity and the ageing process. Vitamin E has much to do with oxygenation of tissues and, therefore, of energy production. Neural structures depend upon it for integrity.

Food sources include wheatgerm; sunflower seeds; eggs; wholegrain cereals; and eggs.

Women with fibrocystic breast problems are usually vitamin E deficient (as well as reacting to toxins in coffee).

Little absolute proof exists as yet for specific roles for vitamin E, although it is frequently reported to be involved in sexual performance and to be deficient in cases involving fatigue.

Toxicity is possible with very high doses, and normal supplementation is around 400IU daily. There is no RDA.

Vitamin K
This is essential for normal blood clotting.

It is found in large quantities in leafy vegetables and cereals.

Deficiency is unlikely since it can also be manufactured in the bowel by friendly bacteria.

It is not usually available separately for supplementation.

If bruising is occurring without much cause and this is associated with fatigue, then vitamin C and zinc should help. If it doesn't it is possible that vitamin K may be deficient. A medical check is necessary to establish this.

Vitamin F
(better known as Essential Fatty Acids)

There are two essential fatty acids, so called because the body cannot make them from other fats, and they are vital to health. These are linoleic acid and linolenic acid. They form vital structural parts of the cells and are essential for the manufacture of specific biological materials such as the prostaglandins. There are more than fifty different prostaglandins identified to date, the roles of which include the prevention of 'stickiness' of platelets in the blood.

Deficiency of EFAs involves chronic degenerative diseases, including arthritic problems; cardiovascular disease; psychiatric disease; diabetes; skin diseases; auto-immune diseases (colitis, rheumatoid arthritis etc.); allergies; PMT; behavioural problems; gastrointestinal problems and recurrent infection.

Low levels of some of the prostaglandins are a specific feature in particular health problems. For example prostaglandin E1 (PGE1), which has an anti-inflammatory role, is found to be low in depressives, allergic people, diabetics, alcoholics, people with hardening of the arteries — all of which are likely to produce symptoms of fatigue.

A further series of substances produced from EFAs derived from a different source, are thromboxanes. These are involved in inflammation and pain production, as well as increased 'stickiness' of the blood. The relationship between PGE1 and the thromboxanes is critical in terms of health and well-being.

The form of EFA which allows increased production of thromboxanes and decreased production of PGE1 is called arachidonic acid and this derives largely from meat. The type of EFA which produces increase PGE1 derives largely from plant foods, notably the oil of evening primrose and blackcurrants, or from cold water fish sources.

The minerals zinc and magnesium, and the vitamins B_3 and C, are essential for adequate PGE1 production. Vitamin E reduces the production of inflammatory substances.

EFA supplementation has been found helpful in the following conditions: eczema; hyperactivity in children; dandruff and dry skin; brittle finger nails; recurrent infections; easy bruising; schizophrenia; increased levels of blood fats; inflammatory conditions; certain kidney conditions; angina; multiple sclerosis; PMT; benign breast disease; diabetes; obesity etc.

Suggested dosage of evening primrose oil suggested is between 500mg and 2,000mg daily. Oil derived from cold water fish may be supplemented at a dosage of 4 to 8 capsules daily.

People with epilepsy should not take EFA supplements without guidance. Nutrients which enhance EFA metabolism are as follows (adult dosage); zinc (15mg); magnesium (200mg); vitamin C (500mg); vitamin E (200IU); selenium (100mcg); vitamin B_3 (50mg); vitamin B_6 (50mg); biotin (500mcg).

Iron

The functions of iron in the body are multiple. It is a component of enzymes, is necessary for the production of haemoglobin in red blood cells, and is a major element in the energy cycles of the body. Deficiency is common in women due to menstrual loss and this leads to anaemia which deprives cells of oxygen and in turn leads to fatigue. In children this leads to hyperactivity, loss of appetite, learning difficulties and headaches.

Sources of iron in food are organ meat; oatmeal; molasses; and dark green vegetables. We tend to absorb approximately a third of the iron in meat and a tenth of the iron from vegetables, although this can be increased by taking vitamin C at mealtimes.

Signs of deficiency may include a smooth red tongue; recurrent mouth ulcers; pale appearance and brittle nails.

Those most at risk include the elderly; premenopausal women; teenagers; people using aspirin frequently; pregnant and lactating women.

Supplemental iron is recommended only under medical guidance, since toxicity is possible (RDA is 18mg daily). As suggested above, increased use of vitamin C at mealtimes enhances iron absorption.

Calcium
Calcium is essential for healthy bones, teeth, nerve and muscle function as well as many other body processes.

Sources from food include vegetables (cabbage family, apples); pulses; dairy produce; fortified bread; and hard water.

Absorption is hampered by lack of vitamin D (sunshine vitamin) or excessive fibre in the diet.

Deficiency leads to muscular spasms and a tendency to cramps. Chronic deficiency results in rickets in children and osteomalacia and osteoporosis in adults. In the early stages of calcium deficiency there would be a tendency for muscles to become easily fatigued.

Those most at risk of deficiency are the elderly; teenagers and those who habitually use laxatives or antacids containing aluminium; smokers; pregnant women; vegetarians; and people using diuretics.

Supplementation is suggested at rates of 1g to 1½g daily. The RDA is variable (more in pregnancy etc.) at around 800mg.

Magnesium
This is an essential element of cells, required for production and function of many enzymes, and it is present in bone. It helps the brain derive energy from nutrients.

Major sources in food include green leafy vegetables; cereals; nuts; pulses; and seafood.

Deficiency leads to depression, lethargy and fatigue, as well as confusion, and sometimes epileptic seizures.

Those most at risk of deficiency include heavy drinkers; people using oral contraceptives; and those using diuretics.

Supplemental levels suggested are 500mg to 750mg (roughly half the amount of calcium supplementation). As a rule when calcium is supplemented magnesium should also be supplemented.

Together with potassium it is suggested as a useful supplement for fatigue (see Potassium for details) (RDA is 300mg). Use magnesium aspartate for best results in fatigue.

Manganese
This plays a major part in the role of insulin which controls blood sugar levels (see Hypoglycaemia and Fatigue) it is also vital for integrity of muscles and ligaments. It is a factor in the supply of energy to the brain.

Food sources are green leafy vegetables; wholegrain cereals; nuts and meat. Deficiencies are associated with glucose intolerance; disc and cartilage problems; reduced brain function; reduced fertility; and growth retardation.

Supplementation is suggested at a rate of 10mg (RDA 2.5mg).

Potassium
This is the commonest deficiency found in fatigued people. It is essential for normal nerve function, is found in most cells of

the body and counterbalances sodium in the body economy.

It is found in most foods, especially dairy produce; potatoes; grapes; bananas; tomatoes; apricots; peaches; walnuts; and vegetables.

Deficiency produces symptoms of weakness; loss of appetite; nausea; listlessness and fatigue. Neuromuscular weakness and fatigue are also noted.

It is reported by many clinicians to help fatigue when supplemented in association with magnesium (Rob Krakovitz MD, *High Energy*, Ballantyne Books, New York, 1987). The form recommended is potassium/magnesium aspartate in a daily formulation containing 400mg magnesium and 200mg potassium.

Those most at risk of potassium deficiency include people taking: laxatives regularly; aspirin in high doses; cortisone type medication; antibiotics regularly; the drug levodopa; certain diuretics (some contain additional potassium to make up that lost, and this will usually be indicated by the letter K at the end of the name of the product. K is the chemical letter for potassium.)

Supplementation is suggested at a dosage of 200mg to 2,000mg. Higher levels are desirable if sodium is high in the diet, as this helps counterbalance some of the negative effects of excessive sodium. Use potassium aspartate for best results in fatigue.

Sodium

This is present in most body fluids and is required to maintain the fluid balance of the body. It is essential for normal nerve transmission. It is found in most foods, with excessive amounts in processed foods. Addition of salt at mealtimes is never necessary.

Deficiency leads to loss of appetite; muscle cramps; headaches; weakness; fatigue; nausea; vomiting and impaired sensory function.

Most at risk of depletion of sodium are those taking certain diuretics, or those drugs which cause fluid retention. Also at risk are people who sweat a great deal, especially if they are also on a low sodium diet.

The RDA is around 4g daily. Most people get about five times this amount due to added salt in food.

Zinc

Zinc is one of the most important trace elements in man. It is also one of those shown to be inadequate in many diets in industrialized countries. Zinc is required for the manufacture and function of over 20 important enzymes. It plays a vital role in wound healing and is a major component of the immune system. It plays an important role in maintaining pancreatic function, an organ which bears much of the strain in dealing with high and low sugar problems, often so much a feature of fatigue. It is also a factor in release of energy for the brain, from glucose and proteins.

Good food sources include oysters; pumpkin seeds; ginger root; muscle meat; egg yolk; wholewheat; oats; soya beans; nuts; shrimps; garlic; pulses; carrots; and potatoes.

Deficiency of zinc can be an element in a number of conditions including: retarded growth and brain development; anorexia; infertility; hair loss; a variety of skin conditions; immune deficiencies; fatigue; behavioural and sleep disturbances; impaired sense of smell and taste; impaired wound healing; dandruff; gastrointestinal problems such as diarrhoea.

Signs of deficiency may include white flecks in the finger nails; poor sense of taste and smell; poor hair growth; night blindness; greasy-red areas on the face/sides of nose; brittle nails; eczema/dry skin.

Phytic acid in cereals may inhibit uptake of zinc from the gut. Iron and copper are antagonistic to zinc (and vice versa), therefore supplementation of any of these needs to be kept apart.

People at most risk of deficiency include those on high fibre diets (especially if a lot of bran is used); those taking iron tablets; those with malabsorption problems; those with weak digestions (inadequate hydrochloric acid); those with liver disease such as cirrhosis, or with pancreatic disease; the elderly; users of contraceptive medication; pregnant or lactating women and vegetarians.

Supplementation of around 20mg to 40mg daily is suggested. Toxic levels are possible, so additional intake is not advised.

Zinc is better absorbed at night and supplementation should be last thing at night on an empty stomach. Supplementation in the forms of zinc picolinate or zinc orotate is recommended.

Copper

Copper is essential for the proper working of major enzyme systems and aspects of the body's immune function. It is needed for availability of energy for the brain, and maintenance of myelin, the insulator of the nervous system.

Food sources include nuts; shellfish; pulses; and fruits.

Deficiency leads to anaemia, and consequently fatigue; musculoskeletal defects; nervous system problems; infertility cardiovascular problems and raised cholesterol levels; immune deficiency.

Deficiency can result from excessive zinc supplementation. Toxicity is easily produced and supplementation should only be undertaken under guidance. Use of the contraceptive pill raises copper levels and thus depresses zinc (as does pregnancy). Postnatal depression may involve an imbalance between these nutrients.

Selenium

The only proven role of selenium in humans is as part of the enzymes which protect cells against oxidative damage (free radicals).

Selenium deficiency is known to increase risk of heart disease (cardiomyopathy and cardiovascular disease) and cancer.

Selenium is found in wholegrain (if soil supplies are adequate); garlic; and fish.

Selenium has an antifungal effect and can be applied directly to lesions such as ringworm. Its use in commercial anti-dandruff products is well known, although why it helps this condition is not known. Selenium is a powerful detoxifying agent against mercury toxicity (see page 69).

It should always be supplemented together with vitamin E, with which it has a synergistic action (they enhance each other's effects). It is itself toxic if used excessively.

Supplementation should not exceed 200mcg daily. People sensitive to yeast should avoid the selenomethionine form, and obtain selenite or selenate instead.

Iodine

Iodine is vital for thyroid production of hormones (see Thyroid Problems and Fatigue), thus having major implications for fatigue.

It is found naturally in seaweed; seafoods; eggs; pineapple; some green vegetables (spinach, green peppers); and wholewheat bread, as well as in iodized salt.

Some soils are deficient in iodine and there will, in consequence, be an increase in the incidence of goitre (enlarged thyroid) in such areas.

Excessive amounts of iodine produce acne and also suppress thyroid function, which allows for its use when the gland is overfunctioning (thyrotoxicosis). Continued high dosage can lead to goitre just as effectively as can deficiency.

A daily amount of 100mcg to 200mcg is more than adequate.

Chromium

This is part of the glucose tolerance factor (see Hypoglycaemia and Fatigue) which keeps sugar metabolism normal. Insulin becomes ineffective when chromium is deficient, leading to fatigue.

Good sources are found in yeast; black pepper; calf's liver; wheatgerm; wholegrain breads; and cheese.

Supplementation should be in the form of GTF (glucose tolerance factor) chromium unless there is a sensitivity to yeast, in which case another form should be found which is not derived from yeast.

A daily amount of 500mcg is adequate for supplementation.

Germanium

This little-known element has been shown to have profound influence on the energy cycles of the body and to have major implications for those with chronic fatigue since it improves function without increasing oxygen demand.

Best food sources are garlic and ginseng.

Germanium has been shown not to accumulate in the body, thus presenting no toxic threat; to have powerful detoxifying properties against both mercury poisoning and radiation exposure; to be immune system enhancing, oxygen enriching, and to have powerful pain-killing properties. It has been successfully used in treating Candida albicans overgrowth. Japanese research has shown it effective when used in treating many serious conditions, including arthritis, senile osteoporosis and cancer, where its dramatic antitumour and pain-killing ability, in high doses, is proven. It is important to obtain germanium organic form. It is a highly desirable addition to the supplementation programme of anyone with fatigue.

Dosage of 100mg to 400mg daily is commonly used therapeutically, although some therapists use levels of 3,000mg or more daily in serious disease. The cost is the main obstacle to high dosage.

This is a brief survey of the vitamin and mineral elements as they relate to fatigue, and there follows a summary of those amino acids with major implications in cases of fatigue. Refer back, also, to the section on Protein in order to become aware of the many ways in which amino acids can influence not just fatigue but so many aspects of health and disease.

Amino acids

Arginine

Major symptoms of arginine deficiency include infertility due to problems in sperm motility.

Its adequate presence enhances acceleration of wound healing; thymus function; glucose tolerance; insulin production; and fat metabolism. Arginine modulates aspects of the detoxification of the body in the urea cycle (see Energy Cycles).

Excess is possible, and restriction is called for in herpes infection, as high levels encourage the virus to replicate.

Major food sources are peanuts; cashew nuts; pecan nuts; almonds; chocolate; edible seeds; soya beans; and cereals.

Schizophrenics should avoid specific supplementation.

Lysine

Lysine enhances concentration and the production of carnitine, and also enhances control of the herpes virus.

Deficiency leads to fatigue, dizziness and anaemia.

Major food sources include fish, chicken; meat; cheese; beans; brewer's yeast; and beansprouts.

Glutamine

Glutamine is a dominant amino acid in connection with the supply of energy to the brain. It readily passes the blood/brain barrier and alters there to glutamic acid, a 'unique brain fuel'.

Glutamic acid is a component of glucose tolerance factor, folic acid, and GABA, a calming agent in the brain. It detoxifies ammonia from the brain, turning it back into glutamine.

Glutamine decreases the desire for alcohol and sugar; and is useful in treating peptic ulcer and depression.

Dosage is 500mg twice daily for a week, then 500mg three times daily for another week, then 1g twice daily for a third week, as a trial of efficacy in fatigue reduction.

Phenylalanine

This gives rise to tyrosine and thence to dopamine, noradrenaline and adrenaline — major hormonal and neurotransmitter factors influencing energy production (see Depression and Fatigue and Stress and Fatigue). Phenylalanine stimulates production of substances which induce satiety, which has major implications in dealing with overweight.

It delays the degradation of the body's own painkillers, endorphins and encephalins, and is, therefore, useful in instances of chronic pain (see Pain and Fatigue).

The form used ideally is DPA; that usually supplied through Health Food Stores is DLPA which is less effective but far cheaper.

It acts as an antidepressant.

Supplemented in doses of 100mg to 500mg daily for some weeks for depression; or weight control (taken before retiring). Pain control requires doses of between 2,250mg and 4,500mg daily in divided doses away from mealtimes. It is not compatible with MAO inhibitor drugs.

Methionine

Contributes to production of vitamin B_{12}. Produces amino acids taurine and cysteine (see below), is a major detoxification agent against heavy metals, and a powerful anti-oxidant agent.

It detoxifies the liver preventing fatty build-up.

Deficiency results in atherosclerosis (degeneration of arteries).

Dosage of 200mg to 1,000mg daily.

Tryptophan

Essential for synthesis of vitamin B_3 in body, gives rise to serotonin a major neurotransmitter. It has an influence on the choice we make of foods, leading to less carbohydrate and more protein selection. Therefore, it is useful in weight control (see Obesity and Fatigue). It also increases brain uptake of vitamin B_6 and vitamin C.

Deficiency leads to craving for carbohydrates and sugars, and there is a direct relationship with emotional complaints.

Assists sleep (when combined with magnesium and vitamin B_6), and acts as an antidepressant in some cases (see Depression and Fatigue).

Avoid supplementation if pregnant. Not compatible with MAO inhibitor drugs. Dosage ranges between 300mg (general) and 1g (insomnia); 2g (pain relief) and 3g (depression). All in divided doses between meals.

Tyrosine

Tyrosine derives from phenylalanine, and itself gives rise to major thyroid hormones (see Thyroid and Fatigue) as well as dopa, dopamine, noradrenaline and adrenaline.

Deficiency leads to low body temperature; low blood pressure; and fatigue.

It aids in altering abnormal brain function through its neurotransmitter influence, and is useful in cases of depression where tryptophan is not.

Small doses are more useful in influencing neurotransmitter function than large ones.

Not compatible with MAO inhibitor drugs.

Cysteine

Together with methionine (which produces cysteine) this is major sulphur containing amino acid, thus has powerful detoxifying potential.

It is a component of glucose tolerance factor (see Hypoglycaemia and Fatigue).

Essential for the body's effective utilization of vitamin B_6.

Cysteine is often deficient in chronic disease.

Supplementation suggested in most chronic disease states, but not in diabetes without supervision.

It removes heavy metals such as mercury, lead (see Toxicity and Fatigue), and protects against the effects of smoking and alcohol. It is also involved in maintenance of insulin and enzyme adequacy.

The texture and flexibility of the skin is enhanced by its antioxidant action.

Dosage of 1g three times daily for a month suggested in chronic ill-health (together with three times this amount of vitamin C to avoid kidney damage) as well as 50mg vitamin B_6. Avoid if diabetic.

Carnitine

Carnitine is synthesized in the body from lysine and methionine, if adequate vitamin C is present.

Men have a greater need, and inadequacy leads to sperm motility depression.

It removes fatty deposits from the liver and heart, and aids in mobilizing fatty deposits in obesity. It aids heart muscles, when these are under stress due to myocardial infarction and necrosis. It is useful in cases of intermittent claudication (inadequate circulation to the legs) as well as muscular dystrophy, and it protects against alcohol damage to the liver.

Dosage of 1g to 3g daily for alcohol protection. In general 200mg three times daily, increasing to double this to improve 'brain energy'.

Glutathione

This is made up of glutamic acid, cysteine and glycine. It is a free radical deactivator and detoxifying agent (heavy metals etc.); and delays the ageing process and enhances the immune function.

Dosage 1g to 3g daily.

This is not a complete and comprehensive list of all amino acid functions but a selection of those most pertinent to fatigue. For further information, see my books *Amino Acids in Therapy* (Thorsons, 1985) or *The Healing Power of Amino Acids* (Thorsons, 1989).

There are, as has been indicated above, special needs for particular nutrients at certain times.

It is not possible to summarize all of the myriad variations, but the list below will describe the major requirements for additional supplementation during particular stages of life:

Special requirements for nutrients

Infancy and Childhood: Adequate protein and complex carbohydrates; EFAs; vitamins A, C, D; calcium and zinc.

Adolescence: Adequate protein and energy foods (complex carbohydrates, unsaturated fats); vitamin C; calcium; phosphorus; zinc. There is a high degree of calcium deficiency in the diets of adolescents.

Menstruation: All B vitamins with emphasis on folic acid; vitamins A and C; EFAs; iron; iodine; magnesium; zinc.

Fertility: Vitamin B complex; vitamins A, C and E; zinc; iodine; selenium; germanium; amino acids arginine and carnitine.

Pregnancy: Protein and complex carbohydrates; vitamin B complex; vitamins C, E and K; calcium; zinc; iron.

Lactation: Complex carbohydrates, proteins and desirable fats; vitamins B_1, B_2, B_3, C and D; iron.

Menopause: Vitamins C, D and E; calcium; zinc; amino acid tripeptide glutathione.

Ageing: Vitamin B complex; vitamins A, C and E; calcium; magnesium; selenium; germanium; iron; glutathione and/or cysteine; carnitine.

In chronic ill-health: Add high dosage, balanced formula, free form amino acids, as described in the section on Protein and Energy, plus B-complex; Beta carotene; vitamin C; zinc; selenium; calcium and magnesium; manganese; Essential Fatty Acids; potassium.

DEFICIENCY CHECKLIST

The following list of signs and symptoms all relate to nutritional deficiencies. If any of them is a common feature in your life then almost certainly you need to change the food you eat and possibly consider supplementation as indicated in this book. Check your answers again six months after changing your diet.

Are your nails ridged and/or do your nails break very easily?
Are there white flecks in your nails?
Do your gums bleed when you clean your teeth?
Do you get mouth ulcers?
Are there stretch marks on your skin?
Do you get cracks at the corners of your mouth?
Do you get dry, irritated skin at the sides of your nose?
Does strong light irritate you?
Are your eyes, mouth or nose dry?
Is your sense of taste or smell poor?
Do you get muscular cramps?
Is your skin very dry, flaky etc.?
Do you have a strong body odour?
Do your feet smell strongly?
Do you bruise easily?
Do you remember your dreams when you wake?
Are the whites of your eyes blue tinged?
Is your tongue bright red and very smooth?
Is your tongue deeply fissured ('geographical tongue')?
Are you very sensitive to changes in temperature?

CHAPTER 9

Toxicity, detoxification and fatigue

When we speak of toxicity it may be in reference to those irritants, poisons and toxins which accumulate in the body tissues as a result of our normal biological functioning which, for one reason or another are not adequately eliminated or detoxified. Or, it may be toxicity which accumulates in the body due to unnatural exposure to substances in the environment or our food.

It is reasonable to assume that most people living in industrialized societies are to some extent contaminated by environmental poisons in this manner, even when good wholesome food is eaten as a norm. If, however, dietary excellence is not a feature of a person's life, then toxicity is usually coupled with nutrient deficiency, resulting in a compounding of negative effects in health terms, with fatigue a major outcome of this.

Over a period of years our bodies accumulate the debris of the toxins in:

● **The air we breathe. Most air in cities and much in the countryside is polluted with heavy metals such as lead and petrochemical and other toxic material.**
● **The food we eat. Most food is contaminated with pesticides, preservatives and other chemicals, unless** organically grown and produced.
● **The contaminated water we drink. Most water in cities or near heavy industry contains petrochemical and heavy metal contamination.**
● **The poison we ingest through junk foods, stimulant drinks and social drugs (e.g. tobacco and alcohol).**
● **The poisons we accumulate from the medical drugs we use.**
● **The naturally occurring toxins (i.e. metabolic waste products) which are not efficiently eliminated because of nutritional deficiencies, sedentary living, inadequate exercise and use of social drugs (coffee, alcohol, etc.).**

All of these build up toxic presence in the body and influence its function negatively, none more so than toxic heavy metals, examples of which include:

Lead
This highly toxic metal is found in the human body of all the inhabitants of the planet, to an extent where levels are some 500 to 1,000 times higher than in people who lived in prehistory.

Lead interferes with vital enzyme functions in the body, especially those dependent upon zinc. Among the effects of lead toxicity are learning and behaviour problems, including hyperactivity in children; delinquent and violent behaviour in adolescents; and depressed immune function.

The major symptoms to be seen in low-level lead exposure are lethargy, tiredness, aches and pains, depression, and suscepti-bility to infection. Assessment of lead toxicity can be performed by a simple hair analysis in which a gram of hair from the nape of the neck is analysed by special techniques. If positive then another sample may be requested, from pubic hair, to confirm the finding.

To eliminate excessive lead from the body, detoxification is required. This should ideally involve both an oral chel-ation programme, as well as intravenous chelation if the condition is serious. If the condition is assessed as low level lead (or other heavy metal) toxicity, then oral chelation should prove adequate, for fortunately there are a number of nutrient factors which have specific detoxifying effects on toxic metals (see pages 71-72).

Aluminium

This toxic metal is widely found in the modern environment. Among the sources which should be avoided is possible are:

Aluminium cooking utensils (it is leached out when acidic foods are cooked in them); aluminium cans used for food and drinks; aluminium salts added to table salt to prevent moisture attraction; in proprietary antacid medication sold freely worldwide, and taken by the ton annually in most industrialized countries; added to flour in the bleaching process; in underarm and deodorant sprays; in city tap water; medical use for people on dialysis.

The toxic effects of aluminium are mainly on the central nervous system, and the major disease with which it is now firmly associated is Alzheimer's disease (presenile dementia) in which the brain substance becomes a tangled mass of non-functioning tissue leading inexorably to total inability to function. Hormonal and liver dysfunction is also a feature of aluminium toxicity.

Prevention is the best approach, and so avoidance is suggested of the various sources outlined above, most notably aluminium cooking utensils. Glass or porcelain is the safest medium.

Cadmium

This toxic metal may reach us from water supplies, breathing tobacco smoke, working with plastics, paints, rubber, plated ware, insecticides and solder. It is present in high levels in some foods such as oysters, coffee and tea, some tinned foods, cola drinks (not all) and gelatine (used in jellies).

The signs of cadmium toxicity include high blood pressure, with a wide variety of other symptoms, including fatigue.

Cigarette smoke is probably the most dangerous source for most people, since when inhaled over half of the toxic metal is retained, whereas only a little is absorbed from the bowel when it is ingested in food form. Second-hand smoke is as toxic as smoking the cigarette itself, so it is wise to avoid smoky atmospheres.

Removal from the system, and deactivat-ing its toxic effects, is achieved by use of vitamin C and zinc. Doses of these should be moderate to high for some time, if cad-mium toxicity is suspected or confirmed by hair analysis. One to five grams of vitamin C daily in divided doses, and 25mg to 50mg daily of zinc.

Mercury

This is probably the most toxic of all metals and the most insidious, in that most adults have had large quantities inserted into their mouths in the form of amalgam fillings from which mercury is now known to leach, and to thus poison the recipient by slow degrees. Some forms of mercury are more toxic than others. Ethyl and methyl mercury which are used in seed dressing to prevent mould development before sowing are extremely poisonous.

Seafood is a major source of mercury since the seas have become contaminated with industrialized wastes containing it.

The results of mercury poisoning are severe nervous system damage, mental incapacity and symptoms resembling multiple sclerosis, often with a major feature being extreme fatigue.

The source of toxicity from amalgams has long been denied by dental authorities although they go to great lengths to warn dentists and their assistants about mercury's dangers. A recent development has at last proved that officialdom has awoken to the risks involved. In 1987 (May) the health authorities in Sweden announced that pregnant women would no longer receive amalgam fillings and that over a period of several years, as alternative materials were assessed, use of all amalgams in the country would cease. This example will doubtless be followed by other countries. This is fine for the future but it still leaves many hundreds of tons of mercury in the mouths of the world's population.

The period of major risk is when fillings are being put in or changed, when large amounts of powdered mercury or mercury in solution are ingested or inhaled. A rubber dam should be used in the mouth to prevent swallowing of such material.

In the USA, and in Europe, there are dental practitioners who have converted their practices to the sole job of replacing amalgams, using gold, porcelain or plastic materials instead. This replacement has to be performed in a special manner since it has been found that some teeth with fillings have a high, and some a low, electrical potential. The teeth should all be measured for this and the quarter (quadrant) of the mouth in which the teeth with the lowest potential lie should have its amalgam fillings changes first, in order to avoid sometimes drastic reactions.

Detoxification (Vitamin C saturation)

Mercury toxicity can be reduced by using high dosage vitamin C and vitamin E (usually coupled with selenium).

There is a caution, however, regarding vitamin C if mercury exposure is continuing, since it seems under these conditions to increase tissue absorption. Thus, if mercury levels are high and the exposure is no longer current an amount of *vitamin C* should be taken equivalent to tissue saturation. This is measured by increasing the dosage until bowel tolerance is reached. Starting with a gram every two hours during waking hours (10g to 12g daily) increase this by 2g daily until there is a looseness of the bowels or actual diarrhoea. This is bowel tolerance and the dose should be reduced to what it was the previous day, when no looseness was noted. This level of intake is maintained until again looseness is noted indicating the body's need for vitamin C is reducing.

This method, based on the research of Dr Robert Cathcart in California, is an excellent one for finding just what vitamin C the body needs at any time of increased demand, such as stress, toxicity or infection. It can lead to intakes of heroic quantities. Up to 40g daily are not uncommon, with much higher levels in some individuals.

Such high dosage would probably not continue for more than a few weeks; bowel tolerance would indicate the time to gradually reduce to normal levels of intake, which could be as low as half a gram daily.

Vitamin E is known to prevent the nervous system damage caused by mercury, and dosages of 500IU to 1,000IU daily, together with 100mg to 200mg of selenium (they act synergistically) is suggested.

The mineral calcium is also helpful in assisting mercury elimination and this should be taken (together with magnesium with which it works in the body) in doses of 1g of calcium daily (plus half a gram of magnesium). This should be taken before retiring to bed, when it will be found to enhance sleep.

Many individuals with Candida and/or post-viral fatigue syndrome symptoms have been shown to improve dramatically once mercury is chelated out of their systems, and they have had their dental fillings changed.

General rules relating to heavy metal toxicity elimination should include:

● **Avoidance of exposure.**

● **A dietary pattern which encourages excellent bowel function. This should, therefore, include a high fibre element (fresh fruits and vegetables, pulses and wholegrain cereals, especially oats) as well as the introduction of live bacteria cultures such as acidophilus (see Candida albicans and Fatigue).**

● **Nutritional excellence is called for, and the general advice contained in this section and the book as a whole should be adopted.**

● **Exercise is essential as long as this is within the limits of your current health status. Building up towards aerobic exercise performance three times weekly is the ideal (see page 21).**

● **Use of oral and/or intravenous chelation (see below).**

● **Fasting (see page 72-74).**

● **Vitamin C saturation (see above).**

Oral chelation

Chelation is derived from the word for 'claw' in Greek, indicating what the intent is. This is that the substance will grab hold of the toxic element and assist it out of the body.

This can be done in a number of ways. For example, the use of oatmeal porridge is a chelating agent, in as much as it assists any metals in the gut to the outside world.

A similar effect is experienced when foods containing pectin or algin (two mucilaginous fibres) are eaten. Thus, apples and seaweed have specific and strong chelating effects on substances in the bowel.

A specific formulation of nutrients has been devised which achieves optimal oral chelation of substances in the blood stream, and which is suitable for home use.

The daily amount which should be taken of this formulation is around 30g, which is equivalent to about an ounce. It is suggested that enough be mixed together to last for a month, and that this be kept refrigerated. It can be eaten mixed in cereal or yogurt, or mixed in a fruit juice.

ORAL CHELATION FORMULA

Quantities for daily use are given next to individual constituents and this should be multiplied to assess amounts required to make enough to last a week, a month etc.

4g lecithin (obtain from health food store, ensuring that this is high in phosphatidyl choline. It may be in the form of capsules or granules).

12g coarsely chopped sunflower seeds (this is a source of linoleic acid and potassium and should be obtained from a health food store).

5g debittered brewer's yeast (this is a source

of selenium, chromium and B vitamins. It should not be used by anyone with a Candida problem or who is allergic to yeasts. It is obtainable from pharmacists or health food stores).

2g bone meal (as a source of calcium and magnesium; obtain from health food stores).

5g raw wheatgerm (as a source of vitamin E, obtainable from health food stores).

500mg vitamin C (in the form of sodium ascorbate; obtainable from health stores or pharmacists in powder form, ideally).

100IU vitamin E (in capsule form from health food stores. Ensure that this is D-alpha tocopherol).

25mg zinc (in the form of zinc picolinate or zinc gluconate, from health food stores or pharmacists).

This mixture should be blended together and refrigerated. Use 30g daily for a chelating effect, as well as aerobic exercises three times weekly for not less than 30 minutes. In addition a daily supplement of methionine or cysteine or glutathione should be taken. These are sulphur-rich amino acids which chelate heavy metal as well as other toxic elements.

Dosage should be 1g daily of methionine or 1½g of cysteine, or 1½g of glutathione, with water, away from mealtimes.

Intravenous chelation

This method is now being used to improve circulatory conditions by removing plaque material from arteries which have become blocked (see *How to Avoid Heart Disease* by Colin Goodliffe, Blandford Press, 1987). It was, however, first developed in the 1940s as a means of eliminating lead from the system, a purpose for which it is still uniquely well suited. It is also excellent for removal of other toxic metals amenable to access from the bloodstream.

The method involves the infusion into the venous system of a liquid containing the chemical EDTA (an artificial amino acid). The process takes some hours, during which time the patient reclines and relaxes. The infusion is repeated several times over a period of some weeks until levels of toxic metals are reduced.

In treating circulatory problems, up to 30 infusions are often given over a period of several months, during which time remarkable improvements in circulatory and heart function are often seen. Goodliffe mentions this as being a safe alternative to by-pass surgery.

There are many centres in the USA where chelation is carried out, but only a few in the UK where it is available under medical supervision, in London and the North of England.

General detoxification fasting and modified fasting

Fasting is a means of general detoxification which is as old as mankind. Most animals when ill will instinctively refuse food until the self-healing mechanisms of their bodies have done their work.

Fasting at home is not suggested for more than a 48-hour period if unsupervised.

The ideal method of fasting is in an institutional setting such as a health spa, where the fast may be undertaken, together with rest and relaxation, in a pleasant atmosphere with treatment staff available in case of need. In such surroundings fasts of 20 or 30 days are not uncommon for serious health problems.

In the context of self-treatment detoxification, a short fast, repeated at regular intervals, provides a safe alternative. But, no one should attempt a self-help fast if they are not adequately nourished. You should be well rested and in a relaxed frame of mind before beginning.

FASTING ROUTINE

• Begin the fast the night before by having a light meal, such as salad, a bowl of yogurt (natural, live) fruit or a vegetable soup.

• Whilst fasting drink at least 4 pints of water (or other liquid, see below for variations on liquids) daily, and not more than 8 pints.

• Liquid should be consumed at roughly two hourly intervals, or whenever desired.

• In order to ensure continued bowel function it is desirable to follow one or other of the following options:

(a) Have a warm-water enema on each day, whether the bowels function normally or not (see method below).

(b) Take a dose of psyllium seed powder (obtain from health food stores) three times per day during the fast. This should be the powdered version of psyllium seeds and not the husks or capsules. Mix in a blender a tablespoonful of the powder with 8 fl oz spring water and drink this straight down. This provides bulk, which is totally non-absorbed, for the bowel.

• Ensure that duties are light when fasting. There is no need to stay in bed, but plenty of rest is needed. A little fresh air and exercise is permitted if no exertion is involved.

• No driving should be done whilst fasting as you may feel light headed.

• Put up with slight symptoms of nausea and headache if they arise. This is evidence of detoxification and should not be treated by any medication.

• Stop all medication during the fast. If medication has been prescribed then take advice as to the advisability of fasting and the cutting off of medication.

• Avoid smoking of all sorts during fasting.

• The first meal after a fast should be a light one, such as yogurt or vegetable soup or a baked apple. When this is accepted and digested a light meal with protein such as an egg (boiled) or a little steamed fish could be eaten. After that return to a normal diet.

If the fast began on Friday evening, for example, and the abstinence period ran until Sunday evening when the fast was broken, a normal breakfast on Monday morning would be acceptable, followed by normal work and eating thereafter.

This pattern of 48 hours of detoxification should be carried out once a month at least.

If a longer period is needed this, too, can be undertaken at home, under the guidance of a qualified practitioner (registered naturopath, or a doctor with experience of fasting such as a clinical ecologist).

NOTE: It is suggested that a coffee enema be used twice weekly, in between fasting periods, as an additional detoxification process.

Details are given on page 75, along with instructions of how to take a conventional enema.

Fasting variations
A water fast
A fast on water only is the best for speedy detoxification. It is also the least comfortable, since as detoxification begins there is, after the first 24 hours, commonly experienced a general feeling of nausea and lassitude, often accompanied by headache. This tends to pass fairly rapidly and, on a long fast, the period after the third day is frequently one in which a renewed sense of energy and well-being is strongly felt.

However, since the self-administered fast ends after two days this good feeling is seldom noted until several such fasts have been undertaken and detoxification is progressing well.

If the moderate discomfort of this detoxification process can be borne, the water fast is the recommended route. If not, then one of the more gentle alternatives suggested below should be tried. Although effective, these are slower in their detoxification effects.

When water is used this must be distilled water or spring water; never tap water. The total quantity should not exceed 8 pints daily or be less than 4 pints daily. It is a good idea to add a teaspoonful of ascorbic acid powder (vitamin C) to each quart of water consumed. Use either calcium or sodium ascorbate powder in this quantity to assist detoxification.

Potassium broth fast
This involves the use of the juice (broth), left after cooking several vegetables, as a substitute for water during the fast. It is tasty and carries a plentiful supply of nutrients derived from the vegetables, making the fast less arduous.

To make the broth wash and chop four large carrots, a few sprigs of parsley, two stalks of celery, six spinach leaves and two of any of the following: asparagus spears, potato skins, courgette (zuccini), lettuce leaves, beet tops, onion, turnip tops. There should be sufficient for four cupsful, and this should be added to one and a half quarts of water in a stainless steel or Pyrex saucepan, with no seasoning apart from a clove or two of garlic, if desired. Bring to the boil and simmer for 30 minutes. Strain the liquid and discard the vegetable remnants, keeping just the broth. Refrigerate, and warm as needed.

If constipation is a problem, then a tablespoon of flaxseed (linseed) and a tablespoonful of bran can be soaked overnight in the broth and the liquid drunk as indicated below. In this case do not chew the bran or seeds at the time of consumption.

If this option is followed then the psyllium seed powder, recommended on page 73, is not needed. Use the broth as the sole liquid intake, or alternate it with plain distilled or spring water during the day, so that at least two pints of broth and two pints of water are consumed daily. Each mouthful of broth should be retained in the mouth for a period of not less than five seconds to mix it well with saliva.

Modified juice fast
Use of a dilute (50/50 with spring water) juice, such as apple, pear, carrot or tomato, instead of water alone, is suggested if low blood sugar is a problem. Drink at least four pints daily at two hourly intervals. Try to keep each mouthful of the juice in the mouth for a lengthy period, even 'chewing' it. This ensures maximum benefit and ease of digestion, and helps avoid gas.

Mono-diet fasting
An alternative to a liquid fast is a mono-diet in which one substance alone is consumed. The most reliable of these, for the purpose of detoxification, is plain brown rice, and a small amount, with no seasoning, should be eaten whenever you feel hungry. If you feel thirsty, drink plain spring or distilled water.

No more than a pound of rice per day

(uncooked weight) should be eaten. This can have a dramatic beneficial effect on high blood pressure, and it is an extremely powerful detoxifier.

Enema instructions
The idea of using an enema is to ensure that toxic wastes which are being released into the bowel do not stay there and become reabsorbed. Thus, whether or not a bowel movement has occurred, it is necessary and desirable for an enema to be taken at least once daily (and twice if nausea is a symptom) during the fast.

You can either use a syringe or a gravity bag. Such a bag needs to be suspended so that the warm (body heat) water will drain down the applicator tube when the clamp on it is released. Whichever method you use it is suggested that you lie, knees bent, on your right side, on a thick towel, and use a gentle lubricant to ease the end of the applicator tube past the anus into the rectum. At this point you release the clamp on the tube which allows the water to enter your lower colon. This will best be achieved if the bag is suspended some two feet above your body level.

If you use a syringe, then the water should be squeezed into the rectum slowly, to allow for absorption without undue discomfort, distension or cramping. About a quart of water should be used, and the process will take several minutes. Do not hurry as cramp could result. If a gas-like pressure or cramp is experienced, then gently rub your abdomen to alleviate it. If water starts to run out of your rectum, raise the lower part of your body to allow gravity to drain the water in the colon upwards to counteract its tendency to run out. Retain the fluid for at least five minutes before voiding it into the toilet bowl.

Enema variations
• Acidophilus enema
If you are suffering from Candida overgrowth (see page 110), then dissolve a large teaspoonful of high potency acidophilus powder (Superdophilus is recommended, see page 115) into the quart of water before insertion into the bowel. Retain for as long as possible, ten to fifteen minutes if you can, before voiding. This helps to repopulate the lower bowel with 'friendly' bacteria which are antagonistic towards Candida.

In addition, a dessertspoonful of aloe vera juice (pure) can be added to the water to further control Candida. This type of enema can be taken once or twice daily when on a fast, and several times weekly at other times until the Candida is under control. It is not intended to be a means of cleansing the bowel, but rather a way of introducing 'friendly' bacteria at the other end of the digestive tract, to support that being taken orally.

• Coffee enema
If nausea is a major symptom, along with tiredness, and you have a history of liver trouble, then it is suggested that you use a coffee enema. This has the effect of stimulating the production of bile from the liver, much of which will carry with it large amounts of toxic debris. This is probably the only reasonable way to use coffee at all.

The renowned researcher into natural methods of treating cancer, the late Dr Max Gerson, used this as a part of his comprehensive detoxification programme (along with juices and other nutrients) with amazing results. His daughter continues to achieve similar results at the Gerson Clinic in Mexico.

Method: Take three tablespoons of ground (never instant) coffee and add to two pints of water. Boil for three minutes and then allow to stand for 15 minutes before sieving. One quarter of this (half a pint) should be used at body heat as an enema and retained in the bowel for not less than ten minutes. The remainder may be refrigerated, and warmed and used as needed. The enema should be administered lying on your right side with your knees pulled up. Coffee enemas should be used for detoxification of the liver and not as a means of cleansing the bowel, which is better achieved via diet (high fibre) and exercise.

Use coffee enemas daily, if needed, for detoxification between fasting periods. A sense of lightness and energy may be noted after their use.

Medically prescribed drugs and fatigue

Most medications have side-effects, and fatigue is a common one. There is also likely to be a problem when you stop using prescription medications, particularly when coming off tranquillizers.

Some commonly used drugs which have the effect of inducing *fatigue* are:

Antidepressants, especially those with a sedating action such as amitriptiline, dothiepin and trimipramine, Lithium, and Triavil.

Sedatives and hypnotics (sleeping tablets) derived from Benzodiazepam, especially in elderly people where a hangover-like symptom is frequently experienced. Some others which produce fatigue are Dalmane, Nembutal and Restovil.

Antihypertensive drugs (those which lower blood pressure) such as Inderal, methyldopa and reserpine.

Diuretics, which cause a drop in potassium and sodium.

Beta blocker drugs used in treating cardio-vascular disease, angina and high blood pressure, as well as migraine headaches. Examples are Inderal and Tenormin.

Anticonvulsant drugs, which are used in epilepsy, all cause a degree of sedation and symptoms of fatigue. Examples are Phenobarbitol and Tegretol.

Diabetic drugs, such as the long acting chlorpropamide, often accumulate and result in

hypoglycaemia (low blood sugar) and its symptoms (see page 144).

Antihistamines, which are used in treating allergies and are also found in over-the-counter cough mixtures and cold remedies, induce fatigue and drowsiness.

Analgesics and salicylates. These are pain-killers, and often produce fatigue, especially when used in large doses.

Antipsychotic drugs, such as Stelazine and Thorazine, produce major reduction in energy, along with their tranquillizing effects.

Contraceptive medication. The 'pill' causes many side-effects, not least fatigue.

Muscle relaxants, used in treating musculo-skeletal problems, such as Robaxin and Valium are likely to produce drowsiness and fatigue.

Narcotics, used in pain relief, such as Codeine and Demarol, are potent sedation agents and cause fatigue.

If you have a fatigue problem and are currently using, or have in the past used, any of these drugs, then it is likely that they have contributed to your condition.

Fatigue and withdrawal from medication

Stopping the use of drugs requires expert advice, and they should not simply be dropped from use as this could cause untoward reactions, especially if you have become dependent on them, or addicted to them.

Brenda Campbell Thomas, a therapist with wide experience of the problems associated with patients dependent on, and coming off, tranquillizers has become an expert on the subject, and many of the facts given below have been collected by her and published in articles or in private correspondence with others who are dealing with this epidemic problem.

The number of people estimated to be

addicted to tranquillizers in the UK varies from a quarter of a million to a million people. Many people become addicted to these drugs after only a short period of use. This fact was established as far back as 1978, and by 1980 it was known that at best they were effective as antidepressants for no more than four months.

Withdrawal symptoms after use of benzodiazepam drugs vary greatly from person to person and may include:

Feelings of extreme anxiety.
Sleeplessness.
Agoraphobia (fear of open spaces and crowds).
Depression.
Inability to concentrate.
Hallucinations.
Visual and perceptual problems.
Extreme sensitivity to heat, cold, light and sound.
Amnesia.
Mania, with the mind racing uncontrollably.
Loss of short term memory.
Nightmares.
Tremors and hot flushes.
Loss of appetite.
Strange tastes and difficulty in swallowing.
Nausea.
Loss of sexual drive.
Withdrawal, lack of interest and feeling.
Hyperventilation.
Hypoglycaemia.
Low blood pressure.
Extreme fatigue.

Medical experts estimate that it may take 40 days of withdrawal symptoms for each year of use of such medically prescribed drugs, before normality is restored. Many people have been taking Valium or Librium for fifteen years or more and have become totally dependent and physically, rather than psychologically, addicted to them; with the drug no longer producing any antidepressant effect. Such people may face years of withdrawal symptoms when they try to stop taking these drugs.

Despite the agony of withdrawal, almost all those people who have stopped use of such drugs declare that it was worth the effort. Many self-help groups have sprung up, and there now exist several organizations such as Tranx, Tranx Release and Release, which help people to come off medically prescribed tranquillizers (as well as other drugs in the case of Release).

It is a very sad commentary on modern medicine that people suffering from problems, which could often have been solved by non-drug means, have become dependent on and often physically addicted to drugs which produce no benefit, and often have left them with symptoms worse than those they originally had.

Fatigue is a major symptom in people using anti-depressants and it is a major symptom of withdrawal from these.

In general, a combination of nutritional supplements, counselling and sometimes methods such as acupuncture can be shown to ease the withdrawal from such drugs. The methods outlined in the sections on Depression and Fatigue and Hyperventilation and Fatigue will give guidance on long-term strategies.

CHAPTER 10

Stress and fatigue

Stress is universal. It represents anything which calls upon you or your body to adapt or to alter or to cope, in any way. We can say, therefore, that most of the things which happen to us during a normal day impose some degree of stress upon us.

Stress is not all bad, for although, let us say, having to get breakfast ready for the family, or driving the children to school, or getting the train or bus to work, or work itself, may be stressful events, they are not necessarily so in a way which causes us distress. It is rather the way we feel about these tasks, and any minor crises which may relate to them (burned breakfast, late train etc.) and our reaction to them which makes them either harmfully stressful or just examples of events which we cope with in an easy manner.

What matters in most cases is not that there is something to adapt to, or to cope with, but the manner in which this is accomplished, and the effect this has on your body.

There are, of course, stressful events which are not just a matter of coping with minor crises. A sudden bereavement, or the loss of a job or other major upheaval cannot be dismissed lightly. But the fact is that the degree of effect of even such a shattering blow as one of these events depends on your attitude. To one person it may represent a burden too great to bear, to another it would present a challenge to be overcome.

Stress is also caused by uncertainty about the future, or it may result from anger or frustration about present or past events, or from feelings of being of little worth or value in the world. It may also be the result of gnawing doubts as to whether tasks can be successfully accomplished; doubts about our ability to handle situations.

It may stem from jealousy or suspicion about the motives or behaviour of others, or from lack of satisfaction with our lives, and feelings of apparently wasted effort or time. It derives from not knowing what to do for the best, indecision, or of knowing what to do but, for any of a thousand reasons, not being able to do it. It comes out of feelings of injustice and frustration, or of being unable to effectively express feelings.

What is common to all these negative and stressful feelings? *They all represent personal responses to situations, and the response is dependent not upon the situation, but upon ourselves.* The same event will affect different people in different ways. The event is not the cause of the problem, although it may be the trigger or focal point. It is the response which matters. Responses which achieve something positive, and which do not reflect harmfully upon ourselves. This is why you should learn how to respond appropriately, both to the event, and in terms of your own best interests.

Responses to stress

Your responses to any threat or happening depend upon your attitude towards that event. You are going to be late for an appointment; miss a train; fail to do a certain job through no fault of your own, or through carelessness, be unable to keep a promise etc. Do you allow this to create in you anxiety, worry, fretting, guilt, feelings of inadequacy? Perhaps, but such reactions may also be dealt with by a rational reappraisal of the situation. A realization that you have done your best. Or even an acceptance of the fact that you have not done your best and will do so next time, and will apologize for your failure this time. In other words, you have the ability to alter the results of a potentially stressful event by altering your attitude towards it.

This, of course, will come easily to some and not so easily to others. Our upbringing, conditioning and background will determine our responses, but our realization that it is a matter of personal attitude will be a great mental leap in enabling us to reduce stress feelings in the future.

In primitive times when people were confronted by a need to adapt, alter or respond, their choices were simple. Faced with the need for shelter, they went and found it or perished. When food was wanted, the hunter-gatherer hunted or gathered, or perished. When attacked they would either run away or stay and fight. Their response was appropriate to the stressful event, and if the response was poor it meant that they perished, and this in turn ensured the survival of the fittest and improved the genetic strain.

Such immediate responses to stress are largely physical. The adrenaline (or epinephrine) flows, blood sugar is released from the liver into the bloodstream to fuel the action; heart rate and blood pressure rise to prepare for the activity to come; stomach juices cease flowing and peristalsis stops so that no energy is wasted on unnecessary activities; the pupils of the eyes dilate and the mouth goes dry; the neck and shoulder muscles tense automatically, breathing becomes more rapid and sweating starts. Thus the well-known 'fight or flight' mechanism comes into action, and stress is met by appropriate action.

New strategies needed

But the simplistic fight or flight option is not appropriate for life today. Tempting though it may be, you may not run away from or attack the traffic warden, your boss, or your husband or wife, etc. Other strategies are called for in these times. Finding shelter and providing food no longer involves piling branches together, or grubbing for roots, or stalking rabbits. The provision of these necessities now involves laborious, often tedious, work, and the filling in of many forms, and dealing with many people and situations. Even so, the reactions to all this 'stress' (the adrenaline release, blood pressure and blood sugar increase etc.) still prepares our bodies for the primitive physical response.

Some people are better than others in coping in the face of stress, and do not produce a classical reaction as described above. They cope calmly with stressful situations as though there were no real threat. The following questionnaire is to establish whether or not you react appropriately to stressful situations.

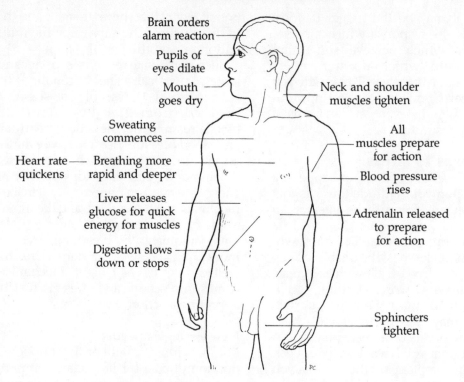

Brain orders
alarm reaction

Pupils of
eyes dilate

Mouth
goes dry

Neck and shoulder
muscles tighten

Sweating
commences

All
muscles prepare
for action

Heart rate
quickens

Breathing more
rapid and deeper

Blood pressure
rises

Liver releases
glucose for quick
energy for muscles

Adrenalin released
to prepare
for action

Digestion slows
down or stops

Sphincters
tighten

Body's reaction to stress 'fight or flight' mechanism

STRESS REACTION QUESTIONNAIRE

Answer the following by ticking (a) or (b).

1 If you have an appointment and you are kept waiting for some time, would you feel:
   (a) Slightly irritated but calm?
   (b) Edgier by the minute, inclined to walk out and/or become very nervous?

2 If you are anticipating something, pleasant or unpleasant, and are keyed up, do you get breathless, tight chested, and find yourself sighing or taking periodic deep breaths:
   (a) Occasionally or never?
   (b) Usually?

3 When upset or angry do you:
   (a) Blush slightly or not at all?
   (b) Go bright red in the face?

4 If you are anxious or frightened would you expect your face to be:
   (a) Slightly pale or unchanged?
   (b) White as a sheet?

5 If you have to speak to a group, or meet new people, or do something in public, do you get either diarrhoea or feel sick:
   (a) Sometimes or never?
   (b) Usually?

6 If you are awaiting an event, and are apprehensive, do you sweat profusely, get a funny feeling in the stomach and/or get goosepimples on the skin:
   (a) Two of these rarely, or only one of these commonly?
   (b) Usually, and then more than one of these?

7 When apprehensive of waiting for something or someone important, does your pulse race and make you aware of a pounding in the heart or head:
   (a) Sometimes and not too strongly?
   (b) Frequently?

8 Does a sudden unexpected sound make you:
   (a) React quickly and strongly?
   (b) Usually not make you react strongly?

The more (b) answers you record the more strongly you are reacting inappropriately to stress factors. The more (a) answers you record the better are your reactions to stress.

Most of us here in the twentieth century have not brought to these changed times equipment capable of dealing with the altered circumstances. Our bodies are still in the Stone Age. Change has been rapid, too rapid for evolutionary and genetic factors to keep pace. The result of our inability to freely use the mechanisms which respond to stress is the abundant presence of stress-induced disease.

The exciting thing is, though, that we can learn to lower our arousal reactions to stressful events by appropriate use of relaxation, and by behaviour modification methods.

The answer to our failure to adapt to new circumstances is that we have to give evolution a hand. We are capable of this because we have intelligence, and can alter our attitudes, and learn new coping skills, so that the new world is dealt with appropriately, and not in Stone Age terms. The irony is that the response which saved the cave dweller's life is today killing their descendents. It is now the individual who reacts slowest and is least aroused by stress who survives.

Identifying the stresses

To learn to cope you must just find out what it is that is creating in you the stress response which can so damage your physical and mental well-being, and the following questionnaire is meant to help you identify just what is happening in you. Knowing the enemy is half the battle won. There are no correct answers, only indications of how things stand with you, and your responses should aid you in identifying the areas which require attention. These are but habits of

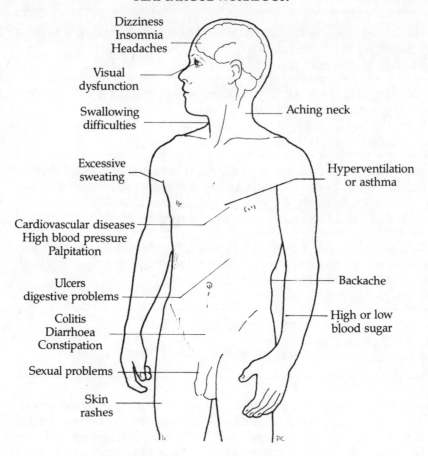

Dizziness
Insomnia
Headaches

Visual
dysfunction

Swallowing
difficulties

Aching neck

Excessive
sweating

Hyperventilation
or asthma

Cardiovascular diseases
High blood pressure
Palpitation

Ulcers
digestive problems

Backache

Colitis
Diarrhoea
Constipation

High or low
blood sugar

Sexual problems

Skin
rashes

Stress related health problems

behaviour and thought, which can be altered as newer ways are learned. Some represent a failure to appreciate the ability you have of coping with situations, and that when challenges are met this can produce a better life. One of the most important lessons you can learn is that you can cope; you really can learn appropriate responses to life's apparent threats and stresses.

STRESS IDENTIFICATION QUESTIONNAIRE

Read each statement and mark the appropriate answer.

1   I tend to worry about things that may never happen.   sometimes/frequently/constantly
2   I have thoughts which disturb and/or frighten me.   sometimes/frequently/constantly

3 I believe myself to be a failure (in marriage, work, life, accomplishments etc.). sometimes/frequently/constantly
4 I feel nervous, restless, edgy, dissatisfied. sometimes/frequently/constantly
5 I feel that there is just too much to cope with. sometimes/frequently/constantly
6 I have little confidence in myself. sometimes/frequently/constantly
7 I find it difficult to express my feelings. sometimes/frequently/constantly
8 I find myself thinking about the past/future. sometimes/frequently/constantly
9 I find it difficult to concentrate. sometimes/frequently/constantly
10 I find myself doing more than one thing at a time. sometimes/frequently/constantly

1 The commitment factor

This is found in people who find it easy to involve themselves actively in whatever is happening around them and in whatever they are doing. They are curious about, and interested in activities, people and things. If this is not a description of you then begin to practise some or all of these elements which make up 'commitment'.

2 The control factor

People who are well endowed with this factor believe and act as though they can influence the events happening around them by means of the way they act, and the things they think, say and do. If you do not feel 'in control', then start thinking that you might be in certain situations. Build on this. Decide when something will take place, however mundane, and see that it is your decision that makes it happen. Make the tea at a certain time. Go for a walk when you decide to do so. Gradually extend this decision making, this control factor, into more important areas of your life. Decide for yourself when you will take a holiday, or visit someone, or begin a new interest. Act in control and you will become more in control of your life.

3 The challenge factor

This involves having an expectation that life will change, and that the changes which take place will be stimulating to your personal development. Whatever happens in life can hold a potential for growth and increased awareness. If change is expected, and welcomed, it will cease to be seen as a negative factor.

The reverse of these three factors is seen in those people who find their lives meaningless, boring and threatening. They feel powerless in the face of the forces of life which they fear may overwhelm them. They welcome a life which offers no changes to routine. They see little prospect for developing positive benefits from such changes as take place.

The first step is to realize the need for new modes of behaviour, and the next is to begin to consciously modify your behaviour accordingly. Change by practising what is desirable and altering what is not. It is slow but sure.

Other stress coping tactics

The following have all been found to be buffers to the effects of stress.

1 Exercise

This has been found to greatly reduce the harmful effects of stress, as it provides an outlet for many of the physiological changes which are stress induced, (see page 79). Walking, running, skipping or any other non-stressful exercise is suggested. At least 30 minutes of aerobic exercise, three times weekly, with never more than a day in between sessions is the ideal.

2 Nutritional support

Many nutrients are used up excessively by the body in stressful conditions. In general vitamin C and the B vitamins are essential. A daily supplement of one gram of vitamin C and a B complex of reasonable strength is suggested (this should contain not less than 25mg of each of the main B vitamins). Attention should also be paid to overall nutrition as outlined in this book. Well nourished people cope better with stress.

3 Relaxation and meditation methods

The use of the mind to help what is a mind-induced set of circumstances, makes sense, and relaxation, meditation and guided imagery are all helpful. They reduce the arousal potential of the body, make it calmer and better able to cope. Repetitive use of such methods pays off.

Stress is with us to stay. It can help us to grow and develop, or it can crush us. Choices occur every day as to which we will allow to happen. Fatigue is a natural outcome of poorly managed stress, just as energetic well-being, and high level health is the natural outcome of well managed stress.

Relaxation exercises

Before starting relaxation or meditation exercises it is important that you read the advice given on breathing techniques (see page 142). Having spent five minutes or so practising these techniques move on to one or other of the two methods of relaxation, presented below. These are not the only two relaxation methods suggested, however they do represent two of the most effective currently available for self-taught application.

Progressive Muscular Relaxation and Modified Autogenic Training are different, and one will appeal more to you than the other. Try them both, for several days each, and then select the one which seems to produce in you the greater degree of relaxation and calmness. Practise this regularly for not less than 20 minutes daily, and ideally twice daily, for several weeks before beginning the meditation/visualization methods outlined. The cumulative effect of breathing, retraining and relaxation exercises will be to reduce arousal. This means that it will take a lot more stress to cause you to become roused. You will become calmer and less easily upset; which at its simplest is what stress reduction is all about.

This can be a major contribution towards your learning the necessary coping skills, for when you remain calm in the face of stress you will have time to produce the conscious elements of commitment, control and challenge which typify the person who handles stress best.

Progressive muscular relaxation

This method involves the systematic, conscious relaxation of all the body areas, in sequence. The position for this exercise should be reclining — either on the floor or on a recliner-type chair. Ideally, there should be no distracting sounds and the clothing worn should not constrict in any way. (A few cycles of deep breathing should precede the exercise.)

Starting with the feet, try to sense or feel that the muscles of the area are not actively tense. Then deliberately tighten them, curling the toes under and holding the tension for five to ten seconds. Then tense the muscles *even more strongly*, for a further few seconds before letting all the tension go and sensing the wonderful feeling of release. Try to consciously register what this feels like, especially in comparison with the tense state in which you have been holding them. Progress to the calf muscles and exercise them in the same way. First sense the state the muscles are in, then tense them, hold the position, and then tense them even more before letting go. Positively register the sense of release. In doing this to the leg muscles, there is a slight danger of inducing cramp. If this occurs, then stop tensing that area immediately and move on to the next. After the calf muscles, go on to exercise the knees, then the upper leg, thigh muscles, the buttocks, the lower and upper back, the abdomen, the chest, the shoulders, the arms and hands, and then the neck, head and face. The precise sequence is irrelevant, as long as all these areas are 'treated' to the tensing, the extra tensing, and then the release.

Some areas need extra attention in this respect. The abdominal region is a good example. The tensing of these muscles can be achieved in either contraction (i.e. a pulling in of the muscles), or by stretching (i.e. pushing outwards of the muscles). This variation in tensing method is applicable to many of the body's muscles. Indeed, at different times, it is a good idea to vary the pattern, and instead of, for example, contracting and tensing a muscle group, try to stretch and tense them to their limit. This is especially useful in the muscles of the face, particularly in the mouth and eye region. Individual attention to these is important. On one occasion it would be desirable, for example, for the 'tensing' of the mouth muscles to take the form of holding the mouth open as widely as possible, with the lips tense during this phase. On a subsequent occasion, the 'tensing' could be a tight-pursed pressing together of the lips. If there is time available, both methods of tensing can be employed during the same exercise, especially in the areas you know to be very tense. The muscles controlling the jaw, eyes, mouth, tongue and neck are particularly important, as are the abdominal muscles, since much emotional tension is reflected in these regions, and release and relaxation often has profound effects.

There are between twenty and twenty-five of these 'areas', depending upon how you go about interpreting the guidelines given above; each should involve at least five to ten seconds of tensing and a further five to ten seconds of 'letting go' and of passively sensing that feeling. Thus, eight to ten minutes should suffice for the successful completion of this whole technique. This should be followed by several minutes of an unhurried return to a feeling of warm relaxed tranquillity. Focus the mind on the whole body. Try to sense it as heavy and content, free of tension or effort. This might be enhanced by a few cycles of deep breathing. Stretch out like a cat, and then resume your normal activities.

Autogenic-type exercises

True autogenic exercises need to be taught

by a special teacher or practitioner, well versed in this excellent system. The modified method outlined below is loosely based on the work of the pioneer in this field, Dr H. Schultz. The distinction between a relaxation exercise and a meditation technique is blurred at all times, but never more so than in autogenic methods which are a blend of the two. At least fifteen and ideally twenty minutes should be given to the performance of this method. At another time of the day, this or another relaxation method should also be performed. This routine should become a welcome, eagerly anticipated oasis of calm and peace in the daily programme. Stress-proofing, without such periods of 'switching off', is not likely to be successfully achieved.

A reclining position should be adopted, with the eyes closed. External, distracting sounds should be minimized. The exercises involve the use of specific, verbalized messages to focus awareness on a particular area. *No effort is involved*, but simply a passive concentration on any sensations or emotions which may result from each message. Imagination or auto-suggestion has been found to have definite physiological effects. By combining a sequence of autogenic (i.e. self-generated) instructions with the passive, focused aspect of meditation techniques, a powerful method of self-help has been created.

The exercise starts with a general thought, such as 'I am relaxed and at peace with myself'. Begin to breathe deeply in and out. Feel the light movement of the diaphragm and feel calm.

Stage I: The mind should focus on the area of the body to which the thought is directed. Start by silently verbalizing 'my right arm is heavy'. Think of the image of the right arm. Visualize it completely relaxed, and resting on its support (floor, arm of the chair, etc.). Dissociate it from the body, and from will-power. See the limp, detached arm as being heavy, having *weight*. After a few seconds the phrase should be repeated. This should be done a number of times, before proceeding to the right leg, left arm and leg, neck, shoulders and back. At each area, try to sense heaviness and maintain a passive feeling in the process.

Stage II: Again, begin with the right arm, concentrating on it as you silently verbalize 'My right arm is warm'. Repeat this and pause to sense warmth in the arm or hand. Repeat this several times. The pause should be unhurried. To encourage this feeling of warmth, it may be useful to imagine that the sun's rays are shining on to the back of the hand, warming it. The sensation of warmth spreads from there to the whole arm.

Proceed through all areas of the body, pausing for some seconds at each to assess sensations which may become apparent. Such changes as occur cannot be controlled, but will happen when the mind is in a passive, receptive state. This exercise increases the peripheral flow of blood, and relaxes the muscles controlling the blood vessels. It is possible to measurably increase the temperature of an area of the body, using these simple methods.

Stage III: This focuses on the breathing cycle with the phrase 'My breathing is calm and regular'. No conscious effort should be made to control the breathing. You should direct your concentration to the slight, even motion of the diaphragm. Nothing should be consciously done about the breathing, which should be completely automatic. Sometimes the verbalized statement can be altered to 'The breathing is calm', or 'I am being breathed', to good effect. Sometimes, quite unconsciously, a deep breath is taken during the otherwise shallow breathing. This is quite normal. Nothing should be done to control the pattern. Simply repeat the chosen phrase, and passively observe and experience the sensations that accompany it. Slow repetition of the phrase promotes deep, slow, regular breathing without effort. Continue for several minutes, repeating the phrase periodically.

Stage IV: The phrase 'My forehead is cool' is repeated for several minutes. This appears to produce a combination of alertness and relaxation. When repeating this phrase, with suitable pauses, try to sense the coolness as a pleasant sensation.

Stage V: The phrase 'I am alert and refreshed' ends the exercise. Breathe deeply, stretch, and continue the day's activities.

During stages I and II, the time spent in each area should not be less than about half a minute; it is, however, quite permissible to spend two or three minutes focusing on any one part, especially if the desired sensation of heaviness or warmth is achieved.

It will probably be found that the desired sensation is more easily sensed in one stage than another, and that some areas seem more 'responsive' than others. This is normal. *It is also quite normal for there to be no subjective appreciation of any of the verbalized sensations.* Do not worry about this. Even if nothing at all is sensed for some considerable time, even some months, there is a great deal actually taking place within the body as a result of the whole exercise. Persistence, patience and a total lack of urgency is all that is necessary for this method to lead to a decrease in muscular tension and a sense of calm and well-being. A 'side-effect' of this particular method is frequently experienced in terms of much improved peripheral circulation, i.e. an end to cold hands and feet!

Meditation exercises

When you have been regularly practising for some weeks the method of relaxation which produces in you the deepest and most satisfying effect, it is time to move on to meditation/visualization methods. At this point the relaxation method can be reduced in time from 20 minutes to 10 minutes at each session, and later, when meditation is effectively being employed, to 5 minutes. It is not essential to make this reduction in time in the preparatory relaxation exercise before going on to meditation, and indeed if you have plenty of time to spare it is better to maintain the full 20 minute period of relaxation (preceded by breathing exercise).

Do not stop the use of the breathing exercise introduction to the relaxation methods, although this too may be reduced in time from five minutes to two minutes at each session (at least once and ideally twice, daily). It is quite important to keep the sequence of breathing-relaxation-meditation going. Ultimately, therefore, the introductory stages, (breathing/relaxation) may be cut down to around seven minutes, before beginning the meditation exercise which suits you best.

A selection of exercises is outlined so that you may try the various approaches and select that which creates in you the greatest effect of deep relaxation. Practise each of the methods for a week or so before deciding which allows you to most effectively calm the mind. It is this objective, a stillness of the mind, which we are seeking.

It is in this stillness that profound physiological changes are noted along with measurable changes in the brainwave patterns. In a state of relaxation/meditation the immune (defence) systems of the body are enhanced dramatically. This has been shown in studies relating to a relatively new branch of science, called psycho-neuro-immunology, which has demonstrated the direct and profound link between the brain/nervous system and the defence systems of the body.

Thus, put at its simplest, a highly stressed person will have much lower resistance to disease than a relaxed person. The stressed person will also be using energy wastefully, at a rapid rate, whilst the relaxed person is conserving it. It should therefore not be surprising to find the stressed, tense person to be suffering from fatigue more markedly than the relaxed and easy-going one.

Relaxation-meditation achieves great energy saving. It is the difference, in energy terms, between using only the lights and utilities in the home which are needed at any time, and having every appliance and light switched on all day and all night. Ultimately the price has to be paid, either in higher fuel bills and fatigue, or in lower bills and abundant energy.

Meditation methods

What all meditation methods have in common is the conscious attempt to focus the mind on one object. In this respect, the relaxation methods already outlined could be seen as forms of meditation. The 'pure' meditation that it is hoped you will be able to add to one of the relaxation methods, provides a different dimension to the programme; for, whilst it is not too difficult to concentrate one's attention on the breathing mechanism and on counting whilst breathing, for example, it requires a greater degree of application to concentrate on an abstract thought or image. What is essential in meditation is a device through which the conscious mind can be diverted from everyday thought processes. In separating the relaxation exercises from meditation methods, I am aware that they do overlap. However, whilst meditation leads inevitably to relaxation and *perhaps* to spiritual awareness, relaxation exercises can seldom lead to more than just relaxation, which is what we are seeking at this stage.

The device or 'distracting object' can be a mental picture or image, a word, a sound, a real object, an idea, an activity, etc. Whatever it is, all other thoughts must thereby be excluded from conscious awareness. There is a form of meditation in which no particular object is selected, but in which the individual attempts to focus on everything that is happening around himself, becoming as fully aware of his internal and external environment as possible during the meditation. This has been called 'open' meditation. All meditation involves a suspension of judgement. The object is observed non-critically. No thoughts about it are encouraged, simply a passive attention to the object. Some methods attempt to combine the use of an object (say breathing or a sound) and the 'open' pattern of meditation' in which thoughts entering the mind are 'watched' but not 'judged' and are then replaced by the meditative object. Research has shown that a variety of physiological changes take place during meditation. Certainly, tension and stress are reduced in the process. Frequently, behaviour patterns involving addiction, such as smoking, overeating and drug or alcohol consumption are improved or controlled by meditation. Such stress-induced conditions as high blood pressure are also markedly affected for the better by the application of successful meditation methods.

In general terms, meditation has been found to produce feelings of greater alertness and ability to concentrate, of being more perceptive, and so on. Many people experience an 'awakening' or a heightening of spiritual awareness. Supporters of these methods often use such phrases as 'cosmic consciousness' and 'transcendental experiences'. These phrases should not put off the would-be meditator for, at the very least, a greater sense of well-being and a more relaxed state should follow meditation. If any of the other benefits or experiences also follow, they should be taken as a bonus. Reduction in stress is difficult to measure. Frequently, the gradual, beneficial changes that do accrue are only measurable by comparison with the previous state of tension. Keeping a record of your results will enable you to make such a comparison after some months of regular relaxation and meditation.

The position or posture adopted for meditation is of importance. The classical poses range from the lotus position to the kneeling at prayer position. Most variations insist that during meditation the spine be kept straight, and this should be remembered, whether you decide to sit or kneel (perhaps using a small meditation stool), or even stand. Many systems and teachers have linked the way we hold and use our bodies with our emotional state. There seems to be a two-way influence, in as much as a physical symptom will usually develop in response to emotional stress, and emotions will be influenced by any tension or 'armouring' in the musculature.

Once the appropriate posture has been adopted, the mind should accept, initially, that you will stay immobile until the completion of the exercise. This stillness is an essential part of meditation and does itself lead to desirable physiological changes, as well as having positive psychological benefits such as increased self-respect and confidence. The self-discipline involved in immobility is enhanced if, during meditation, any irritant such as the buzzing of a fly or an aching of the limbs can be ignored or dismissed and the meditation process continued.

It is known that the meditation experience increases with repetition. Regular meditation requires an element of self-discipline and organization. It is well worth the effort, and once it becomes a part of the daily routine, the oasis of calm and regeneration, which the meditation

period brings, will be eagerly anticipated.

Choose a suitably unhurried part of the day to practise. Morning and evening seem to suit many people. Avoid meditating soon after meals, if possible. Adopt a sitting or kneeling position. (Lying is not suggested for meditation.) Remember to keep the spine straight.

Method I: Concentration
The simplest and probably the oldest form of meditation involves concentrating on one object. It has long been established that by allowing the eyes to roll upwards as you commence meditation, the effect is more speedily achieved. The head is erect and the eyes look upwards as far as they can (towards the eyebrows). This may be accompanied by mild muscular discomfort, which should pass. If this is not found to enhance any of the following methods, then close the eyes from the beginning. Normally, after a short while of maintaining the strained upward-rolled position of the eyes, it comes as a relief and a relaxing experience to gently close the eyes and to then continue the method with the eyes closed.

Breathing in a relaxed, unforced manner, focus the mind on an *imagined* object (a cross, a candle flame, a circle of light, etc.) or, with the eyes looking ahead, focus on an actual object of a similar nature; alternatively, with the eyes gently closed or rolled upwards, repeat a meaningless sound in the mind (not out loud). If visualizing an imaginary or gazing at a real object simply dwell passively on it. Thoughts that intrude should be gently discarded and replaced by the image of the object on which you are concentrating. If a sound is being used ('om', 'aaah', etc.) this should be repeated rhythmically over and over again. It may take on its own rhythm, becoming a continuous drone. The most important point is that concentration should be held on the sound and not directed towards anything else.

Concentrative forms of meditation require persistent practice before they can be maintained for any length of time. At first, the beginner may find that it is not possible to maintain concentration on an image or object (imagined or real) for more than a few seconds at a time before thoughts intrude. Gradually, with patience and discipline, it will be found that minutes at a time will pass in this state and, finally, that it is possible to maintain concentration for as long as is required. This method, by focusing the mind, enhances relaxation, reduces anxiety, and frequently helps in the elimination of psychosomatic ailments. One example of concentrative meditation is a Hindu method known as *tratak*. The object of concentration in this method is a burning flame, which is placed at eye level about a foot in front of the meditator. Breathing is slow, deep and silent. The meditator gazes into the centre of the flame until tears begin to flow, at which point the eyes are closed, and the image of the flame is visualized until it too vanishes.

Another concentrative meditation is that used by raj yogi. They meditate with their eyes closed, focusing attention on the tip of the nose, or the back of the skull. Experiments on meditators who use these methods showed that very soon after starting meditation, alpha waves (a sign of a relaxed state) appeared, and that these were maintained without interruption, despite the following external stimuli being administered: loud banging noises; the meditator's hands being placed in cold water or being touched with a hot tube; bright light; vibration from a tuning fork, etc. In other words, the meditation process was so powerful that none of these stimuli could disturb it or its relaxing effect (as measured by alpha brain wave patterns).

When effectively performed, meditation which makes use of concentration blots out all other sensations and thoughts. This is the key to its usefulness in stress-proofing, for with practice it becomes possible to focus the mind on one thing, be it a sound or an object, and detach oneself from all others. A few minutes in this silent state has restorative and relaxing effects. It is suggested that an attempt is made to spend ten minutes at a time performing such exercises, but that at first only a few minutes be attempted, perhaps tagged on to the end of a relaxation method.

Method II: Contemplation
In many ways this method is similar to the previous one. The object in the mind of the meditator can be an abstract idea, such as 'goodness', 'love', 'truth', etc. or the idea of God. Extension of this can be to use repetitive sounds or phrases, which are repeated rhythmically and silently, for example, 'God is love', or 'Hail Mary full of Grace, the Lord is with thee', etc. Any meaningful phrase will do. As long as the repeated phrase occupies the mind totally, it will have its effect. The constant barrage of thoughts and images, most of them meaningless and useless, that usually occupy our minds needs to be stilled, and these methods are designed to achieve this. The individual's view of the world and of himself, may well be altered as a result, sometimes for only a short time and sometimes permanently.

For those who would rather avoid religious connotations during meditation, the suggestion of Krishnamurti, the Indian philosopher, is that the sound to be repeated could well be 'coca-cola, coca-cola'. There is certainly no reason why this should not be as effective as any other object or sound in silencing thought. Although there are those who maintain that the content and vibrational quality of the 'mantra' or repeated words or sounds, determines their effect, research has tended to support the idea that it is the *act* of repetition and not the actual sound that produces the desired result, at least in so far as relaxation is concerned. Herbert Benson MD, author of *Relaxation Response*, says that the repeated word 'bananas' will do the trick. This, of course, may be seen as an affront to the spiritual connotations of meditating, but in so far as it is our concern to achieve relaxation, 'bananas' or 'coca-cola' would do as well as anything else. After ten minutes of this, allow the mind to become aware of the surroundings and how you feel, and then open the eyes, stretch the body and return to normal activities.

Method III: Meditating on 'bubbles' of thought

Adopt the desired position and induce a state of relaxation. See the mind as the surface of a pond, smooth and calm. Thoughts that enter the mind should be seen as bubbles rising from the depths of the pond. They should be observed, not pursued. In other words, the deliberate following of the thought process is avoided. Simply *detach* yourself and observe your thoughts as they 'bubble' to the surface. Take note of the thought and then gently, without any force, return to your contemplation of the smooth surface of the pond. It is also possible to sink under the surface of the pond, into deeper layers of consciousness as time goes by. As long as thoughts are not intrusive, but are observed and then depart just like the bubbles, the meditation process is continuing. After ten minutes or so, allow the mind to focus on the immediate environment; sense a degree of relaxation and then end the session.

Method IV: Meditating on your corner of heaven

In this method, after adopting an initial posture and relaxing consciously, with the eyes closed or rolled upwards, begin to visualize a place in which you would feel happy and safe. This could be a real,

remembered place. It could be a room or a country or garden scene, or any other place to which you could go whenever you wanted peace and a feeling of security. This place should be so visualized (imagined in the mind's eye) that it can be stepped into and out of as though entering a picture. The picture can be added to as time goes by. If it is a room, then furnishings can be changed or added to or rearranged. Colours should be seen and, if possible, all the senses should gradually be brought into the meditation. Try to hear the sounds (e.g. clocks ticking, bird songs, etc.); smell the various odours (a log fire, newly mown grass, flowers); feel the textures (bark of the tree, velvet upholstery), and so on. There is no limit to the degree of embroidery that is possible in creating this special place. All the powers of your imagination should be employed. This sort of meditation has been called creating a 'safe harbour', and it should be seen by the meditator, whilst conscious of its imagined nature, to be useful as a retreat whenever it is required. This meditation employs all the senses, and is suitable for many who find it too difficult a task to maintain concentration on one object. After ten minutes or so, the meditator steps out of the picture and returns to the normal environment, knowing that the 'safe place' remains untouched and ready for the next visit.

Whichever method of meditation suits you best, it is suggested that you construct such a 'safe haven' for yourself anyway, as it is a valuable exercise in imagery, and is of great use in visualization techniques (see below).

Method V: Breathing and colour visualization

Adopt a reclining or sitting position of comfort in an appropriate room. Breathe deeply several times and sense a feeling of safe, warm ease. Continue to breathe slowly and deeply, but not in a straining manner. As you breathe, visualize the colours red, orange and yellow flowing upwards into your solar plexus. These hues should be visualized one at a time and seen as rivers of colour. The breathing rhythm should not be controlled, but should be allowed to find its own pace and depth. The colours should be seen to flow at a steady, unhurried pace. After spending a minute or so on each of the first three colours, visualize the colour green flowing into the solar plexus from directly in front of you. Spend a minute or so breathing in a slow, rhythmic manner with the image of a river of green light entering your body.

Follow this with blue, indigo and violet, one at a time; these should be seen as being breathed inwards from the air above you. Again, spend a minute or so visualizing each of these colours. The only problem presented by this method is the difficulty some people have in visualizing colours. This becomes easier with practice, although some colours will always be easier to 'see' than others. After completing the colour spectrum, see yourself as being bathed in blue light, and end the meditation with a deep sense of peace and calm before opening the eyes and resuming normal activities.

All meditation methods will assist in achieving relaxation; indeed effective meditation is not possible without it. There is no right or wrong way of meditating, as long as the conscious mind is being stilled. If you have any difficulties, take advice from a teacher of these methods. Regular and patient use of relaxation/meditation methods and the inclusion of visualization exercises can make a marvellous difference to energy levels.

Visualization exercise

Work in the field of chronic disease such as arthritis and cancer, and more recently in AIDS, has shown that if a person can become deeply relaxed and can then visualize aspects of their disease process as altering for the better, measurable changes are often noted.

If we accept that the mind can influence the body for ill, the so-called psycho-somatic diseases, then we have to accept that the reverse is also possible. This is no longer conjecture. Researchers such as radiation oncologist Dr Carl Simonton, co-author of *Getting Well Again* (Bantam), have shown how effective such healing methods can be in cancer cases. I have described this in more detail in my book *Your Complete Stress-Proofing Programme* (Thorsons, 1985) from which the relaxation and meditation methods described in this section are derived.

Once you have achieved relaxation and can still your mind through meditation, you are ready to begin use of visualization methods to enhance health promotion. It is not possible to successfully employ visualization until relaxation/meditation methods are mastered and regularly in use, as the prerequisite of visualization is a still and focused mind, which these preparatory methods produce.

The 'safe haven' meditation is actually an exercise in visualization which will prepare you for the more specific use of this method. In any given condition, disease or state of health it is possible to influence the self-healing, repair mechanisms of the body by such methods. What is necessary is a clearly defined objective. It is probably beneficial to have vague objectives such as 'I want to feel good' but this is not focused enough to achieve marked change. A focus such as a particular function of the body, take the heart rate as an example, is easier to influence.

In this example it is possible for visualization to make the heart beat faster or slower, after very little practice. This may not have general application but to someone prone to palpitation it is indeed very helpful to be able to slow the heart rate down at will. Similar examples can be given for lowering blood pressure and reducing the electrical resistance of the skin.

These methods are being taught in major hospitals worldwide, using biofeedback machines to enable patients to monitor the function they are trying to influence, while they alter their thought processes until the desired changes occur. Thus learned, they can then use these thought process changes to influence natural functions, at will, without the machine. The use of such technology is a means of shortening the process of learning involved in pure visualization. However, most of us do not have access to such training facilities and so must make do with mental gymnastics as described in this section.

Both the examples given above, of lowering blood pressure or electrical resistance of the skin, are means of achieving stress (arousal) reduction, since when aroused (fight or flight mechanism) both blood pressure and the electrical resistance of the skin rises.

If energy is your objective then you need to be able to focus on aspects of the ways in which this is manufactured and used in your body. Work with seriously ill patients has shown that visualization of body processes does not need to be scientifically accurate to be effective. Cancer patients have visualized their tumour cells as any of a variety of things, ranging from grey rocks to enemy soldiers. They may then visualize their natural defence systems as an excavation machine lifting and disposing of the rocks, or as knights in armour galloping out to slay the enemy. What seems to matter is a clear view of the process required to recover.

If you are to imagine energy production and conservation you may need to have an image of the ways in which your body makes energy (see Chapter 4) and in some way which makes sense to you, to be able to visualize this happening in greater degree. Such visualization should be accompanied by positive mental affirmations such as, 'I feel energetic and full of vitality' or 'I feel awake and energetic'. This should, of course, follow on from relaxation/meditation and be a process which lasts for several minutes a number of times daily. The affirmation is important, and it is vital that it sounds comfortable to you, so use your own words. At the same time visualize the result of your goal being achieved. See yourself active and energetic; doing with great ease things which would normally exhaust you: running, working, swimming etc.

This is the desired goal, the intent of the visualization process. By combining for a few minutes this image with the affirmation, you will have begun the process of self-generation of the objective. You are removing negative thoughts, blockages which hinder your progress. It is therefore important that the affirmation be a positive one. It is undesirable to phrase these negatively. For example 'I no longer feel tired' is not nearly as powerful as 'I feel boundless energy'.

Visualize the vital energy of life, manufactured in you with the aid of the many positive things you are doing; the better diet, the cleaner lifestyle, the help from powerful nutrient allies of energy production, the removal of negative influences such as ongoing Candida or poor breathing habits etc. and the use of relaxation/meditation methods. See health as an energy which glows, and feel the golden glow of health and energy. Use the image of this golden light as a means of cancelling any negative thoughts which intrude on this powerful exercise. Continue with this for some minutes, as often as you can daily.

CHAPTER II

Adaptogens and stress

Put at its simplest, an adaptogen is a substance which aids the body in its efforts to adapt to stress more successfully and with no harmful side effects. Another quality of adaptogens is that they have general rather than specific qualities of protection, thus influencing beneficially a number of functions against a variety of harmful influences.

Thus the adaptogen, in a non-specific manner, enhances the body's own powers of recovery and maintenance (known as its homoeostatic or self-balancing mechanisms). Such a non-specific, general aid to adaptation and balance, is of immeasurable value when the body is under general attack from stresses of internal and external origin.

The best known adaptogens are the Oriental herb ginseng, its Siberian cousin Eleutherococcus, and the food of queen bees, royal jelly, as well as pollen. The Russian space programme has brought some of these to prominence in scientific terms, lifting them from the realms of old wives' tales and traditional folk remedies to the very forefront of medical respectability.

They are particularly applicable in stress situations when general non-specific support of body function is needed. They

therefore have a part to play in fatigue reduction.

Ginseng
This ancient plant remedy has long been employed in the Orient as an extender of vitality and life. Non-specific protection against stress of all sorts is reported anecdotally from around the world, and it therefore makes sense to choose such an adaptogen for general, long-term use.

Eleutherococcus
This Siberian root which has many of the characteristics of ginseng, some say more potently, is a powerful antioxidant which has been proved capable of protecting the body against a variety of harmful influences, both chemical, physical and biological.

Royal jelly
This is produced by worker bees to feed the queen bee and has the qualities of an adaptogen. It is one of the world's best sources of vitamin B_5, which itself has been shown to increase animal lifespan and to retard general deterioration. This may have much to do with support for the adrenal glands (source of adrenaline) which suffer so much in stressful conditions.

Pollen

This seems to act in much the same manner as royal jelly. It is a highly nutritious mixture of substances including essential fatty acids and vitamins.

Most adaptogens appear to contain germanium in small but significant quantities, and this too may have something to do with the benefits noted. They all require use for some time before any appreciable improvement in well-being and energy is noticed. Anyone with chronic fatigue should employ one or more of these and should anticipate doing so for a considerable time.

Suggested dosages are:
Ginseng or Eleutherococcus: 500mg to 1,000mg daily.
Royal jelly: one or two generous teaspoonsful daily.
Pollen: 1g-5g daily.

The General Adaptation Syndrome (GAS)

The great Canadian researcher Hans Selye, who has helped us understand stress so clearly, has described what happens to the body over a period of time during which it is exposed to stress.

Initially, as explained in the previous section, there is an alarm reaction, in which the various components of the body's defence and protective mechanisms are mobilized for action (fight or flight). This may be used appropriately to defend the body (running away etc.) and no harm would derive.

If the alarm reaction is repeated many times, however, and there is no appropriate response, the next stage of GAS begins. This is the stage of adaptation. During this stage, which may last for years, the body copes with, adapts to, compensates for and generally puts up with, the strain of repeated alarms and demands. Depending on the general health of the individual, their inherited predispositions, nutritional deficiencies and toxicities, and many other variables, there comes a time when the body can no longer adapt and compensate.

At this point the third stage of the GAS comes into operation. This is the stage of collapse. This is where disease and malfunction become apparent and the individual progresses along a downwards slope towards eventual chronic disease and death unless the causative factors are remedied.

Just which organs and systems will be affected in any person depends upon a vast number of variable elements, with some people coping for longer than others. In the end, though, GAS always produces collapse and disease, unless the organism can be strengthened, or the causative factors removed, modified or altered. Adaptogens assist the body in its efforts to adapt to the demands of any stress factor.

CHAPTER 12

Glandular extracts

The use of raw glandular extracts can provide your body with naturally occurring nutrients in the proportions present in your glands. These extracts contain not only the appropriate quantities and types of vitamins and minerals but also high levels of enzymes, nucleo-proteins, RNA, DNA and hormones. Raw glandulars are so described because they are not heated but are defatted and then freeze dried.

The aim of taking such animal glandular extracts is to provide a complete source of nutrients so that you improve the local nutritional environment of your own body's glands and organs. Put at its simplest, this is meant to boost the function of the depleted organ or gland, not by stimulating it but by replenishing those nutrients which may be deficient.

There does seem to be a degree of 'targeting' possible by these means whereby spleen extract, for example, will encourage spleen regeneration and healing; prostate tissue will assist prostate function; adrenal supplementation improves adrenal function etc. Most of the glandular products on the market are derived from animals from New Zealand and Australia that have lived on open range farms and grazed on non-fertilized grass and have had no hormone or other medication. The fat content of these animals is relatively low.

The organs and glands of sheep have been found to be the least likely to cause allergic reactions, and so they are recommended.

Once removed, any residual fat is surgically trimmed from the glands before they are frozen at $-50°F/-10°C$ and kept frozen until processed. No heat or solvents are used in processing, and only water is extracted in the final stages.

A wide variety of glandular and organ extracts is currently available. Those of particular interest if you are suffering from fatigue are thyroid, adrenal and pituitary concentrates. Some manufacturers combine extracts of different glands or organs together with additional nutrients to increase their potency. One that I recommend is 'Adrenal Tissue Concentrate with Synergistic Complex' from Nature's Best. This includes adrenal tissue, spleen tissue, vitamins A, C, B_1, B_2, B_5, B_6, and zinc.

If you have indications of an underactive thyroid or pituitary, then use of these glandular extracts can be most helpful, but they are not suggested as a sole means of dealing with any problem, rather as part of a comprehensive self-help, self-healing approach.

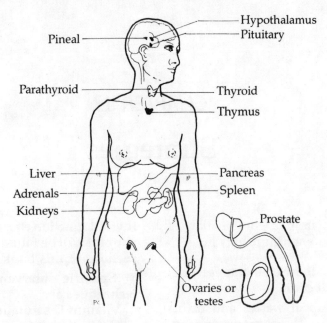

Location of endocrine glands and associated organs

CHAPTER 13

Strategies

Fatigue results from a combination of interacting factors which results in:

- Depletion of those elements essential to energy production.
- The build-up of wastes and toxins which interfere with energy production.
- Alterations in the energy production, distribution and utilization system.
- Negative changes in the self-regulating, self-healing mechanisms of the body (immune deficiency).
- Breakdown of normal communication within the body involving the nervous system and hormonal production/utilization.
- Mento-emotional or psychosocial problems.

By using a combination of the following most cases of chronic fatigue can be helped:

- Optimum nutrition. This means eating as healthily as is possible and supplementing as appropriate. Whether this relates to special needs for the elderly, the young, those who are high or low in blood sugar, suffering from allergy, toxicity, Candida infection, high or low thyroid function etc., a pattern of dietary support will be found in the appropriate sections of this book.
- Specific intervention using such techniques as:
  Vitamin C saturation.
  Controlled detoxification via fasting, chelation methods (oral or intravenous).
  Anti-viral action involving herbal medication.
- Support for the energy cycles, using Coenzyme Q_{10}, glandular extracts and specific nutrients as indicated.
- Stress reduction.
  Relaxation/meditation/visualization methods or biofeedback.
- Use of non-specific help via adaptogens.
- Alteration of lifestyle, attitude and behaviour.
- Environmental manipulation using humidifiers, ionizers etc.
- Aerobic exercise.
- Breathing retraining and postural correction.

The strategies outlined above provide a framework from which to work, and all are explained in this book. Each specific ailment section contains its own variations of these elements. They are not to be taken as being exhaustive of all the possibilities of energy enhancement, but as being comprehensive in that they approach most of the possible contributors to fatigue from a self-help perspective. Additional help can be sought from the professional support of osteopathic practitioners, acupuncturists, yoga instructors etc., but self-help measures in the long run are more important since we must become responsible for our own health and well-being, with recovery of vitality and full energy potential being our objective.

Specific ailments and fatigue

In the following sections I look at the fatigue component of a number of common, and some not so common, health problems. In this way it may be possible to identify your fatigue as belonging to a specific health problem of known cause, and often of known cure. Answer the simple questions and read the

brief description relating to each of the conditions mentioned and see whether you fit into one or other of the pictures thus created.

If there is a clear indication of a connection, you may wish to consult your doctor about what course of action might be appropriate. There may be more than one condition to which you feel identified. Do not become concerned, for what we are discovering in this section is not a way of making a firm diagnosis but of indicating possible links between your fatigue and conditions which may apply in your life.

If in any doubt as to the possibility of such a connection in your case please check with your doctor before assuming that you *have* one or other disease or condition.

The list of conditions which follows is not exhaustive. There are many other possible links with fatigue but for the most part those conditions discussed represent the most likely areas of ill health which relate to this basic problem. These are listed alphabetically and not in order of importance.

CHAPTER 14

Adrenal insufficiency and fatigue

Diabetes and low and high thyroid activity, are all endocrine (or hormonal or 'glandular') problems, which usually have fatigue as one of their major symptoms (see pages 133 and 174).

Another, potentially serious endocrine disturbance which has fatigue high on its list of symptoms, is one which involves a most important hormone-producing centre, the adrenal gland (which lies just above the kidneys). Other than fatigue the symptoms of adrenal gland problems, known medically as Addison's disease, include: weakness; irritability; decreased appetite; loss of weight; discomfort in the abdomen; vomiting and nausea; changes in skin colour (to a bronzed/ brown hue) and loss of hair from head and pubis. Replacement of the adrenal hormones, which are being inadequately produced in such a condition, is required, and should be undertaken by a suitably qualified therapist.

Addison's disease represents about the worst aspect of adrenal dysfunction. However, many people suffer symptoms relating to adrenal dysfunction which are not a result of disease but rather follow from misuse and abuse.

General adrenal insufficiency

The adrenal glands produce adrenaline (or epinephrine) in response to demands made on the body (i.e. stress). The vital hormones which culminate in adrenaline's activity throughout the body may literally make the difference between life and death in response to stress, as adrenaline provides the impetus which allows for the typical 'fight or flight' reaction.

There is an instantaneous mobilization of body responses which causes blood to be diverted to muscles in preparation for action, together with all the alterations necessary for great activity in response to a challenge, including mobilization of stored sugar into the bloodstream.

This is also known as the alarm stage of the General Adaptation Syndrome, and is more fully explained in the sections dealing with Stress and Fatigue (page 78) and Adaptogens and Stress (page 95).

If dietary factors needed for this response are deficient, and/or stress demands are constant or heavy, then there is a likelihood of adrenal exhaustion or deficiency. This leads inexorably to feelings of exhaustion and fatigue as well as a myriad other symptoms.

One of adrenaline's actions is to reduce lactic acid levels in the system. Lactic acid, which results from physical activity, as well as from shallow breathing, makes us feel fatigued, depressed, lethargic and dull. Removal of lactic acid by adrenaline gives the opposite feeling, one of happiness, energy and stimulation.

One activity which releases adrenaline is exercise, which accounts for the 'high' and the general feeling of well-being which athletes experience. However, this only happens if the adrenal glands are functioning well, with adequate nutrients present for that function. Just what those nutrients are can be seen from a brief look at the pathway in the body which results in the eventual production of adrenaline. Each stage of this pathway has to be completed efficiently or the process slows or ceases, leading to dysfunction, disease and loss of energy.

The substance initially involved in this vital chain is an amino acid (fraction of protein) called phenylalanine, which interacts with a specific enzyme to produce another amino acid, tyrosine (which is also vital for thyroxin production by the thyroid, when combined with iodine). Tyrosine then interacts with other enzymes to become a most important substance called L-Dopa. This in turn interacts with phosphorus and vitamin B_6 (pyridoxine) to produce the precursor of adrenaline, dopamine.

In the process thus far, apart from phosphorus and vitamin B_6, the mineral magnesium has to be present in adequate quantities for smooth production to continue. Finally, a complex interaction occurs involving enzymes which are copper and vitamin C dependent, and which eventually result in adrenaline being available to act as the spur which harnesses the multiple body processes every time stress demands a response, i.e. hundreds, if not thousands, of times every day.

This whole complex process, initiated by adrenaline, takes a split second. Dr Robert Erdmann, in his excellent book *The Amino Revolution* (Century) describes the nutrients needed to keep the adrenal gland capable of producing adequate stress-coping substances. These include the amino acids arginine, glutamine, phenylalanine, tyrosine and tryptophan, as well as vitamins A, B_1 (thiamin), B_2 (riboflavin), B_3 (niacin), B_5 (pantothenic acid), B_6 (pyridoxine), B_{12}, folic acid, C and E; together with the minerals and co-factors magnesium, potassium, manganese and choline. Nutrition needs to be optimal to allow for adrenal sufficiency, since these nutrients include a number which are notoriously inadequately supplied by the average diet.

When highly stressed and inadequately nourished the adrenal glands often become incapable of performing their tasks. At such times the common tendency is to 'whip' them into activity by use of stimulants. Every cup of tea, or coffee, or alcoholic drink, or cigarette, results in adrenal stimulation. This is no more health enhancing than the whipping of a tired horse to produce a little more effort before it collapses.

It is the adrenaline which produces the end-product of sugar in the blood in response to these stimulant factors (see Hypoglycaemia, page 144) as it is necessary for the muscles to have available adequate energy-producing sugars to cope with whatever dangers have provoked the 'fight or flight' stress reaction, which is the usual cause of adrenaline release.

Fortunately, or unfortunately, in modern life this response is not usually suitable. We hardly have the opportunity to run or fight as a response to the multiple stress factors which face us daily. Nor does artificial production of adrenaline, stimulated by common drugs (e.g. caffeine, tobacco and alcohol) have any positive outcome. Superfluous sugar from adrenaline release, or from sugar consumption, has to be dealt with by insulin production, with the consequences described in the sections on hypoglycaemia and stress. Thus, the use of stimulants and caffeine-rich foods not only results in damage in terms of the initially higher, and then lower, sugar levels, but also eventually causes the adrenals to begin to malfunction. Once these become inadequate to their normal tasks a number of major health problems emerge and one of the first of these is the development of allergic reactions (which further drain the adrenals); and, of course, fatigue is a consequence.

The alternation of stress and stimulant usage (or use of sugar-rich foods) can thus be seen to be involved in several aspects of fatigue development, including adrenal insufficiency, allergy and hypoglycaemia. Dealing with this calls for various elements to be considered:

● **Nutrition must be excellent.**

● **Stress requires reduction (see page 78).**

● **Specific supplementation should be considered, most notably of the B-vitamins, vitamin C and the amino acids and minerals as outlined above.**

● **Factors such as hypoglycaemia and allergy need attention (see pages 144 and 104).**

● **Glandular extracts may be helpful (see page 96).**

Underactive Adrenal Questionnaire

Complete the Underactive Adrenal Questionnaire, and the Blood Pressure Test (see page 103), in order to ascertain whether adrenal insufficiency is part of your problem.

Answers to the following questions will give an indication of underactive adrenal gland function. Score 2 for a 'YES' (once a week or more) and 1 for a 'SOMETIMES' indicating more than twice monthly but not as often as weekly.

1 Do you lack energy and feel generally fatigued?

2 Do you wake up with headaches?

3 Do you have any allergies?

4 Do you have a noticeable lack of saliva?

5 Is your circulation poor (cold hands and/or feet)?

6 Do you like salty food?

7 Do beans, cabbage, and brussels sprouts give you indigestion?

8 If you get up quickly from sitting do you feel faint or dizzy?

9 Do your ankles swell at night?

10 Do you find yourself yawning a lot, constantly wanting fresh air?

11 Do you have frequent infections, colds etc.?

12 Are your nails ridged?

A score above 6 indicates a probable adrenal insufficiency. If this is confirmed by the Adrenal Blood Pressure test, then you can be fairly certain that an insufficiency exists. Stress reduction is therefore called for, and nutritional advice as outlined in the section on adrenal insufficiency should be followed.

The basic nutrients needed include vitamin B_5 (pantothenic acid, usually marketed as calcium pantothenate); vitamin B-complex; vitamin C and probably raw adrenal gland extract (200mg to 400mg daily). See the section on glandular extracts for more information.

Adrenal Blood Pressure Test

There is a test which is used to indicate whether the adrenal gland is underfunctioning. This requires that someone take your blood pressure after you have been lying down for four minutes, and then again immediately after standing up.

In this test only the systolic pressure is considered. This is the higher of the two pressure readings taken. For example, a normal pressure is usually considered to be 120/80mmHg. Of these two figures 120 is the systolic, and 80 the diastolic pressure. These represent different aspects of the variable pressures relating to heart and circulatory function.

If the higher of the two systolic figures (which should be the one taken standing) is not at least five, and ideally ten, points higher, than that taken when you were lying down, then adrenal function can be considered to be poor. An example might be that the pressure reading lying down is 120/80mmHg, and the standing pressure only 124/80. Of these figures we are only interested in the 120 and the 124. The difference is low (only 4) and indicates poor adrenal function. Had the initial (reclining) figures been 120/80 and the standing figures 128/80 the difference of 8 would indicate that the adrenals were functioning normally. Sometimes the standing figure is actually lower than the lying figure indicating very poor adrenal function.

CHAPTER 15

Allergies and fatigue

One of the major symptoms of allergy to food or inhaled substances is fatigue. Other common symptoms associated with allergy are depression; headache; skin rashes; digestive problems such as cramp, diarrhoea and bloating; frequent 'colds' which are actually attacks of allergic rhinitis (hay fever like symptoms such as itchy eyes, postnasal drip, persistent slight cough, stuffy or runny nose and sneezing which may relate to house dust, animal hairs or dust, chemicals and pollution).

A common sign in allergic people is a dark shadow under or around the eyes. Many allergies can be present without a person having the slightest idea that they are allergic to anything; their only being aware that they feel unwell most of the time, with fatigue the most prominent symptom.

The allergy may be a 'masked' one in which the food or foods involved are eaten regularly and so the reaction is not a violent one, but rather a low grade, continuous one. Depression accompanies this in many instances. Also, a variety of other 'mental' symptoms may be noted, including anxiety, panic attacks and general irritability. There may be obvious fluid retention, especially in women, and this often relates to wheat sensitivity. Weight may fluctuate markedly, mainly related to this factor of fluid retention; and there may be aches and pains in the joints, as well as headaches. Other symptoms commonly found include; hot flushes; digestive and bowel problems; intolerance to alcohol; dizziness; palpitations and sweats; and craving for particular foods almost to the level of addiction.

The last symptom is a clue to the offending food, for it is frequently found that that which is craved is the allergen.

The way to find the culprit food is to go on an exclusion diet, and gradually reintroduce foods until there is a recurrence of symptoms. Ideally, though, if you suspect an allergy you should consult a naturopath or a doctor specializing in food and environment related allergy (see section on Candida, page 110, as this can also be a cause of allergic symptoms).

The foods which have been found to be major causes of allergic symptoms are:

- **Cereals such as wheat, rye and oats.**

- **Dairy produce, including milk, butter and cheese.**

- **Maize (corn).**

- **Eggs.**
- **Chicken.**
- **Sugar of all sorts.**
- **Yeast, and foods derived from it.**
- **Artificial flavourings, colourings and preservatives in food.**
- **Citrus fruits.**
- **Alcohol.**
- **Pork and beef.**
- **Chocolate, coffee and tea.**

It can be seen that many of the commonest allergens are foods which have been introduced to man's diet since farming and food processing began. Previous to this man ate little or no dairy produce or grains, and absolutely no artificial additives.

A return to a 'Stone Age' diet can be beneficial if you suffer from allergies of the sort described. This entails elimination of all dairy produce, all grains, and meat from domesticated animals. What is left includes all vegetables and most fruits (care with citrus is advised) and meat from free-living animals (game) as well as fish.

A warning is necessary as you are likely to suffer withdrawal symptoms as allergens are excluded from your diet. These will be almost as strong as in addiction cases. Therefore, expect to feel pangs of craving for offending foods for a while.

Other dietary methods:

Lamb and pear diet
To assess the effects of exclusion of offending foods on general health and fatigue the following method may serve well. It has been used extensively by tens of thousands of patients with allergy, and works because it includes only a very few, usually safe, foods and substances.

For five to seven days eat only the following:

- **Lamb including any organ meats from lamb (roast, casserole, grill or stew).**
- **Fresh ripe, but not overripe, pears with no skins.**
- **Bottled mineral water.**

Nothing else should be eaten or drunk.

If your symptoms of ill health fade away and fatigue is reduced or absent then this is a clear indication that a food allergy is behind the symptoms. Reintroduction of foods other than the above, one at a time, can then show which the culprits are. However, this needs to be done cautiously since a more violent reaction to the offending food can be anticipated after its five days absence from the diet.

Rotation diet
A rotation diet is one in which foods from the same group or 'family' are consumed only once in four days. This helps to identify the food families which may be most implicated in the allergy, allowing more specific identification of the particular food(s).

This is also an excellent way of altering the diet as a treatment for allergy, since by spacing foods in this way many symptoms abate. As with the pear and lamb diet there is a degree of care required once allergens have been removed from daily use, since their reintroduction regularly in the diet can produce marked reactions.

It is suggested that if you have evidence of food allergies you should take advice as to the best way of altering your pattern of diet.

Exclusion diet
This is a diet which eliminates those foods

which are the greatest overall culprits in food allergy. This is less stringent than the pear and lamb diet, and less complicated than the rotation diet. It is a pattern which should not be modified, but applied strictly so that identification is made of culprit foods.

Safe Foods	Unsafe Foods
Game, lean cuts of lamb, rabbit. Turkey (avoid skin). White fish (eczema patients avoid). All vegetables except those listed opposite. Bananas, pears (no skin), mangoes, pomegranates, papaya. Rice, sago, tapioca, millet, buckwheat and products of these. Sunflower oil, olive oil, safflower oil, linseed oil. Tomor or Vitasieg margarine.	Beef, pork, chicken, sausages, tinned or smoked meat, bacon. Shellfish, smoked fish. Potatoes, onion, soya-beans, sweetcorn. All other fruits. Wheat, oats, barley, corn and their products. Corn oil, soya oil, 'vegetable' oil and nut oils (especially peanut oil). All other margarines. All milk products, whether from cows, other animals or soya. Eggs.
Some herbal teas (camomile, linden blossom). Glass bottled mineral water, filtered or distilled water.	Tea, coffee, decaffeinated coffee, bottled juices or squashes. Alcohol, tapwater.
Sea salt.	Herbs and spices. All food colourings and preservatives and additives. Yeast. Chocolate. Sugar and honey.

Three weeks of this diet will often produce a marked change in health with fatigue being modified or disappearing.

This is an aid in diagnosis of allergens and is not intended as a long-term pattern of eating. Often it is found that symptoms such as headache and fatigue are worse for several days after beginning an exclusion diet. After there is improvement, and the diet has been followed for some three weeks, excluded foods can be added back in to the diet, one at a time, at an interval of two days between each reintroduction.

Good quantities of reintroduced foods should be eaten since small amounts may not provoke a reaction.

If a reaction is noted in the form of a return of symptoms, then you should exclude the culprit food for the present. It may be reintroduced in a rotation pattern (not more often than once in four or five days) after the full period of testing for allergens is complete. If it still provokes a reaction then it should be excluded for six months at least.

Drugs which are being taken under a

doctor's advice should only be stopped if clearance is obtained from the practitioner before beginning an exclusion diet. Smoking should be stopped. Also, food supplements can contain elements which are undesirable in terms of allergens, so it is best to check with a suitable practitioner (naturopath, clinical ecologist or nutritionist) before taking any whilst on the diet.

Reactions to reintroduced foods may occur within a few minutes, or some hours, or even days after ingestion, and they may be a racing pulses and palpitations; sweating; facial swelling and/or a skin rash and aching joints.

Wait until the reaction has settled completely before resuming the reintroduction of excluded foods, and remember to stop the food which caused the reaction. If the reaction is severe it sometimes helps to take a dose of 2g or 3g of vitamin C and/or two teaspoonsful of bicarbonate of soda dissolved in water.

Pulse test

These are dietary methods of assessing food allergens. Another method is to use what is called 'pulse testing'. This is a remarkably effective method for identifying body reactions to food.

First, learn to take your wrist pulse. Sit comfortably and take this for a full minute before you eat a particular food or a meal. Record the pulse rate; eat the food and re-test the pulse 15, 30 and 60 minutes after eating. If an increase or decrease of 10 to 15 beats per minute are noted after a meal then the food eaten probably contained an allergen.

Once suspect foods are identified, re-test them and, once certain as to their involvement in allergy, place them on rotation (that is eat them once in five days only) or exclude them altogether. It is, of course, necessary to avoid other reasons for a rise in pulse rate, such as extreme agitation or exertion. Always do the test when resting quietly.

Allergy can be a major cause of fatigue, and the advice given above should assist you in identification of allergens in your food, and free you of fatigue.

Other forms of allergy, such as to inhaled substances, require expert advice from a clinical ecologist or naturopath to help the body to cope with the problem and hopefully to overcome it. Homoeopathic medicine and acupuncture are also often very useful in such cases.

CHAPTER 16

Anaemia and fatigue

Anaemia literally means 'lack of blood', but in general usage it means a reduction in the levels of haemoglobin (the red, iron-rich, oxygen-carrying component of the blood). Anaemia results in fatigue, lassitude, palpitations — especially on exertion — breathlessness, swollen ankles, and characteristically a 'washed out' appearance.

There are many other reasons for all these symptoms, so anaemia may be suspected if they are mainly present, but it can only be identified certainly via a blood test.

ANAEMIA QUESTIONNAIRE

1 Are you breathless on exertion?
2 Are your ankles frequently swollen?
3 Do you frequently have palpitations?
4 Are your lips pale?
5 Are your fingernails pale?
6 Are the inside linings of your eyes pale?
7 Are the whites of your eyes blue?

These are all common signs of anaemia along with that most obvious of symptoms, fatigue and lack of stamina. When anaemia is more severe there will also be hypersensitivity to cold; nausea; tendency to faint; insomnia; and headaches.

The major causes of anaemia include:

● **Loss of blood (repeated heavy periods, bleeding piles or ulcers).**

● **Insufficient blood manufacture due to low iron levels, low folic acid or low vitamin B_{12} levels.**

- **Inadequate digestive acids (this adds to iron deficiency as well as being aggravated by it).**
- **Inherited diseases which interfere with blood manufacture.**
- **Other serious illness, such as rheumatoid arthritis, cancer or leukaemia.**

Of the above *iron deficiency anaemia* is one of the commonest causes, and signs of this may include:

- **The tongue may be smooth and shiny.**
- **Cracks may be noticed at the corners of the mouth.**
- **Difficulty with swallowing.**
- **Dyspepsia and diarrhoea are common.**
- **Nails may be spoon shaped.**
- **Whites of eyes may have a blue tinge.**

Diagnosis is by blood test, and treatment is by iron supplementation which can be very rapidly effective in dealing with fatigue.

Supplementation with vitamin C encourages iron absorption (500mg to 1g with each meal is suggested). Foods which reduce iron absorption are tea, coffee (especially when taken with a meal, where a reduction of over 50 per cent of iron content of food eaten is possible as a result). Wholegrains and legumes have a slight effect on iron absorption, but on balance should be eaten especially if vitamin C is adequate.

Care should be taken with iron supplements as these can upset absorption of other nutrients such as zinc. The best form for taking it is as iron gluconate. Zinc should be taken as well (ratio of iron to zinc 2:1) with no more than 25mg of iron being supplemented daily. Vegetarians are at some risk of low iron unless a great deal of vitamin C-rich food is eaten.

Iron-rich foods include liver; sardines; egg-yolk; nuts; figs; apricots; lentils; watercress.

Another form of anaemia is that related to lack of vitamin B_{12} and this is called *pernicious anaemia*. This may accompany psychological disturbances or depression. The physical signs are similar to those of iron deficiency anaemia as well as:

- **Tingling in the limbs.**
- **Very red, 'raw beef'-coloured, tongue.**
- **Very smooth yellowish skin.**
- **Dyspepsia.**

Treatment is by supplementation of vitamin B_{12}, often by injection as well as iron and folic acid (another B vitamin). Attention to the status of the digestive juices is also important.

Vegetarians may become deficient in B_{12} more easily than meat eaters. Good food sources are organ meats; liver; eggs; and brewer's yeast. If the symptoms of fatigue accompany some of the signs mentioned (and also include confusion and depression in an elderly person) then a check should be made of B_{12}, folic acid and iron status.

This condition runs in families and is noted more in blue-eyed individuals with hair that is prematurely greying.

CHAPTER 17

Candida albicans and fatigue

In the introductory chapter dealing with the multiple elements associated with fatigue as a health problem we met several individuals who, in their own words, described the sheer hell of their predicament. Among these were people who were afflicted by yeast overgrowth, better known by its scientific name, Candida albicans. This yeast is present in almost everyone from a very young age. It has lived as a parasite inside us from time immemorial, presenting little danger to health as long as the bodily defences were operating efficiently. It normally takes up residence in the lower intestinal tract, and is kept there by powerful bacterial colonies which populate the regions higher up in the bowel, and which are regarded as 'friendly' bacteria, in that they assist in the digestion of our food, and actually manufacture some of the B vitamins we need (such as biotin).

Each of us has a population of bacterial and yeast micro-organisms, weighing between 3lb and 5lb, living happily inside us at any time. Each bowel movement contains a large component of dead bacteria which is thus eliminated. Should anything happen to upset the health of these friendly bacterial colonies, opportunistic yeasts and other bacteria which had been kept in check may proliferate and spread to regions previously barred to them.

Unfortunately a number of factors in modern life have led to just such a disturbing situation. These include the abundant and sometimes profligate use of antibiotics. These are, of course, excellent for the killing of unfriendly bacteria which may be infecting us, but unfortunately they are not discriminating and also annihilate the friendly ones. People on lengthy courses of antibiotics often note the presence of thrush in the mouth or reproductive organs after treatment. This is Candida showing its ability to spread to pastures new when given the chance.

Another contributory factor to the spread of Candida is the use of hormonal drugs, including the contraceptive pill. Others include multiple pregnancies; recurrent infections which lower the efficiency of the immune (defence) systems of the body; and other immune-response lowering factors such as deficient diet and a polluted environment. On top of this, the large amount of sugar that we eat creates ideal conditions for Candida's spread, since like all yeasts it thrives on sugar.

When these yeasts spread to new areas of the bowel they may alter from a simple yeast to a fungal form. This is known as the *mycelial* stage, and in it the fungus puts down root-like structures which can actually penetrate the bowel mucosa. This allows the passage of partially digested food particles, as well as yeast spores and breakdown products, through the bowel wall into the bloodstream. This, in turn, leads to a massive drain on the defence systems of the body — the immune function — and can be the primary cause of allergic-type reactions as the body is confronted with foreign proteins in the bloodstream. A wide variety of symptoms may result including:

Fatigue	Digestive
Nausea	disturbances,
Anxiety	including
Depression	bloatedness,
Lassitude	diarrhoea or
Muscular aches	constipation
and pains	Vaginal irritations
Migraines and	Cystitis
other allergic	Menstrual and
conditions	premenstrual
	problems
	Acne.

There is often, accompanying Candida overgrowth, a strong element of sugar or carbohydrate craving. This, in itself, is a clue to the condition, and will gradually disappear as the normalization process is put into operation.

Fatigue is very frequently a symptom of chronic Candida overgrowth, and this often leads to the increasing use by the sufferer, of stimulants such as alcohol, tobacco, caffeine-based foods and drinks, and a high sugar diet in order to achieve a semblance of energy. Such strategies are misplaced for they actually increase the ultimate degree of exhaustion. Also, of course, increased use of stimulants of the sort described has the short-term effect of increasing blood sugar levels which actually enhances Candida proliferation (see also Hypoglycaemia, page 144).

Many of the mental/emotional symptoms resulting from Candida activity are explained by the action of acetaldehyde, a breakdown product of alcohol which is actually produced by Candida under certain conditions, from sugar, in the body. This substance can be shown to react with a natural neurotransmitter in the brain, dopamine, to produce morphine-like substances which bind to special receptor sites in the brain, producing addiction (to alcohol in many cases) and mental disturbances.

Is yeast *your* problem?
The completion of the following questionnaire will provide evidence as to whether or not Candida is a factor in your current health picture. It is not possible to make an absolute diagnosis by these means alone but a strong likelihood can be suggested. There are a number of medical tests which claim to show Candida activity, and some are more reliable than others, although none are totally accurate.

MEDICATION HISTORY

1 Have you ever had a course of antibiotics lasting for eight weeks or longer; or for shorter periods, more than four times in one year?

2 Have you ever had a course of antibiotics for the treatment of acne for more than one continuous month?

| 3 Have you ever been treated with a course of a steroid drug such as cortisone, prednisone or ACTH? |
| 4 Have you ever taken contraceptive medication for a year or more? |
| 5 Have you ever been treated with an immunosuppressive drug? |
| 6 Have you been pregnant more than once? |

SYMPTOM HISTORY

| 1 Have you had recurrent or persistent cystitis, vaginitis or prostitis? |
| 2 Have you a history of endometriosis? |
| 3 Have you a history of oral or vaginal thrush? |
| 4 Have you had athlete's foot or any fungal infection of the nails or skin? |
| 5 Have you ever had a diagnosis of myalgic encephalomyalitis (post-viral fatigue syndrome)? |
| 6 Are you severely affected by exposure to chemical fumes, perfumes, tobacco smoke, etc? |
| 7 Are your symptoms worse after eating yeasty or sugary foods? |
| 8 Do you suffer from a variety of allergies? |
| 9 Do you commonly suffer from abdominal bloating (distension), diarrhoea or constipation? |
| 10 Do you suffer from premenstrual tension? |
| 11 Do you suffer from depression, fatigue, lethargy, mood swings, feelings of unreality? |
| 12 Do you crave sweet foods, bread or alcohol? |
| 13 Do you suffer unaccountable muscle and joint aches (tingling, numbness, swelling etc.)? |
| 14 Do you suffer from vaginal discharge, irritation, or menstrual cramp or pain? |
| 15 Do you suffer from lack of sexual desire or impotence? |

If one or more of the questions in the first list, and two or more of those in the second list, are answered with a firm 'YES', then Candida is likely to be a part of the background to your problems.

Any symptoms associated with Candida are more likely to be worse when conditions are damp.

Getting the yeast back under control involves a variety of strategies including:

● **A dietary pattern which deprives it of its favourite sugars.**

● **A diet low in yeast-based foods, to**

which the body may have become sensitive.

● **The use of antifungal agents such as garlic, olive oil, the B vitamin biotin.**

● **The use of antifungal drugs such as Nystatin or Capristatin.**

Above all there is a need to repopulate your digestive tract with bacterial cultures which can re-establish the lost control over Candida and restore the balance to your internal environment. This calls for the use of high-potency bacterial cultures such as acidophilus and bifido factor, and for food which will help maintain the balance. Specialized foods such as amino acids (the constituents of protein) may be needed to ensure adequate nutritional levels of vital elements.

Anti-Candida strategy

First, you must change the food *you* eat to deprive Candida of *its* main food: sugar. At the outset this also includes avoiding fruit and fruit-juices for a few weeks.

The other major nutritional strategy calls for the avoidance of all foods based on yeast, derived from yeast or containing yeasts, moulds or fungi. This is recommended because most people with Candida overgrowth will have become sensitized to yeast, and their bodies will react against all forms of this until Candida is under control and detoxification has been achieved. Many foods, of course, have both a high simple carbohydrate level (sugars and refined cereals) as well as having a yeast content, making them particularly undesirable, e.g. white bread and pastries.

Foods which are sugar rich and which should be avoided on an anti-Candida diet include:

● **All sugar, whatever its colour.**
● **Sweets and glace fruits.**

● **Alcohol in all forms.**
● **Refined flour products (cakes, biscuits, pastry, white bread, white buns and rolls, white pasta, etc.).**
● **Foods with hidden sugar, including frozen peas and other frozen vegetables.**
● **Preserves, jams, marmalades, honey, pickles, sauces etc.**
● **Most processed cereal products, unless 'sugar free' is specified.**
● **Fruit and fruit juice (for first three weeks of diet).**
● **Milk, especially pasteurized milk (high milk sugar levels), although live natural yogurt can be eaten.**
● **Coffee, tea, chocolate, cola drinks (even sugarless ones) as these stimulate sugar release into the bloodstream from body stores (see Hypoglycaemia and Fatigue, page 144).**

Those foods which are yeast based or contain elements of yeast, or which are high in mould content, should be eliminated from the diet including:

● **Breads of all sorts, except non-yeasted wholewheat or corn bread.**
● **Cakes and cake mixes, biscuits and crackers.**
● **Buns, rolls, pastries and anything in breadcrumbs.**
● **Mushrooms, truffles.**
● **Soya sauce.**
● **Buttermilk and sour cream.**
● **Black tea.**
● **All cheeses except cottage cheese.**
● **Citrus drinks if canned or frozen.**
● **All dried fruit.**
● **Nuts and seeds unless freshly opened.**
● **All fermented beverages such as beer, wine, spirits, cider, ginger ale.**

● All malted products.

● Any food containing monosodium glutamate (likely to be high in Chinese restaurant foods).

● All vinegars.

● All relishes and salad dressings.

● Sauerkraut and pickles, including olives.

● Most multivitamin preparations, individual B vitamins, B-complex, and selenium supplements, unless 'yeast free' is stated.

● Antibiotics (these should be avoided during anti-Candida treatment unless absolutely essential.

These lists, on the face of it, leave little food to choose from, but this is, in fact, not so, as the suggested menu will show.

Suggested anti-Candida menu

Breakfast: High fibre intake is found to help control Candida, and this leads to a suggested breakfast of either a muesli type dish (non-sugar) or oatmeal porridge. A high protein intake is also desirable. Choose from:

● Oatmeal porridge. Flavour with cinnamon and/or ground cashew nuts. Make porridge with water, not milk. Use no honey or sugar.

● Mixed seed and nut breakfast. Combine sunflower, pumpkin, sesame, flax (linseed) seeds with oatmeal or flaked millet. These can be eaten dry or soaked overnight in a little water to soften them, or moistened with natural live yogurt. Add freshly milled nuts and/or wheatgerm if you wish.

● Three times weekly; two eggs, any style except raw.

● Bread or toast made without yeast or sugar.

● Brown rice kedgeree (fish and rice dish).

● Wholewheat rice or oat pancake (no sweetening).

● Natural live yogurt (add wheatgerm or cinnamon if you wish).

● After three weeks, add fresh fruit to the diet. Papaya is particularly recommended as a fruit which aids digestion.

● Fish (not smoked).

● Wholewheat or wholerice flakes and yogurt; or shop-bought sugar free muesli, plus yogurt.

Drink: Herbal tea or mineral water.

Main meals: Commercially produced meat tends to contain residues of antibiotics and/or steroid preparations with which the animals are dosed in order to produce rapid growth and weight-gain, and to keep down diseases. Therefore, such meat should be kept to an absolute minimum in the diet during Candida treatment.

Instead use free-range poultry, game and fish as sources of animal protein, or lamb which is little affected in this way, or choose a vegetarian type dish in which pulses and cereals are combined to give adequate protein intake (see the section on Protein and Energy for an explanation of this in detail).

A variety of fresh vegetables should be eaten to keep nutritional status high as well as to provide excellent forms of fibre.

One of the main meals each day should include fish, poultry, game, lamb, or a vegetarian combination together with a large mixed salad. The other main meal should be a suitable source of protein together with cooked vegetables.

Garlic is a potent antifungal agent, and as much fresh garlic as is manageable should be used in food preparation. Fresh is more effective than cooked, although there are still benefits to be obtained from cooked garlic.

With a choice of proteins, as outlined,

together with brown rice, wholemeal pasta, and the whole range of vegetables and pulses it is possible to create imaginative and tasty meals and dishes. Soups, stews, risottos and pasta dishes offer no shortage of ideas for anyone with a little patience and imagination. A plethora of cookbooks which can help in this are available, including several Candida cookbooks.

Supplements to control Candida

The most important supplements are those which repopulate the bowel with bacterial cultures which control Candida.

● Three times daily, between meals, and dissolved in a little tepid water, a quarter teaspoonful of *Lactobacillus acidophilus* powder. The brand I recommend is Superdophilus for reasons of potency and known quality. Take for at least three months.

● Three times daily, between meals, and dissolved in a little tepid water, a quarter teaspoonful of Bifido factor, another bacterial culture with similar properties which also aids liver detoxification. Take for at least three months.

● Once or twice daily, 500mcg biotin.

● High potency garlic capsules (if fresh is not being prolifically eaten). Three capsules twice daily after meals (Kyolic deodorized version recommended).

● Oleic acid, which derives from olive oil is an antifungal agent. At least a dessertspoonful of olive oil should be added to food daily. Ensure that this is first pressing (virgin, cold-pressed is ideal).

● Juice of aloe vera is an antifungal agent. Two or three teaspoonsful of pure aloe vera juice daily should be added to water and consumed.

● A non-nutrient element, derived from the coconut plant, caprylic acid, is a powerful antifungal agent and is recommended in the form of Caprycin capsules or tablets. Three to six capsules daily should be taken.

● Germanium is a known antifungal agent and is highly recommended (see Deficiency and Fatigue, page 64 for more information on this amazing element). A daily dose of 300mg is suggested.

Immune system enhancing nutrients

In addition to antifungal treatment it is necessary to boost your natural immune function. The following supplements are recommended for this purpose.

● Vitamin C. One gram three times daily.

● Arginine. Three grams daily with water on an empty stomach before retiring. If herpes or other viral conditions are current use Ornithine instead. Take either of these for no more than a month continually.

● One high-potency B-complex capsule/tablet containing no less than 50mg each of major B vitamins. Ensure that this is a yeast-free form.

● Additional 50mg of pyridoxine (vitamin B_6), taken at a separate time from B complex.

● Selenium, 50mcg to 100mcg and vitamin E, 200IU, daily.

● Zinc, 50mg daily.

● Magnesium 500mg daily.

● Free Form Amino Acids, 10g to 20g daily. (See also the section on Protein and Energy.)

● Vitamin A in the form of beta-carotene, 15,000IU daily.

● EFA (vitamin F) as oil of evening prim-

rose. Two 500mg capsules daily.

For further information on this topic read my book *Candida Albicans: Could Yeast be Your Problem?* (Thorsons, 1985) which gives greater deail on anti-Candida strategies.

In conditions such as myalgic encephalomyelitis (ME) also known as postviral fatigue syndrome, Candida is frequently a factor in the symptom picture.

ME has been dubbed 'closet AIDS', since it has so many symptoms in common with that major immune function collapse, which is also always preceded and accompanied by rampant Candida activity. In dealing with the complex symptoms of ME it is essential at the outset to take Candida seriously in hand, and to thus begin the process of rebuilding bowel integrity. A short-term effort will not produce real results in such cases, for it may require many months of diligent application of the elements required to control Candida.

NOTE: Associated with an anti-Candida programme there will frequently be a period of what is known as 'yeast die-off' or 'burn-off', during which the body is called upon to detoxify the breakdown products of the destroyed yeast. This may produce symptoms which are as bad as those previously endured and may last for some days.

Awareness of this possibility will help prepare for this unpleasant stage which is replaced by a steadily increasing sense of well-being. When this is experienced there is often a tendency to 'kick over the traces' with an abandoning of the careful nutritional strategy, leading to a swift return of the Candida symptoms.

Only a steady application of the programme will yield the desired results. Stick it out and enjoy renewed energy. There may, however, still be other elements in the pattern to sort out and this will often include longstanding viral infections.

CHAPTER 18

Cardiovascular disease and fatigue

Oxygen is a key element in the economy of the body, and its deficiency generally or locally results in a reduction in energy. Blood is the medium in which oxygen is carried to all parts of the body, and its adequate presence is, therefore, dependent upon a sound means of transportation. If the major pumping mechanism of the body, the heart, or the channels through which the blood travels, are impaired structurally or functionally, then circulation will be inefficient and oxygen will fail to arrive in adequate quantities to meet the needs of the tissues.

Other factors come into this, including the efficiency with which oxygen is brought into contact with the blood, in the lungs. Thus, the way we breathe is important. Also important are the secondary pumping mechanisms of the blood. As we move our bodies, muscles contract and relax. This has a pumping effect on the blood vessels which lie in those muscles. If we do not move adequately then circulation becomes impaired. This emphasizes the need for exercise, especially what has been termed aerobic exercise (see page 21).

The major muscles of the heart can themselves become deficient in oxygen due to partial blockage of the vessels supplying them with blood. This is the condition which produces angina pain and heart attacks, and which is termed cardiovascular disease. It is a major cause of fatigue and may be associated with symptoms such as a tingling, numb sensation in the arms, usually the left one; a tightness or choking sensation noted in the throat; a feeling of pressure on the chest; pain in the jaw, neck, throat, arm and shoulder.

When the heart muscles are inefficient, and oxygen levels in the body in general are low, sensations of general fatigue as well as shortness of breath will be experienced, especially when lying down. There may be a swelling of the ankles, light-headed feelings and a tendency to faint. There may also be a non-productive cough, palpitations and the face and hands may have a blue tinge.

One of the major underlying causes of all this is a narrowing of the arteries known as atherosclerosis. Among the factors which contribute to, or are associated with this, are:

- **High blood pressure.**
- **High blood sugar levels (diabetes).**
- **High cholesterol and fat levels in the blood.**

- **Obesity.**
- **Inactivity (inadequate exercise).**
- **Smoking (which should be stopped).**
- **Physical and emotional tensions (reaction to stress).**

Following the nutritional, exercise and stress reduction advice contained in the other sections of this book, will assist in preventing such a state from occurring, and will help in remedying aspects of it if it does exist. Nutrition, especially, is important in terms of lower levels of refined carbohydrates and fats, and higher intake of complex carbohydrates and other nutrients, as described in the sections, Fat and Energy, Carbohydrates and Energy, Obesity and Fatigue, Diabetes and Fatigue, and Hypoglycaemia and Fatigue.

Stress reduction, as described in the section on that topic, as well as in the section on Depression and Fatigue, is particularly applicable to cardiovascular disease and high blood pressure.

Specific nutritional assistance via the use of vitamins C and E, as well as the minerals and trace elements magnesium, selenium and, most importantly, germanium, as well as the amino acid carnitine, should be investigated, as should use of essential fatty acids such as MaxEpa. All these are described in the section Deficiencies and Fatigue. The nutrient Coenzyme Q_{10}, as described in the Energy Cycles section, should also be considered as this, in particular, has been found to assist in cardiovascular distress.

Chelation therapy and cardiovascular disease: the fatigue factor

The method of oral chelation described in the section on Toxicity and Fatigue is highly recommended for removal of arterial plaque which is restricting circulation in people with atherosclerosis.

Chelation is a process whereby one material locks on to another and transports it. This happens in the bloodstream constantly where haemoglobin chelates with oxygen and transports this to the tissue. In just such a manner detoxification of heavy metals, such as mercury and lead, can be achieved by nutrients such as calcium.

An artificial amino acid called EDTA has been used for some forty years to chelate lead out of the system by orthodox medicine. It has for years been realized by some practitioners that in doing so it also tended to begin the break-up of the cement-like deposits of plaque which obstruct the arteries of people with atherosclerosis. These deposits contain not only fatty deposits, including cholesterol, but also calcium. Once this has been 'softened' by the EDTA infusion, and a degree of chelation of the salts in the deposits achieved, the body seems quite capable of removing the fatty materials on its own. Thus a gradual restoration occurs of the integrity of the blood vessel, and improved circulation follows.

This therapy is controversial inasmuch as orthodox medicine tends to discount the amazing results achieved by their fellow doctors who are employing chelation. As with so much in medicine, the gentler less invasive approach seems to be denigrated by those who favour more direct intervention. In this case the proponents of by-pass surgery see chelation as a poor substitute. However, the more than a million people who have enjoyed its benefits thus far in the USA, and increasingly in Europe, may see a different aspect of the situation, for they are saved serious surgery and not inconsiderable expense.

CHAPTER 19

Chronic ill-health, old age and fatigue

It is not within the scope of this book to give specific advice as to the many ways of dealing with, or of modifying, chronic diseases such as bronchitis, emphysema, cancer, multiple sclerosis, arthritis, liver or kidney disease, all of which would probably have associated with them the symptom of fatigue and exhaustion.

In general terms, though, all or any of these can be made less troublesome by judicious use of the advice associated with:

Stress reduction (relaxation, meditation, visualization etc., see page 78).

Nutritional excellence (see various sections relating to energy such as carbohydrate, protein, fats and energy cycles pages 47, 42 and 30).

Supplementation of individual nutrients as indicated (Deficiency and Fatigue, page 52), and especially of free form amino acids (see Protein and Energy, page 47).

Specific nutrients related to energy production, such as selenium, germanium and vitamin C, in most cases of chronic ill-health (Deficiency and Fatigue, page 52) and individual amino acids as outlined in that section and the Protein and Energy section (page 47) as well as Coenzyme

Q_{10} (Energy Cycles, page 30).

Detoxification should be applied to all states of chronic disease, and the judicious use of fasting and other detoxification methods should be studied and employed as applicable (Toxicity and Fatigue, page 68).

Use of Adaptogens as non-specific aids to health enhancement (see Stress and Fatigue, page 78).

Bowel health. Most cases of chronic disease involve to a greater or lesser degree the health of the bowel. The section Candida albicans and Fatigue (page 110) should be well examined to see whether, as part of any chronic disease process, this is a factor. If so, appropriate attention, as described in that section, should be given. In all cases of chronic ill-health bowel health will be enhanced by use of periodic detoxification methods, high vegetable fibre intake and use of Superdophilus supplementation.

Pain control, as described in the section Pain and Fatigue, should be employed wherever this relates to chronic disease. It can be seen that there are multiple ways in which the advice relating to other areas of ill-health can be modified for use in a variety of chronic diseases. The body is a self-regulating, self-healing mechanism and the methods outlined, such as stress reduction and nutritional excellence, simply remove obstacles to that self-healing mechanism. Complete recovery is not always possible due to damage to structures and tissues. However, within the framework of what is reparable, almost anything is possible if we can learn to co-operate with our bodies, to release negative patterns of thought and behaviour and, above all, to love ourselves and give our mind/body complex a chance to heal itself. More often than not this is achieved by a combination of the removal of blockages within our emotional/psychological make-up and reforms of lifestyle, diet, and habit. This impetus, together with specific assistance (physical therapy, surgery, exercise, relaxation-meditation-visualization, supplementation etc.) should be the aim of all those afflicted with chronic ailments.

The elderly

Fatigue relating to age usually comes on slowly and is characterized by a general slowing down in the ability to perform simple everyday tasks; the need for more sleep and rest; slower recovery from illness and exertion. These are all indications of a general decline in vitality rather than evidence of actual ill-health.

Many illnesses are more likely in the elderly, such as cardiovascular disease or cancer, and these are usually associated with fatigue. It is important, therefore, to establish reasons for what appears to be an unnatural degree of tiredness.

Many physical and mental ailments may be associated with fatigue, but very often in the elderly psychosocial factors such as those listed below are likely to be involved, either alone or as part of a complex of interacting elements:

● Social isolation.

● Boredom.

● Lack of purpose in life.

● Bereavement.

● Longstanding stress, such as nursing a sick relative or spouse etc.

● Depression.

Most of these elements can be modified by altered attitudes, and this is talked about in both Depression and Fatigue and Stress and Fatigue (pages 122 and 78). Certainly, any such factors would be less likely to produce symptoms such as fatigue, were nutrition at optimum levels and adequate fresh air and exercise obtained.

Among the commonest physical conditions associated with fatigue in the elderly, all of which require proper diagnosis before advice being given or taken, are:

● Hypothyroidism (See page 174).

● Circulatory deficiency, especially of the brain (see Deficiency and Fatigue, page 52 and Cardiovascular Disease and Fatigue, page 117 with particular note of chelation therapy, also oral chelation as described in Toxicity and Fatigue, page 68). Amino acids and other nutrients such as vitamin E, germanium, and vitamin C can assist in such conditions.

● Cardiovascular disease and respiratory disease, including low and high blood pressure and breathing difficulty. The sections on Cardiovascular Disease and Fatigue (page 117), Hyperventilation and Fatigue (page 138), Exercise and Fatigue (page 20) and Deficiency and Fatigue (page 52), can all assist in awareness of strategies which can help to improve these conditions via lifestyle and nutritional changes. All will benefit from stress reduction as described in Stress and Fatigue (page 78).

● Poor nutrition. This can benefit from application of the concepts and suggestions found in the sections relating to energy (Protein, Carbohydrate and Fat and Energy, as well as Energy cycles pages 47, 36, 42, and 30 as well as Deficiency and Fatigue, (page 52) and Hypoglycaemia and Fatigue (page 144).

● Drugs. See Toxicity and Fatigue, page 68.

● Chronic pain. See Pain and Fatigue, page 164.

● Immobilization due to arthritis etc. Consulting an osteopath, chiropractor or physiotherapist for treatment and advice as well as application of the self-help measures in the various sections of this book can assist in pain reduction and improved mobility.

● Chronic degenerative diseases. The fact is that some people cope better with disease than others and this has to do with social customs, culture and personality.

Application of the concepts as outlined at the outset of this section should help in physical/chemical and psychological improvement being achieved inasmuch as this is possible.

In elderly people it is estimated that organic causes (physical disease) account for a third of all cases of chronic fatigue. Psychosocial factors account for a further third (social isolation, boredom, lack of purpose etc.) and the rest relate to the physiological aspects of growing older.

Inevitably there is a degree of overlap in these elements. In many people with ill-determined psychosocial causes it has been found that chronic hyperventilation is involved in the associated depression, anxiety, lassitude and fatigue. See Hyperventilation and Fatigue, page 138. Among the vague symptoms noted in such people are chest pains and palpitations; dizziness, lack of concentration and numbness; dry mouth and shortness of breath, and cramps and spasms.

There is clearly no universal advice which can be given relating to fatigue in relation to ageing or chronic disease. What is most important is identification of the many possible elements which make up the causes of the condition. Apart from the psychosocial elements which can be helped by stress reduction and counselling, there are multiple possible organic (physical, chemical) causes.

A useful mnemonic has been coined to help us keep track of these variables. This is the word MEDICINE.

M = Metabolic (body energy and detoxification cycles, hypoglycaemia, diabetes).

E = Endocrine (hormonal factors such as thyroid, adrenals etc.).

D = Deficiencies (nutritional, fresh air, exercise, etc.).

I = Iatrogenic or poisons (caused by drug medication or toxicity).

C = Cardiorespiratory (heart and breathing problems and body oxygenation).

I = Infections (viral, fungal, bacterial etc., resulting in immune decline).

N = neoplasms (cancer) and blood diseases (anaemia etc.).

E = Etcetera (rheumatic and other chronic diseases, neurological problems etc.).

CHAPTER 20

Depression and fatigue

Fatigue is one of the key elements in depression; a feeling of lethargy, tiredness, apathy, disinterest, weakness, lack of energy or direction; a feeling of oppressive weight and often of difficulty in breathing properly, together with a sense of everything being too much bother; a feeling that no effort of any sort is worthwhile. Depression is primarily a disturbance in mood. Mood being considered a prolonged emotional state, or tone, which dominates a person's outlook. It has been described by the American Psychiatric Association as a condition in which are noted:

● **Poor appetite with weight loss; or increased appetite with weight gain.**

● **Insomnia or excessive sleep patterns.**

● **Agitation or retarded activity.**

● **Loss of interest or pleasure in usual activities, or decreased sexual drive.**

● **Loss of energy and feelings of fatigue.**

● **Feelings of worthlessness, self-reproach or inappropriate guilt.**

● **Diminished ability to concentrate or think.**

● **Recurrent thoughts of suicide or death.**

If five of these signs or symptoms are present for not less than one month, then depression is considered definite. If four are present for not less than one month the patient is considered probably depressed.

The list is not an easy one to apply to oneself. The following questionnaire will help to identify the elements more clearly. Answer the questions with a simple 'YES' (if current and constant for at least a month, in which case score 2) or 'SOMETIMES' (if current and present for less than a month or intermittently, in which case score 1) or 'NO' (if not current and only rarely present, in which case score 0). Each question deals with a major symptom commonly found to be operating in depressed individuals. The questions are based loosely on the Beck Depression Inventory, a standard medical assessment tool.

1	Do you feel a strong sense of sadness?
2	Do you have a strong feeling that the future is hopeless or holds little to look forward to?

3	Do you have a sense of having failed in life?
4	Are you bored and dissatisfied with most elements of daily life?
5	Do you have strong feelings of guilt?
6	Do you have feelings that you hate yourself/your behaviour and are deserving of punishment?
7	Do you have feelings of self-disgust/self-disappointment/self-loathing?
8	Are you critical of yourself, blaming yourself for negative events?
9	Do you have suicidal thoughts?
10	Do you cry a lot, or did you cry a lot and now find that you can no longer cry, even if you wish to?
11	Do you become irritated and annoyed easily, or did you once become easily irritated and annoyed but now find that this does not happen (a sense of withdrawal and indifference)?
12	Have you lost interest in other people and their doings?
13	Do you have difficulty in making decisions?
14	Do you believe that your appearance has altered for the worse, or that you look old and/or unattractive?
15	Is all work an effort?
16	Is your sleep disturbed?
17	Do you get very tired without good reason?
18	Has your appetite become poor?
19	Have you lost weight without trying to?
20	Have you developed physical symptoms which cause you anxiety?
21	Has your interest in sex diminished markedly?

The highest score possible on this test would be 42. A score of 7 or thereabouts indicates that depression is not a factor. A score of around 14 indicates mild depression. A score of 18 or so indicates moderate depression. A score over 20 indicates severe depression.

Mild depression (a score of 15 or 14 or less) may be considered within the range of normal daily alterations in mood. Even this level should cause some concern if most of the symptoms have applied for more than a month. Anyone with a moderate depression, say a score of 16 or above should seek help for their condition and should take heed of the various aspects discussed in this section.

Anyone with severe depression should seek immediate professional help, and apply as much as possible of the advice in this section. However, we should not lose sight of the fact that, at times, depression is a perfectly normal reaction to life events such as marital problems, bereavement or job loss, for example. It would be abnormal in the face of tragedy to be happy and carefree. **It is the length of time which depression lasts, and its degree of appropriateness or otherwise, to life events and circumstances, which decides whether it is harmful.**

There are a number of clearly defined patterns of thinking and behaviour, which are more likely to lead to states of depression and anger (these two elements are very close, as we will see), which can be modified by means of your coming to recognize that there are choices to be made in the manner of your response to life events and stress factors.

Depression can exist alone, known as 'unipolar', or it can exist with mania (a condition in which great agitation would be apparent, for example), in which case it is known as 'bipolar' (a term also used when mania exists alone).

There is a great divide between doctors who consider that depression is a result of mental/emotional factors and those who see it as resulting from biochemical alterations which affect the brain, thus causing the mental emotional changes leading to depression.

The first school of thought argues that depression is best treated by drugs, which control the symptoms, and/or counselling which helps the person to learn to have insights into their problem with better coping skills. The doctors who see biochemical changes as the cause argue that nutri-

tional treatment or medication is required.

In many instances a complex interaction exists in which both psychological and environmental/nutritional factors are operating. It is well established that nutritional deficiencies, as well as certain toxicities, can produce depression, as can the actions of a number of common drugs, or the presence of a hypoglycaemic or allergic conditions. Other common causes include hormone imbalances and some infections, such as Candidiasis (see page 110).

Even where the major elements in a depressed state are seen to result largely from psychological factors there is strong evidence that, by attention to simple dietary strategies, the overall ability of the person to cope becomes better, and often the depression lifts spontaneously.

Such nutritional strategies are listed later in this section. But first I will briefly examine some of the major possible elements which can commonly be shown to produce depression, which in itself is a major cause of fatigue.

NOTE: Anyone currently on anti-depressant durgs should take a long hard look at just what the drugs they are using may be doing to them. These, however, should not be abandoned out of hand, for a great deal of dependency, or even addiction, may have taken place, requiring skilled help in the stopping of their use.

Nutritional deficiency and depression

It is possible for depression and, therefore, tiredness/fatigue to result from most nutrient deficiencies. The major changes though are related to a few of the important vitamins and amino acids. Some vitamins which have been shown to influence mood and behaviour dramatically when deficient include:

Vitamin C: lassitude; depression; hysteria; excessive concern about health.

Biotin: depression; extreme lassitude; constant desire for sleep.

Vitamin B$_{12}$: depression; psychosis; irritability; confusion; loss of memory; hallucinations; delusions; paranoia.

Folic Acid: forgetfulness; insomnia; apathy; irritability; depression; psychosis; delirium; dementia.

Niacin (vitamin B$_3$): apathy; anxiety; depression; hyperirritability; mania; memory loss; delirium; dementia; mood swings.

Pantothenic acid (vitamin B$_5$): restlessness; irritability; depression; fatigue.

Pyridoxine (vitamin B$_6$): depression; irritability; sensitivity to noise.

Thiamine (vitamin B$_1$): mental depression; apathy; anxiety; irritability; forms of psychosis.

Serum levels of many of these may be tested for in medical laboratories. Normal serum levels do not, however, indicate that levels in other tissues and areas are normal. This is especially true of B vitamins which may show normal levels in blood, but be extremely low in the areas of the central nervous system, for example.

Folic acid is the commonest nutritional deficiency in the world, with studies showing that over 65 per cent of patients admitted to psychogeriatric wards were grossly deficient. Studies have also shown that vitamin B$_{12}$ and folic acid supplementation has a beneficial effect in many cases. In some instances this is all that is required, whereas in others such supplementation is seen to enhance other therapeutic measures. Vitamin B$_6$ is especially important in the metabolism of tryptophan, and a test for this (tryptophan loading test) can be conducted to ensure that adequate levels are present. However, since the B vitamins are safe in even fairly large doses, such testing may be an unnecessary, time consuming, and often expensive, exercise. Simple supplementation as advised below cannot harm anyone and is likely to have general benefits, and sometimes specific ones relating to depression.

It is clear, therefore, that high potency B-complex supplementation, plus vitamin C, is indicated as a general measure in cases of depression. It is interesting that biotin is also very much called for in cases of Candidiasis. It is essential, if this yeast overgrowth is active, that any B vitamins taken are not themselves derived from yeast.

It is desirable to supplement vitamin B$_6$ separately from the B-complex supplement since it is found to be better absorbed in this manner. Also, as we will seen, the amino acid tryptophan is often a useful nutrient in depression, and this depends upon adequate B$_6$ for its metabolism.

Amino acids and depression

Tryptophan, phenylalanine, tyrosine, glutamine and methionine are all amino acids. That is to say they are fractions of protein, of which the body needs 20 to allow it to make protein, and each of which has unique attributes of their own, including powerful therapeutic effects.

There is great complexity in the ways in which amino acids function, and the rules of when and how they should be taken should be strictly adhered to, as should warnings when not to take them.

For example tyrosine and phenylalanine (which produces tyrosine in the body) should never be taken by anyone who is taking MAO (monoamine oxidase inhibitor) drugs. These are antidepressants and could well be prescribed for anyone with depression. Before trying to use amino acids, such as these two, in self-treatment, it is essential that you discover just what drugs you are taking, and if these are MAO inhibitors you should not take the amino acids.

Similarly, tryptophan should not be taken by a pregnant woman.

Amino acids used therapeutically should be taken away from mealtimes, and ideally with a small carbohydrate snack (a biscuit for example). Take amino acid supplements separately, if more than one is being used, and stick closely to the quantities recommended.

Studies have shown that the daily taking of 3g of tryptophan, and 1g of vitamin B$_3$ (nicotinamide) had profound antidepressive effects in unipolar depression. Often trials have been less convincing, however, and this is thought to relate to the fact that some forms of depression are better treated this way than others, and selection is necessary for best results.

It is not always easy, however, for the layman to know which group they belong to in this categorization.

Robert Buist Ph.D. has defined the method of selecting who will benefit from tryptophan and who from phenylalanine/tyrosine supplementation. He has noted that those who respond poorly to the drug amitryptaline and have low levels of the breakdown product of norepinephrine, MHPG, in their urine, will probably respond well to trycyclic drugs and should, therefore, respond well to supplementation of phenylalanine and tyrosine, but not to tryptophan.

Another subgroup are those who do respond well to amitryptaline, poorly to trycyclic drugs, and have high levels of MHPG in their urine (and, therefore, in their brains). These people should respond well to tryptophan supplementation.

The only way to know which of these amino acid strategies will work is to have a medical assessment of the urine to see whether there are high or low levels of MHPG (metabolite of norepinephrine), or to know which anti-depressant drugs have been used and whether they were effective. Another clue to the possible need for tryptophan is insomnia.

Amino acid supplementation
● **If tryptophan is indicated by your history (see above), 500mg three times daily should be tried at first, increasing to not more than 6g daily. Always take at least 50mg of pyridoxine (vitamin B$_6$) and 1g of nicotinamide (vitamin B$_3$) with the tryptophan as this assists in its metabolism. Take these daily in three divided doses with water and a carbohydrate snack, well away from mealtimes.**

If insomnia is a feature of your condition, then 1g of tryptophan together with vitamin B$_6$ should be taken half an hour before retiring.

● *Phenylalanine*. Up to 500mg daily or *tyrosine* 200mg to 400mg daily in divided doses, if these are indicated by your history.

● *Amino acids suitable for all depressed individuals*: In general people with symptoms of fatigue, especially if this is related to depression, will benefit from supplementation of all the amino acids in what is known as 'free form'. A balanced formulation of all 20 amino acids in this free form will be readily absorbed and will provide the raw materials for your body from which it can make the myriad proteins necessary for normal function. This is virtually predigested protein since the individual amino acids in such a formulation are separate and easy to absorb, not as in a protein such as meat, fish or egg where, although all of these amino acids would be present, they would be linked to each other and thus require a sound digestive process to break them into their component parts. This is already done when a free form amino acid capsule is taken.

Individual capsules contain between 500mg and 1,000mg, depending on the brand. In order to obtain positive results fairly rapidly, as many as 10 to 15 of these should be taken at a time, up to three times daily. This would provide not less than 15g of pure protein daily and as much as 45g, depending upon dosage and quantity. Experimentation may be needed to find what level of intake gives the best results in terms of improved energy levels. Take these away from mealtimes (the amino acids would be less well absorbed if other foods, especially of a protein nature, were competing for uptake) and with water or diluted fruit juice.

It should be noted that there are a number of brands of amino acids marketed which have less than adequate quality control.

Glutamine is another amino acid which can help depressives as it provides a detoxification effect on the brain, removing ammonia which may have accumulated. It is popularly known as a brain energy food, and it boosts brain function.

One of the interesting uses of glutamine is as a means of reducing sugar craving, which may be a particular feature of hypoglycaemic people whether depressed or not.

A three times daily dose of 300ng to 500mg is suggested (with water/diluted juice, away from mealtimes).

Methionine is another important detoxifying amino acid and should be used if there is any evidence of heavy metal toxicity (see below) at dosages of 1g daily.

Together with amino acids certain nutrients are recommended, such as vitamin C ($\frac{1}{2}$g) and Vitamin B_3 (200mg) with glutamine; and vitamin B_1 (100mg); zinc (25mg); vitamin B_3 (200mg); vitamin B_6 (200mg); and vitamin C (500mg) with the other amino acids listed above.

Depression and drugs and other toxic factors

Social drugs, such as tobacco, alcohol and caffeine, are capable of disturbing the normal balance between biochemical processes in the body which profoundly affect mood. There is a class of substances called neurotransmitters which enhance or retard the interaction between nerve endings, and which influence brain function and nervous system function dramatically. If there is an imbalance between those which enhance, and those which retard, major behavioural and functional changes take place, accompanied by mood altera-

tions. Thus, if those which enhance are predominant, to an unnatural degree, there will be hyperactivity (mania), and if those which retard are predominant, to an unnatural degree, then lethargy and indifference, and probably depression, will be a feature. These are all affected by nutritional balance as well as by drugs and toxic elements in the environment and diet.

Other commonly used drugs which alter the fine balance between neurotransmitters include cocaine, marijuana, steroid (hormone) drugs including the contraceptive pill, medication used in high blood pressure conditions, and many drugs employed in treating cardiovascular disease such as beta-blockers.

Caffeine

The daily use of caffeine-rich drinks and foods is a major element in the disruption of normal function. A cup of coffee contains between 50mg and 150mg caffeine. Tea contains around 50mg, and a cola drink 35mg. Studies have shown a direct link between the severity of symptoms in psychiatric conditions and the amount of caffeine consumed. Caffeine has a direct effect on the chemistry of the brain as well as having the feature, described in the section on adrenal exhaustion, of stimulating this hormone-producing organ. It causes sugar release into the system, which is followed by insulin production to control the higher sugar levels, and subsequently low blood sugar. All these elements interact creating a picture of a system which is malfunctioning and out of control, restoration of which depends upon your rebuilding your nutritional status by stopping the drug influence. No one who has depression or a tendency towards it should have any caffeine at all. This means no coffee, no tea, no cola drinks and no chocolate or cocoa.

The Pill

The use of oral contraceptives can lead to major nutrient imbalances, and to decreased levels of vitamins C, B_{12}, folic acid, B_2 (riboflavin), B_6 (pyridoxine) and zinc, which can be directly contributory to depression. Among the major influences is vitamin B_6 deficiency. Anyone who has taken or is taking contraceptive medication should supplement with this all important vitamin.

Tobacco
The use of tobacco poses a serious threat to vitamin C levels. Among the effects of low vitamin C are depression, hypochondria (overconcern with health and symptoms) and hysteria. Vitamin C deficiency also leads to specific changes in nerve function.

Tobacco smoking has an effect on adrenal function similar to that of caffeine; the pattern being, first adrenal stimulation, then sugar release, followed by compensating insulin release and subsequent low blood sugar levels, by which time the body seeks a further boost through a sugar snack, a caffeine drink or another cigarette. This cycle continues until exhaustion of the adrenals sets in, or marked hypoglycaemia or diabetes becomes a feature; and depression may be apparent as well. A vast number of interlocking hormonal and biochemical changes result from smoking.

Stopping smoking may involve any of a number of strategies, including nutritional support (notably vitamins B and C) as well as acupuncture, hypnosis, nicotine chewing gum and herbal treatment. Whatever it takes, smoking should be stopped. All or any of these strategies can work only if you have a real desire to quit smoking. The knowledge that the habit is not only killing you but also making your reduced lifespan a far from happy period, should enhance your desire to break it.

Other toxic factors and depression
Anything which 'poisons' the body can create changes leading to biochemically induced depression; for instance, toxic heavy metals such as mercury, lead or cadmium (see page 68). I also include such recent introductions as aspartame as an artificial sweetener. This is used in many proprietary drinks and foods as a replacement for sugar. Its formulation is aspartic acid, phenylalanine and methanol. The intake of phenylalanine, and therefore of tyrosine (derived in the body from phenylalanine), will dramatically increase if a lot of aspartame is consumed. This will have the effect of depressing tryptophan levels (these amino acids compete with each other for uptake) and could lead to low levels of brain serotonin, the substance which tryptophan contributes to the biochemistry of the body. This could have severe repercussions in depressive situations. The methanol content of aspartame is large and it poses a toxic threat which could have a profoundly negative impact, especially on sensitive individuals or children. Aspartame-containing food and drink should be avoided.

Summary
If you are suffering with depression/fatigue you should follow the general advice given below:

● **Stop intake of all foods and drinks containing caffeine. There may be withdrawal symptoms for up to three days, including headache and lethargy.**

● **Stop or drastically reduce intake of sugar, refined carbohydrates and junk foods.**

● **Avoid alcohol completely. There may be withdrawal symptoms which should be helped by taking the vitamins B and C suggested below, together with 1g of calcium, ½g of magnesium and 50mg of zinc daily as well.**

● **All social drugs should be stopped. Assistance in dealing with withdrawal symptoms can be obtained from nutri-**

ents such as those mentioned for alcohol, as well as by electro-acupuncture.

● Eat regular meals. This means at least three meals daily, and more if hypoglycaemia is a factor (see page 144).

Strategy

● To begin assessment of nutritional elements which may be deficient and thus affecting depression, start with a survey of the deficiency symptoms outlined in the section Deficiency and Fatigue (page 52) introduce appropriate supplementation.

● At the very least, you should take a high potency formulation B-complex (containing not less than 50mg of each of the major B vitamins) as well as 500mg to 1,000mg vitamin C.

● Supplementation of all the amino acids combined in a balanced formulation (free form amino acids) is suggested, as well as individual amino acids according to requirements. Vitamins B_6 and B_3 should also be added.

● Food allergy should be checked for and, if present, dealt with as outlined on page 104.

● Premenstrual tension syndrome should be assessed and dealt with as outlined on page 170.

● Hypoglycaemia and diabetes should be assessed and, if necessary, dealt with as outlined on page 144 and page 133.

● Thyroid function should be assessed, and professional advice taken about treatment, as well as following the general advice on page 174

● Candidiasis should be checked for and dealt with as outlined on page 110 if found to be active.

● Heavy metal toxicity should be checked for using hair analysis and, if present, dealt with as outlined on page 68.

General lifestyle changes

Exercise has a marked antidepressant effect since it brings about biochemical changes of a highly desirable sort. Regular exercise and adequate sleep are two key features in recovery of energy and the elimination of depression. You should exercise until pleasantly tired at least three times weekly for not less than 30 minutes. See the section on aerobic principles on page 21 and follow the guidelines. Sleep, for not less than 6 and not more than 8 hours, each night is health enhancing. A midday or early afternoon siesta is an excellent way of topping up a short night's sleep. Half an hour to an hour of complete rest at this time (not reading or watching TV) can promote a regeneration of energy. If sleep does not come easily to you, tryptophan can prove a great help in its enhancement. Avoid sleeping tablets.

Note: Anyone with post-viral fatigue syndrome (see page 153) should avoid exercise which tires them.

The mind, the emotions and depression

The effect of the stress we are exposed to in daily life is not so much due to the level of the stress as to our individual reactions to it (see pages 78-9). What causes ulcers in one person may result in no reaction at all in another. No matter whether it involves students under high examination pressures, or bus drivers dealing with traffic jams, or people facing the future after be-reavement or loss of a job, or people work-ing under constant pressure such as air traffic controllers.

In all such examples, some will pass through the multiple and major stresses with no signs of mental or physical ill-effects, while others will develop a variety of emotional, behavioural and physical conditions which can sometimes be life threatening in degree. Much work has been done to identify what the variables are, and whether the desirable responses of those who are unaffected by stress can be learned by those who react poorly to it, and the evidence is that to a large extent this is possible. This is talked about fully in the section on stress, but I mention it again here to reinforce an aspect of depres-sion which is little understood, that there are similar variations in response to de-pression and that we have choices which we can learn to exercise when faced with the complexities of life. Some of the re-sponses we make have become habitual and can lead inexorably to depression.

Dr Wallace Ellerbroek, an internationally renowned psychiatrist, has argued along these lines most forcibly ('Depression as Behaviour', *Journal of Energy Medicine*, Vol. 1, No. 1, pp 63-9, 1983), and many of the thoughts presented below are derived from his hypothesis which can be of prac-tical value to depressed people.

Let me pose a few questions and see how you respond:

● **When events are seemingly unpleas-ant, is it because we are viewing reality and finding that it falls short of our ex-pectations of how things ought to be?**

● **Can we accept that when everything is peeled away there are in life only two basic 'emotions'; what we 'like', and what we 'do not like'?**

● **Can this be expressed a different way, by saying that, taking account of all the** degrees of these emotions, there is, in re-sponse to anything in life, only that which makes us happy, and that which makes us unhappy?

● **If the world as you perceive it, and your fantasy of the world as you believe it 'should be', matches, does this produce a good feeling in you?**

● **If the world as you perceive it, and your fantasy of the world as it 'should be', do not match, does this produce a bad feeling in you?**

● **Can we express depression as 'my fantasy of reality does not match my fantasy of how it should be, and there is nothing I can do about it'?**

● **Can we express anger as 'my fantasy of reality does not match my fantasy of how it should be, but I think there is something I can do about it'?**

● **Is it possible that the only difference between depression and anger (which in-cludes irritation, rage, frustration etc.) is that in one we feel impotent in the face of elements we do not like, and in the other we feel potent (i.e. we can do some-thing about it)?**

● **When we become aware that there is a difference between our fantasies and the reality which we perceive, and we react by adjusting our fantasy to match reality, are we behaving in a rational, real-istic, non-neurotic, survival enhancing manner?**

● **When we recognize a difference be-tween our fantasies and reality as we per-ceive it, and insist that the reality should be altered to match the fantasies, are we behaving in an unrealistic, irrational, neurotic and anti-survival manner?**

● **Have we a choice in the manner in which we perceive events, whether we see them as pleasant or unpleasant (like/dislike; good/bad; happy/unhappy etc.)?**

● Is it possible, when faced with something unpleasant, for us to choose one of three responses?:

1 *It should not have happened.* (This is a denial of reality and may be altered to a somewhat less psychotic response by saying 'it would have been nice if it had not happened', although this too is not a positive response.)

2 *It happened.* (This acceptance response is less negative than No. 1 but may still not be helpful in avoiding negative effects.)

3 *Considering all the factors of which I am aware, and the many of which I am not, and since it apparently did happen, obviously it should have happened.* (This response is the healthiest, for it tends to control, prevent and correct any chance of negative emotional after effects.)

● Is it possible that given such a response as No. 3 above we can see that we don't necessarily have to 'like' what happened, in order to accept that it was what should have happened, thus denying the chance of staying with a fantasy in the face of reality?

● Is it possible that depression or anger, although often apparently justified in the face of the life events/environment of the individual, represent useless and futile responses, which are often the most dangerous thing the person could be doing to themselves?

● If we can see that depression produces visible and audible changes in terms of posture, facial expression, tone of voice etc., that if we consciously alter these from slumped to upright posture, to broad smiles and cheerful voice, we might begin a subtle feedback which can alter the depression?

● Is a way of avoiding depression outlined in the thoughts above, indicating that we should adjust our vision of the world towards a recognition of reality, and that we should carry on in a manner which is other than funereal?

The answers to all these questions should ideally be 'yes', and it is suggested that counselling and psychotherapy may lead us to a better awareness of just how much damage we do to ourselves by trying to cling to behavioural patterns and ways of reacting which are harmful to us.

All we need to do is accept things as they are, not as we would wish them to be, unless, that is, we can do something positive about changing reality.

This is possible in many ways. If I fantasize that life would be better if I were not a factory worker living in the North of England, I can either stay with the frustration of a job and place I do not like, or I can do something about moving to, say, Australia and becoming the sheep farmer I always wanted to be. This is altering reality.

The other way is to alter fantasy and to see that the job is not so bad after all and that it allows for free time in which I can go and look at sheep in the countryside, or whatever.

Either altering the fantasy or altering the reality is acceptable and rational and reduces the likelihood of depression. What needs to be avoided is a continuance of the situation in which fantasy and reality are not matched and are thus leading to stress, anxiety, frustration, anger and depression.

All of these are anti-life, anti-health, anti-survival, and all are self-induced to the extent that we *do* have choice. Depression is at times a behavioural response which can be unlearned, if that is what we want to do. It is not easy and often it is not necessary, since the depression is also often likely to be the result of one of the myriad interacting factors referred to earlier in this section. Other factors of which we should not lose sight include the need to admit the fact of depression to ourselves and to those close to us.

This should be done in a non-judgemental manner. Depression thrives on guilt, and this should be avoided. Most people become depressed for short periods many times in their lives. Whilst we have seen that there is probably an element of choice involved how we react to events, once we understand the truths explained above, we are not usually aware of these factors and when we are depressed we are unlikely to have the desire to do anything much about the situation without a great deal of tender loving care, and this needs to come from others as well as being directed from within.

Confide and share your feelings with others who care for you. Follow the general advice given above and know that in almost all cases the depression will pass, especially if you undertake those positive elements described above which are available to you. Holding on to that thought can be a major element in recovery.

Seasonal depression

There is a form of depression directly related to seasonal changes, especially as these relate to greater or lesser light exposure. There are conditions known as summer mania and winter depression which depend upon biochemical changes in the brain resulting from the activity of the pineal gland, which is light sensitive. The most effective treatment for this, if going outdoors more frequently in daylight is not possible (as in a bedridden individual or someone in a northern clime where daylight is very restricted) involves use of what is known as full-spectrum lighting. This is fluorescent lighting which has most of the elements of natural daylight, unlike most commercial lighting which is deficient in these.

Depression is a major cause of fatigue and sometimes depression results from fatigue. If so, attention to the points mentioned, as they apply to you, should ensure that depression lifts, and with it fatigue.

CHAPTER 21

Diabetes and fatigue

When, for any of a variety of reasons, the body loses its ability to control the levels of sugar in the blood (and this may include pancreatic exhaustion as referred to in the hypoglycaemia section) diabetes mellitus exists.

In many patients, usually the older onset diabetics, insulin is being produced but seems unable to influence the muscle and fat cells to burn the energy which sugar represents. If insulin is not present in sufficient quantities or is unable for other reasons to reduce blood sugar by means of its usual ability to enhance cellular uptake of the sugar, then serious health problems, often involving the cardiovascular system and the eyes may result as diabetes progresses.

The two main types of the disease involve what are known as insulin dependent (about 40 per cent of cases) and non-insulin dependent diabetes (most of whom use drugs to control their condition — about 40 per cent — and some who manage this by dietary manipulation — about 20 per cent).

Whether or not the condition can be totally controlled by diet, all diabetics need to pay attention to what they eat and drink in order to avoid a worsening of the condition.

The classic symptoms of diabetes include:

● **Excessive thirst.**
● **Excessive urination.**
● **Loss of weight.**
● **Appetite increase.**
● **Excessive fatigue.**

The major recommendations for diabetics include:

● **Making sure that weight reduction occurs if obesity if a factor.**
● **Ensuring that food eaten matches energy requirements, in other words not overeating.**
● **Excluding from the diet, as far as is possible, simple sugars (sucrose, glucose, etc.) and refined carbohydrates (white flour products, for example).**
● **Ensuring that at least half of the intake of energy comes from fibre-rich, unrefined carbohydrates, such as wholewheat bread, brown rice, wholewheat pasta, oatmeal porridge, etc.**
● **Ensuring that fats are reduced in the diet since this has been shown to greatly aggravate diabetes, especially when com-**

bined with a high sugar diet. This is especially true of saturated animal-derived fats, such as those found in milk, cheese, butter and meat. Levels of fat intake in many instances amounts to around 40 per cent of the food eaten, and this should be restrictedto around 30 per cent, with much of this in the form of monounsaturated oils (e.g. olive oil) or polyunsaturated oils (sunflower oil, for example) and only a small amount coming from saturated sources (animal fats).

● Following a dietary pattern recommended for diabetics.

● Reducing or avoiding salty foods, and the addition of salt on foods, since this substance is known to aggravate sugar sensitivity if too richly present in the diet.

● Reducing or eliminating alcohol.

● Reducing and avoiding stress.

There are a number of special nutrients which have been shown to be able to help in diabetes such as:

Chromium. This essential element is known to be part of what is called the Glucose Tolerance Factor which greatly enhances the body's ability to handle sugars. Unfortunately chromium is poorly absorbed from supplements and so can best be taken in the form of brewer's yeast at a rate of 20 or so tablets daily with food (unless there is a Candida problem, in which case chromium itself should be supplemented, ideally as chromic chloride). This is obtainable from pharmacies (on prescription), and taken in doses of 5ml daily under medical supervision, not because of toxicity, which is not a factor, but because it may alter requirements for other diabetic medication.

Another option is to take Chromium GTF (Glucose Tolerance Factor) obtainable from Health Food Stores. Use in doses of 200mcg daily. This should be combined with amino acids and vitamin B_3 (nicotinic acid) for effective usage, and the package should be checked to ensure that such a formulation is in fact present.

Vitamin C, in doses between ½g and 1g daily is a most useful supplement for diabetics in whom this vital substance is usually deficient. Additional supplementation with vitamins B_6, zinc, magnesium and potassium, as well as essential fatty acids (EFA) from sources such as oil of evening primrose may all assist in stabilizing or controlling a diabetic state. Expert advice from a nutritional counsellor is advisable for dosages.

Another factor which is often associated with diabetes is food allergy, which, as we have seen in the section on hypoglycaemia, can trigger sugar release into the bloodstream. This possibility should be considered and dealt with if noted (see page 104 on allergy).

Stress factors should always be dealt with by counselling and relaxation/meditation methods (see page 78) since stress can severely and adversely affect diabetics.

NOTE: DIABETES IS NOT A CONDITION SUITABLE FOR SELF-TREATMENT. IT REQUIRES EXPERT MEDICAL GUIDANCE, ALTHOUGH A VAST AMOUNT OF HELP IS POSSIBLE BY JUDICIOUS CARE IN DIET SELECTION, SUPPLEMENTATION AND STRESS REDUCTION. The fatigue element in diabetes should improve if the guidelines listed above are followed.

CHAPTER 22

Headaches and fatigue

There are many variations of headache
which incapacitate many people and
which carry with them the feature of exhaustion. Those which are commonly
known as 'tension' headaches can best be
dealt with by following the advice given
in the Stress and Fatigue section as well
as general lifestyle and dietary changes
outlined throughout the book. Migraine
headaches are, however, different from
other headaches and deserve special consideration.

Types of headache
Cluster headache

● Affects mainly males, occurring usually at night.
● Accompanied by stuffy nostrils and
red eyes, on one side of the face only.
● Attacks last 20 minutes to 2 hours.
● Alcohol is a common predisposing
factor.
● Pain is often so severe that the person
affected may be unable to stay standing
or sitting, or to even be able to lie still.

Tension headaches

● Often daily occurrence.

● Sometimes almost continuous.
● Vice-like sensation of pressure on top
of head or base of skull, or both.
● Often described as 'halo' of pain.
● Often accompanies depression or
anxiety.
● Not usually incapacitating.
● Not associated with gastrointestinal or
visual symptoms as is migraine.
● Unaffected by painkillers.

Muscle pain headaches

● Usually result from tension in jaw,
neck or head muscles.
● May result from joint dysfunction
(neck, etc.)
● Muscles will often be tender to touch.
● Movement of head seems to aggravate.
● May last hours. More common in
morning than evening.

Migraine

● Always involves one side of the head
only.
● Has a paroxysmal nature (i.e. violent
and acute symptoms).

● Frequently preceded by aura which may taken the form of flashing lights, inability to speak normally, numbness etc.

● Nausea, diarrhoea, vomiting may precede or accompany migraine.

● Either *circumstantial* (related to particular circumstance, food, etc.,) or *periodic* (falling into pattern of weekly, monthly etc.)

● Last from 2 hours to 3 days.

● Can be incapacitating, leaving bedrest as only option.

● Often associated with:
  — particular foods (food sensitivity)
  — lack of food (hypoglycaemia)
  — emotional stress
  — periods
  — alcohol
  — particular activity (exercise, etc.)
  — use of contraceptive pill
  — Candida albicans overgrowth.

In all cases of regular headache the following questions should be answered for guidance as to patterns:

● When does it begin?

● How long does it last?

● Where do you feel it?

● How often does it happen?

● Does it travel to other areas?

● Is it deep or on the surface?

● What seems to start it off?

● What makes it worse?

● What makes it better?

● What sort of pain is it?

● How much pain is there?

● What other symptoms are there?

● What treatment has been used?

● Was it helpful?

● What do you think of the headache and its causes?

● Why do you think you developed a headache at this particular time?

Fatigue is often an accompanying or subsequent symptom associated with headaches, especially migraine.

Treatment

For *tension* and *muscle pain* headaches stress reduction is called for, as outlined in the section on Stress and Fatigue (page 78) and Depression and Fatigue (page 122) usually together with physical treatment, as outlined in the Posture and Fatigue section (page 167). For *Migraine* headaches, factors such as: food sensitivity (see Allergies and Fatigue, page 104); stress, (see Stress and Fatigue, page 78); Hypoglycaemia (see Hypoglycaemia and Fatigue, page 144); Candida (see Candida and Fatigue, page 110), should be investigated as possible causes and treated accordingly if found to be involved.

If migraines relate to monthly periods then the section on Premenstrual Tension and Fatigue (page 170) should be studied for associated symptoms and possible nutritional deficiencies.

Migraines in children have been clearly shown in studies at Great Ormond Street Hospital for Sick Children to be related, in the main, to food sensitivities. When the irritant food(s) is/are removed from the diet the headaches tend to cease occurring. There is no single culprit, however, with dairy produce, eggs, wheat, food additives and certain meats all producing migraine headaches in some children and not others.

The general advice in the section Allergies and Fatigue (page 104) should be followed. Specific help is possible by the use of the herb feverfew (*Tanacetum parthenium*) a member of the chrysanthemum family. Studies at the City of London Migraine Clinic have proved the safety and efficacy of the use of this plant in treating migraines in most sufferers.

If you grow your own feverfew plants, then between one and five leaves eaten daily (in salad or a sandwich) will be found to be effective. Tablets are available from heath food stores and herbalists, and these are equally effective. Follow instructions on the pack, which is usually to take one tablet daily as a preventive measure. They do not act as a painkiller during an attack. During an attack rest is the best medicine.

Drugs can abort migraines if taken at the outset of aura symptoms, but the effects of these is often worse than the headache, leaving the sufferer free of pain but washed out. Acupuncture has proved effective in dealing with migraine in many cases, but may require a regular pattern of treatment. When the headaches are controlled the fatigue factor usually abates.

CHAPTER 23

Hyperventilation and fatigue

When we breathe, a variety of biochemical states are affected in the bloodstream. When rapid breathing occurs, interspersed with deep sighing, the levels of carbon dioxide (CO_2) in the bloodstream are decreased at a rapid rate leading to what is called hypocapnia, low CO_2, and consequent symptoms of a wide-ranging and often bizarre nature. Such a breathing pattern, which is often associated with emotional reactions, but which may become habitual, is called hyperventilation. This is defined as an increase in ventilation greater than that required for the metabolic needs of the body, and the result is a reduction in what is called the *partial pressure of arterial carbon dioxide* ($_pCO_2$), and this in turn is the cause of a variety of symptoms.

Experts used to consider that the effects of hyperventilation were more related to increased oxygen, whereas nowadays they lay the blame for the symptoms on the decrease of carbon dioxide in the blood, which can at times be life threatening. Profound fatigue is a major symptom in this condition.

There is a complex interaction between the conditions of depression, hypoglycaemia and hyperventilation which is often difficult to unravel. In some instances, when hypoglycaemia is dealt with appropriately (see page 144) hyperventilation improves or vanishes. In others, when appropriate anti-depressive action is taken (see page 122) there is a marked decline in hyperventilation. In yet other cases the hyperventilation appears to be primary, and to actually be the cause of the panic/anxiety/depression state, which may be associated with it. In such cases breathing retraining and stress reduction/relaxation techniques are excellent ways of improving many of the symptoms found with the problem.

A recent study (published in *The Journal of Psychosomatic Research* (Vol. 31, No. 3, pp 401-12, 1987) showed evidence that not only does anxiety, panic and phobic behaviour sometimes appear to result in hyperventilation, but that in many cases hyperventilation appears to be the real cause of the anxiety and panic, often leading to such phobic states as agoraphobia (fear of open spaces).

A study reported in *The Lancet*, (22 September 1984, p 665) showed that when agoraphobics, people with such a fear of open spaces that they could often not leave their homes, were taught to breathe correctly, they could overcome the panic attacks more easily, and could then slowly begin to regain their confidence in going out, thus returning to non-phobic, normal behaviour.

The sequence seems to be that because of a number of factors — not least extreme muscle tension, often associated with poor body mechanics and stress, as well as hypoglycaemia (which may itself be related to depression and/or allergy) — a person might have an anxiety/panic attack when out shopping or in the street. Once this has happened the fear of the same thing occurring again is so great that, faced with going out (or facing any other phobic situation such as height, or enclosed space etc.) muscle tension, combined with bad habits of use, triggers hyperventilation, which then sets in motion the biochemical changes which lead to further panic attacks and sometimes fainting.

After this it is not surprising that such a fear exists of a similar state of helplessness in a public place (or other feared situation) that the person cannot bring herself/himself to go out of the front door. Sometimes as soon as such people even think of doing so, tension and hyperventilation begin, and a panic situation with phobic (intense fear) overtones begins.

Tuula Tuormaa, a researcher into this field of medicine, has studied the complex changes which take place in response to hyperventilation, including the drop in levels of bicarbonate normally found in the bloodstream, leading to increased acidity of the blood through accumulation of lactic and other acids.

She summarizes methods which could reduce the effects of hyperventilation rapidly, and these include:

● **Inhalation of carbon dioxide rich air (breathing into a brown paper bag and** **rebreathing the exhaled air is a good way of doing just this, and this method is often suggested as first-aid for hyperventilators).**

● **The taking of bicarbonate of soda in order to deacidify (alkalize) the bloodstream and short-circuit overbreathing, thus helping increase retention of carbon dioxide.**

It is interesting to note that taking bicarbonate of soda in solution is also often suggested as a means of cutting short an allergy attack. The interconnection between allergy, hyperventilation and hypoglycaemia is indeed profound.

Hyperventilation syndrome
Hyperventilation syndrome (HVS) has been shown to present with the following symptoms (percentage of cases is in parentheses). The figures are from *The Journal of the Royal Society of Medicine*, Vol. 79, p 448, August 1986. Giddiness (59 per cent); difficulty in breathing (53 per cent) palpitations (42 per cent); numbness and tingling (36 per cent); loss of consciousness (31 per cent); visual disturbance (28 per cent); headache (22 per cent); nausea (18 per cent); difficulty in walking (18 per cent); tremor (10 per cent); noises in the head (3 per cent). In addition exhaustion is present in many cases.

These symptoms result from severe and diagnosed hyperventilation. For many people the symptoms they suffer, including fatigue, are not obviously caused by hyperventilation. This factor can be shown to be operating, though, by the simple expedient of having them overbreathe for a minute or so, in order to prove that their symptoms come into play very rapidly.

NOTE: Such challenges are never to be carried out without expert supervision.

Mild hyperventilation is common and may relate to any combination of the following factors:

- **Poor posture.**
- **Muscular tension.**
- **Food or inhaled allergy/sensitivity.**
- **General stress and tension.**
- **Structural problems (spinal or thoracic joint dysfunction due to injury, habitual or occupational use patterns, etc.).**
- **Poor habits of breathing (thoracic rather than diaphragmatic breathing).**

Symptoms may be transient and could include a number of unexplained problems including:

- **Gastrointestinal disturbances.**
- **Dizziness.**
- **Visual disturbance.**
- **Tingling hands, feet or face.**
- **Difficulty in swallowing.**
- **Muscular cramps and pains (especially in the neck and shoulders).**

Apart from these variable symptoms the major complaints are:

- **General exhaustion.**
- **Lack of concentration.**
- **General dissatisfaction with the ability to function normally.**

Other commonly associated problems include:

- **Sleep disturbances.**
- **Nightmares.**
- **Profuse sweating.**

One interesting by-product of lowered carbon dioxide levels is that pain is usually dramatically diminished, which may account for an almost instinctive tendency to overbreathe in response to intense pain. Another side-effect is that when hyperventilating, and thus creating low carbon dioxide blood levels, the reaction of the individual to alcohol will be dramatically increased. This has been noted on planes, where hyperventilation is common through suppressed fear, and where, after a drink or two, some passengers become difficult to control.

- **Anyone who hyperventilates should never drink and drive.**

It has been found in studies that as many as 40 per cent of all patients referred for hospital investigation of undiagnosable symptoms suffered from hyperventilation.

It is important to realize, though, that under certain conditions hyperventilating is not only normal, but essential to survival. Faced with a major challenge, say a wild animal from which we would have to flee or confront, it is essential for greater oxygen requirements to be met by greater intake of breath. Faced with stress the body prepares for action. As we have seen, this also entails the release into the blood of additional sugar to meet the anticipated needs of the 'fight or flight' response to danger. In just the same way the body prepares by increasing the rate and depth of breathing. Unfortunately, though, this is not appropriate in many stress situations in modern life.

Faced with a traffic jam, a difficult boss or employee, or an unpleasant situation in the family, we cannot react as we would were we faced with an obvious challenge such as that represented by a wild animal. We cannot fight the boss or employee; we cannot run from the traffic jam or the family situation. Nevertheless, our body is primed for such action and continues to overbreathe and to react as though it was the needed response. The end-result is a disturbance in blood-gas levels and the sequence outlined above. Such behaviour may become habitual. We may begin to sigh and breathe badly whenever we are stressed, as well as developing tension in muscles, and postural habits which make correct breathing almost impossible anyway.

It is not surprising, then, that health problems arise from such changes. Stress reduction; relearned habits of use; and awareness of this possible sequence of events is a major part of the answer to hyperventilation. Ideally, together with this, should come changes in lifestyle and better ways of coping with stress.

A report in *The Journal of the Royal Society of Medicine* (Vol. 74, pp 1-4, January 1981) tells of 1,735 patients with hyperventilation, treated at Papworth Hospital, Cambridge, of whom more than 1,000 received instruction in relaxation exercises and breathing re-education. Symptoms usually vanished within one to six months and, in many instances (the younger patients), within weeks. Of the group of more than 1,000 patients treated in this way, over 75 per cent were symptom-free when re-examined after 12 months, and a further 20 per cent had only mild symptoms at that time. This is a remarkable result by any standards, and all achieved without drugs.

Less than one patient in 20 with hyperventilation is seen to be intractable in their condition when treated in this manner.

A recent study reported in *The Journal of Psychosomatic Research* (Vol. 31, No. 2, pp 215-21, 1987) discussed the major symptom of acute chest pain found in people attending emergency rooms in hospital, and being found not to have any sign of cardiac problems or other organic cause for the pain. In a group of 70 such cases, all under the age of 40, a detailed study was made of the factors which had contributed to chest pain symptoms, so severe as to have led the individual to seek emergency attention. The common factors were found to include, in women (the patients in the study were divided evenly between the sexes) what the researchers defined as 'neuroticism'; an inability to cope well with uncontrollable major life-events (such as death of a relative, loss of a job, etc.). Most were found to be suffering from what is termed 'vital exhaustion'. Many of the males and some females were found to be what is called 'Type A' personalities, who strive for success and are sometimes obsessive in their behaviour. **All** were found to have tense musculature in the chest region.

The researchers concluded that 'like tension headache, enhanced tension in the thoracic (chest) muscles can cause chest pain. An altered respiratory pattern with predominantly thoracic breathing will lead to increased tension in the intercostal muscles (between the ribs). This is often seen in patients with hyperventilation syndrome.'

Here we can see an interaction between personality (the busy, striving, ambitious, non-relaxed person) often with major stresses in their lives with which they do not cope well, and suffering from 'vital exhaustion' which can mean a general depression or fatigue.

It is logical that such stresses should lead to their developing physical tensions in the muscles between the ribs, with consequent pain and/or hyperventilation and all that this can mean. The cure lies in learning to relax, diminishing stress by developing coping skills and altering negative habits and, above all, by correct breathing.

Breathing techniques

There are a number of methods by which breathing can be improved in a self-help manner:

Yoga pattern breathing

One technique which has been tried and tested for many thousands of years in yoga methodology was recently put to scientific scrutiny and found to be of great value. In 1984 research at the University of Kansas showed that if the yoga method of taking slightly longer to breathe out than to breathe in, all within the context of a general slowing of the breathing rate, is adopted, a marked reduction occurs in anxiety symptoms (*The Journal of Psychosomatic Research*, Vol. 28, No. 4, pp 265-73, 1984). The study involved groups of people who were given different patterns of breathing to follow whilst confronted with varying degrees of distraction, threat and stress. They were monitored for a variety of responses and the different patterns of breathing were then assessed in relation to these responses to stress.

The pattern which emerged as an overall stress reducer involved slowing the pattern of breathing to six cycles per minute, that is a ten second overall timespan for a complete cycle of inhalation and exhalation. The cycle itself was broken into a swift two second inhalation and a slow eight second exhalation phase. This requires practice but can be seen to offer an excellent means of coping with an anxiety producing situation. This is especially true if there is a history of hyperventilation and/or panic attacks.

It is suggested that this be practised on a daily basis for several minutes at a time, so that the rhythm becomes comfortable and familiar. It can then be used when, and if, a situation is experienced which might be expected to generate stress or anxiety.

Abdominal (diaphragmatic) breathing

This method also has its roots in traditional yoga techniques. Most hyperventilation breathing is found to involve use of the upper chest and to neglect the abdominal or diaphragmatic component of the chest/lungs. Ideally, as breathing begins, there should be an outward bulge of the abdomen just below the ribs, as the diaphragm falls and the capacity of the lungs increases to allow air to enter.

The ribs in the lower chest should move outwards (sideways) as this occurs. There should be a co-ordinated and immediately subsequent movement of the ribs of the upper chest thereafter, in which the lower ribs move laterally (sideways) and finally, as the lungs fill, the upper ribs move forwards. As exhalation occurs there is a reversal of these movements with a final doming of the diaphragm associated with the flattening of the stomach region and a collapsing together of the lower ribs. Practising this requires that the full cycle of breathing be put through its paces in both a sitting and a lying (face upwards) position, for several minutes, ideally daily and at least every other day.

Sit, or lie face upwards. Place hands, fingers forward, to rest on the lower ribs so that the tips of the fingers rest on the abdomen. Concentrate on just this region.

As a slow, deep breath begins feel the abdomen push forwards (towards the ceiling if you are face upwards) slightly, immediately followed by a lateral (sideways) movement of the lower ribs.

Inhale to a count of three or four.

After filling the lungs, exhale and feel the ribs of the region on which the hands lie begin to come together, and then finally note the abdomen flatten. Take a count of four or five to exhale before repeating the cycle. Always breathe through the nose and take a second longer to exhale than you took to inhale.

It is most important that exhalation is seen to take longer than inhalation.

If the regions which you want to move do not appear to do so in the desired direction or sequence, then there should be a conscious movement using the muscles to make the desired motion, until this becomes automatic. You may wish to concentrate on just the abdominal movement for a number of breaths, and then just the lateral chest movement, so that the components become familiar to you before you once again try to put them together, as described above.

Do this exercise for a total of 20 cycles and then lie or sit still before changing position or standing, as dizziness may be noted with rapid movement.

Relaxation exercises are described in the section dealing with Stress and Fatigue (page 78). These should be practised on a daily basis for not less than 20 minutes, after the breathing exercises have been performed. By paying attention to all the variables which might be involved in hyperventilation, such as hypoglycaemia, allergy etc., as well as the stress and breathing elements, a sound basis for recovery will have been made. Energy and vitality will return when these negative factors are dealt with.

CHAPTER 24

Hypoglycaemia and fatigue

In order to understand the significance of hypoglycaemia (low blood sugar) we need to define the term as we are using it. Strictly defined, we are speaking of what is called 'reactive hypoglycaemia', in which the level of sugar in the blood falls dramatically in response to one of the following factors:

● **Ingestion of sugar-rich foods (refined sugars or refined carbohydrates or fruit juices, etc.).**

● **Ingestion of substances which trigger a sugar release into the blood, such as caffeine-rich foods or drinks (coffee, tea, cola drinks, chocolate etc.).**

● **Use of stimulants, such as tobacco or alcohol.**

● **Allergic reactions to inhaled or ingested substances to which the subject is sensitive.**

● **Excessive exercise or stress.**

Among the other names used to describe this condition are hyperinsulinism, functional hypoglycaemia and idiopathic postprandial syndrome. It is distinct from another form of low blood sugar which occurs when fasting, and which is indicative of liver or pancreatic problems. In order to function at all normally we require a constant level and supply of sugar in the blood. This allows for strength, energy and activity to be normal.

If sugar levels become low the nervous system in general, and the brain in particular, react badly since glucose is the major brain fuel. Just how important it is can be noted by the fact that, although the brain accounts for merely three per cent of body weight it utilizes over half the glucose used by the body to maintain its functions.

One of the first symptoms of low blood sugar is a general weakness, often coupled with shakiness, cold sweats, inability to co-ordinate properly, muzzy headache, walking and speech difficulty, panic attacks, and often faintness.

Now, it may appear that since low blood sugar is so damaging (and it is) all we need to do to maintain its levels would be to keep eating sugar-rich foods. This is not so. Indeed such action is the very reason for many cases of low blood sugar. This requires explanation.

The opposite of low blood sugar is not, unnaturally, high blood sugar, also known as diabetes, a thoroughly unpleasant and dangerous situation which the body normally protects against (see Diabetes and Fatigue, page 133). In order to maintain levels of sugar in the blood at an optimum level, never allowing it to get too high, the pancreas produces insulin which reduces these high levels. Every time a sugar rich food is ingested there is a sharp rise in blood sugar which the pancreas deals with by producing adequate amounts of insulin. This restores normal levels.

Whenever a stimulant is used, whether this be alcohol, caffeine, or tobacco, or any other stimulant drug, there is a release into the bloodstream of sugar which had been stored in the liver or elsewhere in the body. High levels in the blood are again prevented by the pancreas, as with sugar-rich food intake.

Whenever we are highly stressed, or roused to anger, we automatically release sugar from stores into the bloodstream, in order to prepare us for action, this is the so called 'fight or flight' reaction which allows us to cope with dangers and challenges. If the sugar thus released is not used by appropriate action, running or physical response, for example, then once more the high levels have to be dealt with by insulin.

If we put this altogether and visualize the common situation in modern society we can see that, on an average day, a person may consume sugar-rich foods, refined carbohydrates (white bread, etc.) as well as tea, coffee or cola drinks, partaking of chocolate and often smoking as well, all in the midst of a rushed, stressed lifestyle and job environment. We can see that the pancreas is going to be working pretty hard to maintain levels of sugar where they belong under such circumstances.

Ultimately, as with any overworked organ, it may become inefficient and start to over-react, bringing blood sugar levels too low, leading to hypoglycaemia. Or it may stop producing adequate levels of insulin, resulting in rising levels of blood sugar, and the onset of diabetes which may call for artificial insulin being used.

One of the major symptoms of low blood sugar is weakness and fatigue. The taking of a stimulant when this occurs, which is the common response, only adds to the likelihood of the problem becoming worse. Thus, whenever a dip occurs in blood sugar, and fatigue or shakiness sets in, the person may eat a sweet, drink some coffee/tea/cola, smoke a cigarette or eat a cake, or any combination of these. The result is an immediate lift, as the sugar thus released, or ingested, hits the bloodstream, followed by an inevitable dip again as the insulin arrives to modify it.

The swings of energy and mood in which this results, are experienced by many people, and because it is so common it is considered normal. It is definitely not normal, and is in fact very dangerous, leading ultimately to collapse of the pancreas and a variety of unpleasant chronic problems, including a long string of symptoms, which may include all or any of the following. Note: the figures in brackets represent the percentage of patients affected in studies of some 900 hypoglycaemics (*American Practitioners Digest of Treatments* 971-7, June 1959; and *The Journal of the National Medical Association*, Vol. 58, pp 12-17, 1966).

Neurological symptoms
Tremors (54 per cent); numbness (51 per cent); headache (45 per cent); incoordination (43 per cent); blurred vision (40 per cent); loss of balance (34 per cent); fainting (14 per cent); convulsions (2 per cent).

Somatic symptoms
Gastrointestinal (68 per cent); palpitations (54 per cent); pains in muscles and joints (53 per cent); sweating (41 per cent); gasping for air/feeling of being smothered (37 per cent).

Psychiatric symptoms
Nervousness (94 per cent); irritability (89

per cent); *fatigue/exhaustion* (87 per cent); dizziness (86 per cent); depression (77 per cent); sleepiness (72 per cent); confusion (67 per cent); anxiety (62 per cent); insomnia (62 per cent); antisocial behaviour (47 per cent); crying spells (46 per cent); inability to concentrate (42 per cent); phobias (31 per cent); suicidal feelings (20 per cent); nervous breakdown (17 per cent); psychosis (12 per cent).

Depression and fatigue can be seen to be major elements in the response to low blood sugar. This is a very widespread phenomenon, affecting, it is estimated, some 10 per cent of the populations of industrialized societies such as the USA and Western Europe. It is often associated with other problems such as allergy, which also triggers a sugar release, leading to addiction in some instances. It is markedly aggravated by stress, both physical and mental, leading to the need for a stress-reduction programme as well as the dietary strategies outlined below.

Because the condition often leads to, or is associated with, depression this can severely complicate the treatment. Tuula Tuormaa, a leading researcher into this complex area writes as follows ('Nutritional Therapy and Counselling as an Alternative Medicine for Affective Disorders', unpublished manuscript, 1987):

> In my experience in treating people suffering from hypoglycaemia, the same basic pattern of symptomatology in any one person is usually constant, only the severity of attacks may vary from time to time. Apart from the fact that there are individual differences as to the level of blood sugar at which symptoms appear, the rapidity with which the blood sugar falls is of prime importance; that is, the more rapid the fall, the more severe the symptoms of anxiety, which are directly caused by the massive increase in adrenaline (epinephrine) secretion which helps to release stored glycogen from the liver in order to rectify the hypoglycaemic state. It has been established that during

> rapid fall of the blood sugar, plasma and urinary levels of adrenaline can increase as much as 10 to 50 fold, depending upon the degree and severity of the fall.

> Also the greatest variations in the blood sugar level are usually associated with either an excessive anxiety or marked depressive state. In short, most of the hypoglycaemic symptoms can be explained in terms of the reaction of the following:

> (a) A rapidly decreasing blood sugar concentration.
> (b) The final lowered level when the body, including brain, has less fuel to function optimally.
> (c) The compensatory reaction to the low blood sugar, especially the secretion of adrenaline and other counter-regulatory hormones, such as glucagon, cortisol, and growth hormones.

> What interests me here is that tranquillizers such as benzodiazepines are at first potent growth hormone activators, thus helping the blood sugar to rise but apparently, after long-term therapy, tolerance seems to develop to this growth hormone releasing effect.

> Findings suggest that the first therapeutic action of tranquillizers (benzodiazepines) may be their blood sugar releasing potential, which after long-term therapy can depress growth hormone release, which in turn could lead to a chronic hypoglycaemic state.

> A fact which could support my hypothesis is that the symptoms of hypoglycaemia and benzodiazepine addiction and withdrawal are similar.

Thus we have a picture in which, because of any of a variety of often controllable elements (diet, sugar consumption, stress), a low blood sugar pattern develops which includes depression as one of its symptoms. This is treated by substances which reduce the depression, partly through release of more sugar via hormonal influences. Ultimately these become ineffective, by which time the person is often addicted to them. The withdrawal from, or continued use of, these drugs leads to even greater low blood sugar.

Diagnosis
It is usually possible to recognize the pattern of symptoms and their timing. This in itself can be diagnostic.

A more formal route is the use of what is called a six hour glucose tolerance test, which gives a characteristic pattern of blood sugar, after a high dose of glucose is taken on a fasting stomach.

HYPOGLYCAEMIA QUESTIONNAIRE

Answer the following questions with a 'YES' (3 points); 'SOMETIMES' (2 points) 'SELDOM' (1 point); or 'NEVER' (0 points). In this context 'YES' means more than once a week, 'SOMETIMES' means at least once a week, 'SELDOM' means less than once a week, but more than once a month.

1 When you wake in the morning do you feel lethargic and unwilling to get up?
2 As mealtimes approach do you feel shaky, lightheaded, faint, very irritable, headachy?
3 Does eating a meal give you a lift in energy terms?
4 Do you find yourself craving sugar-rich or carbohydrate type foods (cakes, cookies, bread, etc.)?
5 Do you feel unnaturally exhausted around mid-morning or mid-afternoon?
6 Do you find yourself using tea, coffee, chocolate, cola drinks or tobacco to 'give yourself a lift' during the day?
7 If you miss a meal would you feel physically or emotionally ill?

If your score on this test is five or more with at least one 'YES' answer, then you are probably hypoglycaemic and need to follow the self-help plan outlined below.

Treatment of hypoglycaemia should entail all or most of the following:

● **The stopping, or severe curtailing, of the use of sugar-rich foods and drinks, including fruit drinks or very sugary fruits such as melons.**

● **The stopping, or severe curtailing, of the use of refined carbohydrates, including white flour products such as cakes, biscuits, bread etc. (see Carbohydrates and Energy page 36).**

● **The stopping, or severe curtailing, of all stimulant drinks such as coffee, tea, colas, and alcohol.**

● **The stopping of tobacco usage.**

● **The eating of four or five small, snack type meals daily rather than one or two large ones.**

● **The ensuring of an adequate breakfast, the most important meal of the day for the hypoglycaemic individual (and everyone else). This must contain a reasonable level of protein such as egg, fish, lean meat, yogurt or a vegetarian source such as nuts and seeds (sunflower,** pumpkin, sesame, etc.)

● The identification and elimination of allergic factors, whether these are foods or chemicals in the environment (see page 104).

● The avoidance of excessive exercise or of stress (see page 78).

● The carrying of a high protein snack (nuts, cheese, etc.) at all times to be eaten when and if symptoms begin. Never use sugar-rich foods for this purpose. The body uses proteins to make sugar and does this at a pace which does not cause severe fluctuations in blood sugar, such as occur when sugars are taken directly.

● The use of nutrients, e.g. chromium as outlined in the Deficiency and Fatigue section (page 52).

Remember that once hypoglycaemia exists it can usually be controlled by the sort of strategies outlined above, but it is unlikely ever to be completely 'cured'. Thus, a return to the habits which allowed it to develop will ensure a rapid return of the symptoms which came with it. It may accompany Candidiasis, allergy, hyperventilation and other factors discussed in this section. It seldom exists in isolation of other health problems.

CHAPTER 25

Infections and fatigue

Ongoing, low-grade infections have a thoroughly debilitating and exhausting effect on the immune (defence) systems of the body, producing lassitude, exhaustion and fatigue in most instances, as well as lowered resistance to further infection.

I have covered one particular form of infection in detail in the section on Candida and Fatigue (page 110). I have also covered the long-term possibilities of viral involvement in the condition known variously as myalgic encephalomyelitis and post-viral fatigue syndrome (page 153), but a wide range of other possible infectious agents exist in relation to chronic fatigue. Among the clearer general signs of this being a factor are:

● **The sudden onset of fatigue and other symptoms.**

● **Recurrence of continual fever.**

● **Intermittent chills.**

● **Aches and flu-like pains.**

● **Congestion and swelling in the lymph glands, especially in the neck-throat region.**

● **Digestive/bowel disturbances.**

● **Nausea and lack of appetite.**

When a low-grade on-going infection, such as often occurs in the genito-urinary tract of women, is operating, all or any of the symptoms listed above may be noted along with pain on passing urine, often associated with a degree of urgency and frequency.

These may all be vague symptoms which would become far more dramatic were the infection to spread to the kidneys, a not uncommon occurrence. In such a case, not only would there be frequency, urgency and pain associated with urination, but also fever, chills, diarrhoea, vomiting and nausea. Fatigue would almost certainly be felt.

Candida albicans infestations are often associated with whatever infecting agent is operating in such infections, and sometimes act alone. Symptoms of this sort can play havoc with domestic life and sexual behaviour. Unfortunately, the normal medical care for such conditions — antibiotics, effective as they usually are — leads to increases in yeast and fungal overgrowth which can set the scene for even more widespread infections later. One woman in five experiences at least one episode of painful urination each year, which may hang on and not resolve itself, leading to low-grade infection.

Vitamin C treatment

One approach which has been shown to assist dramatically is the use of high dosage vitamin C. Using the method designed by Dr Robert Cathcart, and described in the section Toxicity and Fatigue, relating to mercury toxicity (page 68), is advocated for urinary tract infections, once Candida control has been instituted as explained in the section on Candida and Fatigue (page 110). When there is an infection in the urinary tract the object is to saturate the system with ascorbic acid so that the overflow reaches these regions and acts against the infecting agent.

Starting with 1g of vitamin C every two waking hours produces an intake on the first day of 8g to 10g. Increase this by 2g daily until diarrhoea is noted. If this is already a feature then it becomes difficult to assess precisely when bowel tolerance of vitamin C has been reached. In such a case stick at around the first day's intake for a week. If there is no initial diarrhoea, but this appears after several days of increasing vitamin C intake this is considered to be the level of tissue saturation.

The dosage taken on the day previous to the onset of diarrhoea is then maintained until symptomatic improvement is felt. Once symptoms of urgency, frequency and pain ease, begin to slowly reduce the intake of vitamin C by 2g daily until a maintenance dose is reached, of 1g to 2g daily.

The coil and local infection

Women using the intrauterine coil as a contraceptive device often develop another fungal infection, involving *actinomycetes*.

This can lead to pelvic inflammatory disease which produces pain locally as well as:

fatigue	mild fever
general malaise	night chills and sweats.

Somewhat later there is the appearance of foul-smelling vaginal discharge and often acute pelvic pain. This can also result from a variety of sexually transmitted diseases which are dramatically on the increase.

Infections of this sort may involve bacteria, fungi, viruses or protozoa. At this time over twenty different types of these are recognized as being widespread in the population. If not contained these can lead to serious damage to the region, involving infertility and often the need for surgery. Sexually transmitted diseases usually involve all or some of the following set of symptoms: itching; burning and swelling of the vulvar region of the vagina; offensive discharge; increased discharge; painful intercourse.

If these are accompanied by abdominal or pelvic pain and a marked change in the nature of menstrual bleeding, then pelvic inflammatory disease is probable. Candida may take part in any of these variations, and the approach suggested for this is recommended.

Those factors which increase the likelihood of pelvic inflammatory disease and ongoing sexually transmitted disease, resulting in infectious vaginitis include:

● **Immune depression resulting from serious illness, recurrent pregnancies, nutritional deficiency, toxic load or use of social or medical drugs (tobacco, alcohol, marijuana, cocaine, etc. and prescription medication including antibiotics, steroids and the contraceptive pill).**

● **Sugar imbalances such as diabetes.**

● **Use of synthetic material in underwear.**

● **Lack of personal hygiene.**

● **Numerous sexual partners (sperm is an immune suppressing material, it has to be for the sperm to remain unaffected in foreign territory; multiple sexual partners result in lowered immune efficiency** in the recipient of the sperm, leading to increased likelihood of infection). Thus, barrier methods of contraception are both less likely to allow this, or to interfere with local ecology, than the coil or the pill.

● **The major infecting agents in these conditions include Candida, as previously mentioned, as well as Trichomonas vaginalis, Gardnerella vaginalis, Chlamydia and Herpes simplex.**

Candida can be dealt with as described in its own section, most notably by the use of a low sugar/low yeast diet, and appropriate nutrients and anti-fungal agents.

Herpes and other viral agents can be controlled to some extent by use of the amino acid lysine, as described in the section Deficiency and Fatigue (page 52). This leads to fewer and less acute outbreaks. A diet low in the amino acid arginine is equally effective (see page 49, ornithine).

The use of AL721 and various herbs described in the section on post-viral disease syndrome (page 153) is suggested as a means of raising resistance to viral agents such as herpes. Nutrients which are particularly effective in boosting immune function to assist in control of such infections include (note that quantities suggested in brackets are daily intakes and for acute infection conditions):

Vitamin A (15,000IU) and its precursor Beta carotene (100,000IU).
Vitamin C to bowel tolerance for acute urinary tract infections. Dosage of ½g to 1g every four waking hours for sexually transmitted infections. Add bioflavonoids, 500mg daily.
Vitamin B complex providing 50mg of each of the major B vitamins (see Deficiency and Fatigue section, page 52).
Zinc 15mg if picolinate; 30mg if other form.
Vitamin E 200IU.

Wherever vaginal infections are current, the insertion into it of Lactobacillus acidophilus in high potency form has a speedy effect in reducing local irritation and helping control other micro-organisms. Yogurt is frequently advised for this, but is a particularly messy method, despite being effective if the yogurt is a 'live' one. Lactobacillus acidophilus internally ½ teaspoonful twice daily is suggested.

Herbal control of viral and bacterial infection is possible by the use of botanical extracts from the plants hydrastis, echinacea and phytolacca, as described in the section on post-viral fatigue syndrome (page 153). A combination of tinctures of these in a ratio of 2:2:1 can be made up by a medical herbalist. From 20 to 60 drops of this mixture every two to four hours is suggested. Local treatment using douches and applications on tampons is useful.

Materials which have been helpful in local infections/irritations such as those mentioned, include the herb hydrastis; two tablespoons of tincture in a cup of hot water as a douche; lactobacillus acidophilus as described above; chopped garlic may be added to the douching solution for its antibiotic effects, or a peeled clove may be wrapped in gauze and inserted as a local vaginal suppository. If irritation is noted (unlikely) then remove.

On-going viral problems including 'glandular fever' or mononucleosis should be dealt with by the high lysine/low arginine diet; use of AL721 and all other appropriate nutrients for immune boosting, as outlined above and in the section on Deficiency and Fatigue and Post-viral Fatigue Syndrome (pages 52 and 153).

Chronic dental disease may also be a factor in fatigue and should be checked for. The general dietary and nutritional supplementation recommendations for this condition are not any different from those suggested for other ongoing infectious conditions. Use of flossing and good dental hygiene as well as periodic checks with a dentist can prevent the infection in the mouth from doing major local damage, and seeding the entire system with infecting agents and toxic products.

This section is not intended to comprehensively cover all possible infectious conditions relating to fatigue. It should, however, indicate some of the options open for self-help measures.

CHAPTER 26

Myalgic encephalomyelitis/ Post-viral Fatigue Syndrome

This condition has become for many a symbol of modern disease, representing as it does an example of a condition resulting from multiple causation, with wide-ranging symptoms and almost no recognition or treatment by the majority of the medical profession. It just does not exist to many doctors. Others, however, have fought long and hard to bring it to the consciousness of their fellow practitioners creating hope to which the tens of thousands of affected individuals have clung. Many of these having been told that they were imagining their symptoms, which are often of disabling proportions.

These are the words of Toni Jeffries, author of *The Mile High Staircase* (Hodder and Stoughton, 1982) who, after several years of effort, had at last been found to actually have something objectively wrong with her after a liver function test.

> After he [the doctor] left I stared at the little piece of paper. And of course I was crying. Anything in those days would make me cry. Because it was this little piece of paper which was saying to me, 'Everything's all right now. You are "allowed" to be ill. After two years, you are "allowed" to be ill.' It was September 1979.
> Why had it taken 40 years since the first major outbreak of ME for a test to be found

which could prove that these desperate people, many with fatigue so bad they could hardly walk across the room, actually had something wrong with them.

Any illness difficult to diagnose is likely to be swept under the carpet when psychiatry has provided such an easy way out. Only a few dedicated doctors, some of whom had once suffered illness themselves, and some still ill with it, have fought for years to enlighten the profession.

Susan Finlay, an ME sufferer (see Chapter 1) and Dr Edward Hamlyn write as follows in (*The Journal of Alternative and Complementary Medicine*, September 1987):

> It has been estimated that there may be 100,000 people in Britain suffering from ME. Many of these people remain undiagnosed by their doctors, or worse still misdiagnosed as hypochondriacs or neurotics.
> Damage to the immune system by a virus, a poison or by a combination of these factors is likely to emerge as the mechanism which gives rise to the clinical symptoms [of ME]. As many as 60 different symptoms may be associated with ME besides the overriding muscular fatigue with which it is chiefly associated. These include digestive problems, difficulties with balance, sight and hearing, loss of memory and powers of concentration, and in some cases inexplicable and persistent pain.

Other symptoms which are common are extreme sensitivity to cold, with very cold extremities being a feature. Headaches, too, are common and may be severe. General emotional unpredictability may also be a strong element in the symptom picture. Finlay and Hamlyn rightly point to changes in our environment as the cause of what they describe as an example of the changing pattern of illness in our society. In this they are not speaking of acid rain and disasters such as Chernobyl, as important as these are, but rather to changes in our immediate environment.

'Our most intimate and sustained contact with the environment is the food we eat. Denatured food with chemical additives is the No. 1 pollutant of our society. Next come drugs, including tranquillizers, antibiotics, steriods, contraceptive pills, smoking, alcohol and caffeine,' they say.

Other environmental factors which have been shown to influence the condition include the presence in the system of heavy metals such as mercury or lead.

A hair analysis is, therefore, a good idea (see Toxicity and Fatigue, page 68) for anyone with ME in order to establish or rule out such toxicity.

Reports exist of people with chronic fatigue who, having established that they also have a mercury toxicity problem, found great benefit by having their amalgam fillings removed and replaced with inert materials. It is of interest that the Swedish government, after years of denouncing opposition to amalgam usage, has announced (March 1987) its intention to phase out the use of amalgams in dental practice over the next decade, and to immediately ban its use in pregnant women.

About ME

ME can occur in epidemic forms, where hundreds of people are affected, or in individual isolated cases. It may be contagious for a very short period, but after a few weeks certainly is not so.

It often starts as a mild flu-like condition, or with respiratory or gastro-intestinal symptoms, not everyone necessarily having the same starting symptoms. It may slowly or rapidly proceed to the point of producing the characteristic fatigue. One of the severest stresses for the person afflicted with ME is the often dismissive attitude of medical advisers who discount the degree of disablement, and who may label the sufferer as 'neurotic' and the condition as being of 'psychosomatic origin'. The viral agents most often blamed for the condition are Coxsakie-B virus and also, frequently, Epstein-Barr virus.

Only about 5 per cent of people thus affected recover completely and spontaneously. Others have varying degrees of fatigue and extreme weakness, accompanied by extreme malaise (and often depression) with a cyclical pattern of recovery and relapse.

Other common features include muscles twitching uncontrollably; sleep disturbances; mood changes, including panic attacks, and great difficulty in concentrating. Often a return of symptoms is experienced whenever a new mild illness, such as a cold, appears, or when under stress or overworked. Immunoelectrophoresis may (in about half of cases) show abnormalities which are diagnostic. In the remainder there is no definitive test as yet.

ME has been seen in epidemic form for over fifty years, the first being recorded in Los Angeles in 1934 where nursing and medical staff at several hospitals were affected (nearly 5 per cent of the staff) with over half of them still ill after six months.

Other episodes which have helped to give the disease so many names include outbreaks at London's Royal Free Hospital in 1955 ('Royal Free Disease') which affected nearly 300 of the staff, causing the closure of the hospital. Only 12 patients were affected.

Another major epidemic occurred in Iceland in 1948 which involved some 500 people, over half of whom were still ill seven years later ('Icelandic disease').

There is no way of knowing how many individual, undiagnosed, isolated cases there have been but there are probably far more than have been involved in epidemics.

Rest and adequate nutrition are two of the major elements in recovery of ME patients. Specific nutrients and other factors (such as AL721, and certain herbal products described below) may also help.

What is certain is that concurrent infections such as Candida (which very often accompanies ME) and hypoglycaemia, both of which are dealt with in other sections of this book, must be considered and dealt with as first priorities, if recovery is to be achieved.

Recent New Zealand studies (reported in *The Journal of Alternative and Complementary Medicine*, September 1987) show a beneficial response by ME patients to nutritional supplementation combined with an anti-Candida programme, and these elements will be talked about below.

The ME-AIDS connection

Both AIDS and ME involve a depleted immune function. The difference between these conditions may only be one of degree, with AIDS involving a few more viral and/or fungal/parasitic infections to make the difference between the chronic ill health of the person with ME, and the chronic and usually terminal ill health of the person with AIDS. An article in *The New York Native* (27 July 1987) entitled 'The Real Epidemic' by Charles Otleb asks:

Is AIDS actually an acute form of Chronic Epstein-Barr Virus (CEBV) disease?

Do chronic Epstein-Barr Virus Disease and AIDS have the same cause, but different outcomes? Does every person with AIDS have chronic Epstein-Barr virus disease and not vice-versa?

The article goes on to report on the findings of Dr Anthony Komaroff, of Harvard Medical School, who calls Chronic Epstein-Barr Virus Disease by a more familiar name, Chronic Viral Fatigue Syndrome (CVFS). He has stated that, after examining over 300 patients with the condition of chronic mononeucleosis (mononucleosis is a disease caused by Epstein-Barr virus [mainly in people aged 15-25] and popularly known as 'glandular fever'; this condition may also be caused by another virus called Cytomegalovirus [mainly in people aged 20-35]). He was convinced that this was a 'real organic disease', characterized by chronic fatigue, and with features which included recurrent pharyngitis and other symptoms of upper respiratory infection; recurrent cervical adenopathy (swollen lymph glands in the neck) and low grade fevers; as well as striking neurological features, in the early stages especially. The onset of the disease, according to Komaroff was typically as follows: 'They were fine until one day they developed what seemed to be a simple cold or flu, with sore throat, cervical adenopathy, myalgia [aching muscles] (sometimes), gastrointestinal symptoms, fever and profound fatigue. But unlike any previous cold or flu the illness never went away.'

Whilst Epstein-Barr virus is found in many patients with chronic fatigue conditions, it is not found in all.

The AIDS comparison with CVFS is made because the symptoms are so similar, and indeed what is known as AIDS Related Complex (ARC) is almost indistinguishable from CVFS. Some scientists have even called CVFS 'Closet AIDS'. Other scientists have linked both AIDS and ME (CVFS) with viruses as diverse as African swine fever virus (see *The Lancet*, 8 March 1986) and a 'new' virus discovered by Dr Shyh Ching Lo, called the DNA virus, with which AIDS-like conditions have been produced in monkeys who were free of the so-called AIDS virus, HIV.

Thus, it seems that with ME, as in AIDS, a number of ongoing or predisposing elements are required to produce the condition, including most often Epstein-Barr virus infection and Candida albicans.

The methods best suited to dealing with this conundrum appear to be:

- **Enhancement of immune function, via lifestyle and nutritional reform; meditation and visualization techniques (see Stress and Fatigue, page 78).**

- **Control of other ongoing conditions which may be depleting immune function, such as Candida infestation.**

- **Rest and relaxation.**

- **Measures which in a non-toxic manner retard the virus's activity in the system (e.g. AL721 and certain herbal products. See below.)**

If you have chronic fatigue which is very much worse for any physical effort and which is related to all or any of the symptoms described above regarding mononucleosis or ME, then it is worth asking your doctor to have tests which may show some or all (or none) of the following features:

- **White blood count: some abnormal findings may be seen.**

- **Erythrocyte sedimentation rate: normal or slightly raised.**

- **Urinary creatinine: increased excretion is noted with fatigue.**

- **Serum myoglobin: increased.**

- **Serum creatine phosphokinase: normal.**

- **Glucose tolerance tests show a 'flat' response.**

- **Total serum immunoglobulin M (IgM): raised.**

- **Total serum immunoglobulin G (IgG): low.**

- **Complement C4 and C1Q: lowered.**

Circulating immune complexes are present in around half of patients with ME. Electromyogram and electroencephalogram readings may show abnormal patterns.

In studies carried out by Dr P. Behan and others ('Post-viral fatigue syndrome: analysis of 50 cases', *Journal of Infection*, Vol. 10, pp 211-22, 1985) a number of significant findings were elicited. In patients in which the condition was considered acute there was often noted a decrease in what are called T-suppressor cells, as well as some decrease in T-lymphocytes. Other factors were found to be normal.

When a chronic state existed, however, T-suppressor cell levels returned to normal, while the ratio between these and T-helper cells altered, indicating a depletion of helper cells in relation to suppressor cells. Other changes noted in the acute stage included increased levels of immunoglobulin A (IgA).

When physical exercise was carried out by these individuals it was found that acidosis increased rapidly, indicating that lactic acid was being produced in excess and not adequately cleared from muscles. It was also noted that hypoglycaemia and allergy played a part in the picture which, combined with ongoing viral activity, led to the level of ill-health experienced.

Even if all tests come back normal, and yet you are severely fatigued and often depressed, in a cyclical pattern, sometimes better than others but never 100 per cent; very much worse for physical activity, with or without any of the multiple other symptoms mentioned above, then you may well be suffering from ME and should follow the outlines of the strategy given below. These can only enhance general well-being and cannot do any harm.

General strategy

● **Deal with general dietary improvement along the lines described in the section Candida and Fatigue (page 110), Obesity and Fatigue (page 161), as well as the sections on Carbohydrates, Fats and Proteins and Energy (pages 30-51).**

● **Rest a lot and, above all, don't try to push yourself, as recovery time is slow with ME.**

● **Use meditation/visualization regularly, as outlined in Stress and Fatigue (page 78).**

● **Deal with the Candida problem which almost certainly accompanies ME (page 110).**

● **Use some or all of the antiviral methods discussed below (AL721, herbs).**

● **Use some or all of the energy-enhancing nutrients outlined below (Germanium, CoQ_{10}, etc.).**

● **Check out the possibility of allergies being involved (see page 104).**

● **Investigate the patterns discussed in relation to hypoglycaemia and hyperventilation for involvement (pages 144 and 138).**

● **Take appropriate action if any of these seems to be playing a part in your condition.**

● **Above all have a determined resolution to recover normal health and energy. It can be done.**

Diet

This should be a high-protein, high-complex-carbohydrate diet, low in refined carbohydrates (sugars, white flour products, etc.) as outlined in the Candida and Fatigue section (page 110). There should be minimal or no use made of stimulants (tea, coffee, alcohol, chocolate, cola, tobacco).

Antiviral strategies

A combination of substances, developed in Israel in the early 1980s, is known as AL721. This stands for 'Active Lipids' in a ratio of 7:2:1. The three ingredients of this are neutral lipids (butter will do) which makes up 7 parts out of 10 of this mixture; phosphatidyl choline (a major ingredient of lecithin found in egg yolks, etc.) which makes up 2 parts out of 10 and phosphatidyl ethanolamine, another lipid substance, which makes up 1 part in ten.

The initial use for this, as devised by the Weizmann Institute, was in treating cancer. The basis for the effectiveness of AL721 is its action in modifying cell membranes throughout the body, making it harder for viruses to attack them. Thus it does not treat the infection, as such, but strengthens the resistance of the body. This has been called 'membrane engineering' and is explained scientifically in a two volume book called *Physiology of Membrane Fluidity* by a cancer researcher Dr Meir Shinitzky (VCRC Press, Boca Raton, Florida). This has been patented and is now undergoing trials for safety by the Food and Drug Administration in the USA.

An underground network has developed for its private, and probably illegal, manufacture whilst it goes through this laborious and lengthy process (several years) before it is officially available. Thousands of people with AIDS are now using it to slow down virus activity in their bodies. The first medical reference to the substance was made in *The New England Journal of Medicine* (14 November 1985) by Dr Robert Gallo the co-discoverer of HIV, the purported AIDS virus. He reported that AL721 could prevent the infection of human T-cells by the AIDS virus in laboratory conditions.

Since then many American AIDS

victims have used AL721 by travelling to
Israel for treatment, and even more have
used it, and are using it, by making a mixture which approximates AL721 in their
kitchens. *The AIDS Treatment News*, an
underground newsletter published fort-
nightly in San Francisco (Issue 24, 30
January 1987) states:

> Theory suggests that in addition to AIDS,
> AL721 might also help against other lipid-
> coated viruses, such as herpes, CMV, and
> Epstein-Barr. It was found to be effective
> against herpes in one animal test, reported
> October 1986 at a symposium in New
> Orleans.

Clinical trials at St Luke's/Roosevelt
Hospital Center, New York, on patients
with lymphadenopathy showed an 80 per
cent drop in viral activity when AL721 was
used in five out of seven patients.

Unsubstantiated reports from many
people with AIDS indicate that AL721 is
effective, but that it has to be continued as,
once stopped, virus activity returns dramatically quickly.

Since AL721 is no more than a selection
of fatty substances in a particular combination, with no side-effects whatever (unless
there is an allergy to eggs) this seems a
reasonable suggestion. But, once you start
taking it, do not stop.

Of course, when we are dealing with a
condition somewhat less severe than AIDS
the repercussions of a relapse are not so
disquieting. In addition the health enhancing, immune supporting, actions which
would be going on at the same time as
AL721 is being used, would hopefully
allow for the body to regain control of its
defences and, thus, to be able to keep virus
activity down.

Recipe for mixture similar to AL721

AL721 is patented (US No. 4,474,773, 2

October 1984) and the mixture described
below will approximate it, but is not exactly
the same.

Obtain high-strength lecithin concentrate. Twin Laboratories Inc, Ronkonkoma,
New York, manufacture such a product
called PC-55. This contains two of the ingredients, phosphatidyl choline and phosphatidyl ethanolamine in a ratio of 5:2
which is close enough to the 2:1 ratio used
in AL721 to be acceptable.

The only other ingredient needed is
butter (neutral lipid): 6 tablespoonsful,
plus one teaspoonful of plain unsalted
butter should be placed in a container, and
then melted.

> An earlier home recipe used
> vegetable oil instead of butter in
> quantities of five tablespoons plus
> one teaspoon of oil, and 10 table-
> spoons of water to the same amount
> of PC-55.

To this add five tablespoonsful of PC-55
(or other similar lecithin with suitable ratio
of ingredients as specified above).

Add 12 tablespoonsful of water, and
whip the mixture thoroughly for five
minutes.

Divide the mixture into ten equal parts,
each weighing a little over 30g (1.06oz).
Place these doses into separate plastic
freezer bags and freeze.

Remove one dose daily from the freezer
and place in refrigerator a few hours before
use. It must be a cohesive blend and not
melted at the time of use. It spoils rapidly
at room temperature. This may be eaten
spread on bread, or mixed in a juice, or put
on a cereal. The breakfast should otherwise
be fat-free (that is, no other dairy produce
or oils). An additional dose may be taken
before bed.

If the use of an ounce or two a day of this lipid mixture can assist in keeping ongoing viral activity depressed this should allow for a release of energy. This seems to be the experience of many AIDS patients.

Herbal control of virus and fungal activity

A number of traditional plant remedies have been proved in recent studies to have enormous potential as controllers of virus activity. Antibiotics, so commonly used, are ineffective against a virus, they only act against bacteria and fungi.

Traditional Chinese medicine has given us several of these herbs, and Western tradition the others. As with AL721, so with the herbs. AIDS has been the catalyst which has led to investigation and validation of their usefulness.

Echinacea species (American coneflower)

Echinacea angustifolia or *purpurea* are powerful antiviral herbs. They both enhance macrophage activity and general deactivation of invading bacterial or viral micro-organisms by 40 to 50 per cent. They are particularly able in their control of the herpes group of viruses. (Wacker, A., 'Virus Inhibition by *Echinacea purpurea*', *Plant Medica* 33:89-102, 1978).

Dosage of either of these is suggested at 500mg of freeze dried root powder, three times daily between meals, for any ongoing virus activity.

Hydrastis canadensis (goldenseal)

This is shown to enhance macrophage activity by the immune system. *Hydrastis canadensis, Berberis aquifolium* and *Berberis vulgaris* are all similar in containing substances which are powerful antimicrobial, antiprotozoal and antifungal agents, acting largely in the gastrointestinal tract. If there is any evidence of Candida activity or of ongoing bacterial activity in the bowel then a mixture of fluid extract of these three

plants (equal parts) should be consumed in doses of a teaspoonful three times daily between meals; or 2 tablets of freeze dried root of a mixture of these three plants, or of any one of them, should be taken three times daily between meals.

Glycyrrhiza glabra (licorice)

This is a widely used plant worldwide, with demonstrable antiviral and antimicrobial activity in humans and animals. It has the potential in laboratory conditions to inhibit herpes group viruses irreversibly, as well as inhibiting a number of other viruses, known to affect DNA and RNA. It also protects the thymus gland, a major element in immune function. Dose of 15 to 20 drops of fluid extract three times daily between meals is suggested.

Lactobacillus acdophilus

If Candida is a factor then this will be an automatic part of the programme (see page 115). If Candida is not a factor, supplementation of a quarter teaspoonful of superdophilus is suggested, twice daily between meals, as a means of enhancing bowel resistance to micro-organisms.

Energy enhancing factors
Free form amino acids

These have been discussed in other sections (Protein and Energy page 47 and Deficiency and Fatigue page 52). For anyone in a state of chronic fatigue, between 5g and 30g daily of free form amino acids (total formulation of all amino acids in balanced ratios) should be taken, whilst other elements of the recovery programme are introduced. Dosage will depend upon the degree of exhaustion and other factors such as digestive and bowel competence, and ongoing infections etc. A gradual reduction in their use can be instituted once energy returns.

Germanium

This has been discussed in the section Deficiency and Fatigue (page 52). Dosage of not less than 300mg is suggested for anyone with ME, and higher doses are preferred. Expense is the only barrier to higher dosage.

CoEnzyme Q_{10}

Lengthy supplementation of this energy cycle factor is suggested for ME patients at a dosage of 50mg to 100mg daily. It takes anything up to eight weeks for results to be seen. This is discussed further in the section on Energy Cycles (page 30).

General immune function and systemic nutrients for ME

● High dosage B-complex formulation (yeast-free source, if Candida is active) which provides not less than 100mg daily of vitamins B_1, B_2, B_3, B_5, B_6. See the section on Deficiency and Fatigue (page 52), plus 400mcg of vitamin B_{12} and 400mcg of biotin. The ideal is for this formulation to be provided in two or three separate doses at mealtimes.

● Additional 50mg pyridoxine (vitamin B_6) at a separate time to B-complex.

● Vitamin E 400IU.

● Vitamin C. Between 1g and 10g daily, depending upon bowel tolerance, for normal care. See the section on Toxicity and Fatigue (page 68), where it is used to deal with mercury toxicity.

● Flavonoids (obtainable at Health Stores). These important cofactors of vitamin C should be taken in doses of 100mg to 200mg three times daily with meals. See also Premenstrual Tension and Fatigue (page 170).

● Beta carotene; divided doses of between 20,000IU and 100,000IU. Higher dosage when active infection.

● Zinc, 20mg daily as zinc picolinate, if available. If not, use zinc orotate in a dose of 100mg (of which only 15mg is zinc).

● Selenium. As selenium citrate or selenate 100mcg to 200mcg at the same time as vitamin E.

● Calcium. A dose of 1g to 1½g daily, together with magnesium, preferably before bedtime.

● Magnesium. In dose of ½g daily.

● Iodine. As potassium iodide, 225mcg.

● Manganese. As picolinate, if possible, in a dose of 15mg daily.

Chromium, may be required, especially if there is indication of sugar intolerance or imbalance. See section on Diabetes and Fatigue (page 133) and Hypoglycaemia and Fatigue (page 144).

Iron may be required. See section on Anaemia and Fatigue (page 108). Specific amino acids may be needed. See section on Deficiency and Fatigue (page 52).

The massive degree of supplementation is necessary to restore normal function to a system which is depleted. Ultimately these nutrients will be slowly reduced and then dropped to a mere maintenance level.

CHAPTER 27

Obesity and fatigue

There are a number of possible reasons for being overweight to the point of obesity (defined as carrying 10 per cent to 20 per cent more weight than the level considered acceptable for height, sex, and age. This condition affects almost a third of all adults in industrialized western societies.

One of obesity's chief symptoms is fatigue, resulting from a variety of causes, but mainly the sheer effort of trying to function with excessive weight.

The major reason for excess weight is excess eating. This does not necessarily mean that obese people eat more than their thin counterparts, but rather that their particular metabolic processes require less food, and they therefore may be eating too much compared only with themselves. The much-debated relevance of metabolically active fat known as 'brown fat' seems to explain the difference between the thin and fat person in many instances. It is thought that nutritional factors such as minerals and vitamins may be able to influence brown fat which is underactive and which is, therefore, resulting in accumulations of fatty deposits.

There are other possible causes of obesity, most notably low thyroid activity (see page 174). If thyroid deficiency is responsible for excess weight, then a supplementary amount of thyroid extract can often deal with the problem, leading to restored energy and weight loss.

If, however, excess weight is the result of dietary factors, then a long and careful campaign is required, using basic common-sense approaches to slowly reducing to a more acceptable level. This does not necessarily mean reducing to lean, model-like proportions, for we should realize that there are racehorses and carthorses, greyhounds and bulldogs. We are not all born to be slim. Some of us are born to be large, which does not mean that the degree of largeness should not be within some degree of control.

Basic rules which can assist in weight reduction, if eating is the major element, should include the following:

● **Reduce the amount of food eaten, but not by sacrificing nutritious foods (see below).**

● **Avoid foods rich in fat; this means cheeses (except low fat ones); milk (except skim milk); butter (use polyunsaturated margarine instead, but sparingly); yogurt (except low fat versions); most meat from cows, sheep and pigs (replace with fish, eggs, poultry and game).**

Nomogram for calculating body mass index

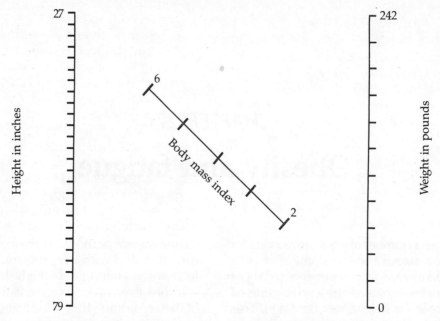

Draw a line with a ruler from your height to your weight. Where it crosses the line in the middle gives your Index number. Men should be between 3.4 and 3.9. Women should be between 3.2 and 3.7. If over the higher number you are overweight.

● Severely restrict sugars (and foods rich in these, such as jams, sweets, cakes, biscuits, chocolates, puddings, honey and alcohol). Use minimal amounts of artificial sweeteners until taste can be trained to not want sweet things. Also avoid refined carbohydrates (white flour products, white rice, etc.) and replace with unrefined carbohydrates such as wholegrain foods and brown rice. Refined foods have lost most of their essential food factors such as vitamins and minerals, and provide what are called 'empty calories', filling us up but not feeding us.

● Eat wholefoods, rich in fibre and nutrients, such as vegetables (fresh rather than canned or frozen, if possible); pulses, such as lentils and beans which are nutritious and high in fibre.

● Avoid dieting as such; rather try to adjust and reform your diet as outlined above, but continuing to eat three meals daily; using some of the 'tricks' suggested below if necessary.

● Attend to any other health factors which may be associated with obesity, most notably high or low blood sugar (see page 144) and allergy (see page 104) which is a frequent element, often involving cereal foods and dairy produce. The diet of our forefathers, before man became a settled creature, involved a very small amount of grains (oats, barley, wheat and rye) and also very little, if any, dairy produce. Most allergies, and many health problems in general, can be helped by adjusting to what has been called a 'Stone Age diet' in which grains, dairy produce and domesticated meats are avoided and replaced with a diet rich in vegetables, pulses, fruits and meat from free ranging animals (fish, free-range poultry, and game such as rabbit or venison which have a very low fat content compared with farmed animals).

● Use a nutritional supplement programme as this is often an aid to weight reduction, especially if this involves the supply of substances in which you might be deficient, such as zinc, chromium, manganese and vitamins C and B-complex.

● Take regular exercise. This means twenty to thirty minutes at least three times weekly, walking briskly, cycling or swimming. This is a major element in recovery from obesity.

● Use simple nutritional tricks such as:
— Taking 300mg to 500mg of the amino acid tryptophan twenty minutes before meals, with a small amount of carbohydrate (a bite of bread, for example). This has the effect of altering the foods you will select at mealtimes from carbohydrate to protein, by affecting the appetite centre in the brain. It is safe apart from for pregnant women.
— Taking a gram daily of the amino acid glutamine. This reduces sugar craving (and alcohol craving in many people). This, as with all amino acids, should be taken with water well away from mealtimes.
— Taking regularly 500mg to 1,000mg of phenylalanine, another amino acid. This, too, assists you in selection of desirable foods. This is not suitable for anyone with very high blood pressure or who is taking drugs for anxiety/depression known as mono-aminoxidases (MAO).

Both tryptophan and phenylalanine are known to reduce the symptoms of depression as well as having pain-relieving and appetite-influencing roles. Glutamine is a 'brain' food and can increase alertness and concentration.

CHAPTER 28

Pain and fatigue

From whatever source, chronic pain can be exhausting. It is a subject that has been deeply researched, and a number of interesting discoveries have been made, not the least of which being that the pain we feel is determined, not simply by mechanical or chemical factors, but that our anticipation of it and attitude towards it, colour the degree and intensity of the pain perceived. Pain is far more variable and modifiable than was previously thought. Unique factors such as the culture we come from, the sort of upbringing we had, and the meaning we give to the pain, all alter its degree of relevance in our lives.

An example of this can be seen when people from different cultural backgrounds are exposed to the same pain factor. Radiant heat is commonly used in such experiments. The reactions vary markedly, depending upon whether the subject is of Mediterranean origin who may describe such heat as painful, or North European, who would usually describe the same intensity of heat as 'warmth'. (*The Challenge of Pain*, Drs R. Melzack and P. Wall, Penguin, 1982). This has to do with pain perception. When studying tolerance (the level at which people will not tolerate an experimental electrical shock, for example) other features emerge.

In a fascinating study it was found that Jewish and native American women tolerated higher levels of pain of this sort than did Italian women. In subsequent studies, when women of Jewish origin were compared with Protestant women, the Jewish, but not the Protestant, women were able to tolerate more pain after they had been told that their religious group tolerated pain more poorly than other groups.

Family influence is a great factor as well, with some making a fuss about, and others putting up with, pain. Such attitudes influence future behaviour in children.

After studying pain in different surroundings, physicians have been astounded by the variations in response to serious injuries. In war situations wounded men were noted to ask for pain relief from morphine in only one case in three, whereas similar degrees of injury in civilians produces requests for morphine relief in four out of five cases. The interpretation as to why this should be is given as follows:

The pain is in very large part determined by other factors, and of great importance here is the significance of the wound. . . . In the wounded soldier the response was relief;

thankfulness at his escape alive from the battlefield, even euphoria; to the civilian, his major injury was a depressing calamitous event.

Thus we have pain influenced by race, culture, family and situation, and all these factors indicate that perception of pain is highly coloured by the mind. The relevance of pain is altered by what we perceive it to 'mean'. If abdominal discomfort is known to be the result of gas then it is discounted and put up with. If, however, the same person hears of a friend with stomach cancer, the gas pain takes on a new sinister significance, and may well become a major issue until reassurance is given that it is, after all, only gas, at which time it is once more relegated to mere nuisance value.

If we are distracted, pain becomes easier to bear. A footballer, injured quite seriously in the midst of a game, may continue playing, oblivious of the seriousness of the damage, until a rest period comes and the distraction of activity is gone.

Anticipation of pain increases the intensity of it by allowing the development of anxiety. It has been clearly demonstrated that the degree of pain perceived is far greater when anxiety exists. The same stimulus under relaxed circumstances may be hardly noticed. Chronic pain sufferers can learn to distract themselves from the pain by concentrating on activities which become absorbing. This reduces perceived pain. This strategy is found to be true only if the pain is a steady one, or one which is increasing gradually. It does not apply to a sharp or rapid increase in intensity.

People taught to have an element of control over their pain, cope with it far better than others who are not taught control. People about to undergo serious surgery will handle the subsequent pain better if they have the whole procedure explained and the anticipated pain described, as well as being told that this can be minimized by use of relaxation and breathing-type exercises, which are taught to them. Such patients report significantly less pain and require much less medication (often less than half the usual amount) as compared with patients unprepared for the pain. They also have reduced hospital stays.

A sense of control has the effect of reducing both anxiety and pain perception. This, together with distraction, should be considered a valuable self-help measure. Even taking dummy (placebo) tablets helps pain considerably, especially in chronic pain conditions. This is because the anticipated relief reduces anxiety and results in less pain, even if the tablet is no more powerful than chalk.

Hypnosis, self-hypnosis (deep meditation), biofeedback and pain relief have been much studied, and the conclusion is that these methods are capable of producing enormous degrees of pain control and relief, in some but not all people, since only about 30 per cent of people can reach deep hypnotic states, a further 30 per cent a moderate state, another 30 per cent no more than a drowsy state, and 10 per cent are incapable of being hypnotized or of self-hypnosis. It is considered that distraction and decreased anxiety are the major reasons for the results of hypnosis, which makes them amenable to self-induction via relaxation/meditation-type exercises. See Stress and Fatigue (page 78).

There is a two way traffic between pain and what are termed neurotic symptoms. Pain is often considered to be the result of neurotic attitudes and behaviour. A chronic emotional problem, for example, may manifest as pain. However, recent research has proved that the opposite is also true, that the pain element can be the cause of the emotional state. When the pain goes the emotional condition may be seen to disappear. There are many types of pain, ranging from burning to stabbing, cramplike gnawing, nagging, smarting, itching etc.

The causes of pain which most often produce a response of exhaustion or tiredness are:

Menstrual pain
Described as cramping (44 per cent of participants); aching (44 per cent); tiring (44 per cent); sickening (56 per cent); constant (56 per cent).

Arthritic pain
Described as gnawing (38 per cent); aching (50 per cent); exhausting (50 per cent); annoying (38 per cent); constant (44 per cent); rhythmic (56 per cent).

Labour pain
Described as pounding (37 per cent); shooting (46 per cent); stabbing (37 per cent); sharp (60 per cent); cramping (40 per cent); aching (40 per cent); heavy (40 per cent); tender (50 per cent); tiring (37 per cent); exhausting (46 per cent); fearful (36 per cent); intense (46 per cent); rhythmic (91 per cent).

Disc pain
Described as throbbing (40 per cent); shooting (50 per cent); stabbing (40 per cent); sharp (60 per cent); cramping (40 per cent); aching (40 per cent); heavy (40 per cent); tender (50 per cent); tiring (46 per cent); exhausting (40 per cent); unbearable (40 per cent); constant (80 per cent); rhythmic (70 per cent).

Cancer pain
Described as shooting (50 per cent); sharp (50 per cent); gnawing (50 per cent); burning (50 per cent); heavy (50 per cent); exhausting (50 per cent); unbearable (50 per cent); constant (100 per cent); rhythmic (88 per cent).

Post herpes pain
Described as sharp (84 per cent); pulling (67 per cent); aching (50 per cent); tender (83 per cent); exhausting (50 per cent).

Dealing with pain should involve both physical modalities and variations on the theme of decreasing anxiety and adopting control over your pain. Acupuncture is an excellent method of easing chronic pain. Nutrients, such as DLPA (DL phenylalanine), and germanium are useful in some instances but not all. See Deficiency and Fatigue (page 52). Practising relaxation/meditation and visualization exercises as described in Stress and Fatigue (page 78) will enable a reduction in levels of anxiety to be achieved, with consequent reduction in perceived pain.

Biofeedback methods produce similar benefits to other anxiety reducing methods.

If visualization is being employed for pain reduction, then the particular wording of affirmations used should differ from those described in Stress and Fatigue (page 78) which relate to energy enhancement. The use of expressions which are comfortable to you should be found, such as: 'I feel safe, comfortable and well', or: 'My arm/leg, head (or anything else which is hurting) feels comfortable and warm'. Avoid negative affirmations such as: 'My pain is no longer so strong', as this would tend to confirm the potency of the pain. At the same time visualization of the area being bathed in a soft light and the pain melting away will support the affirmation. The section on relaxation, meditation and visualization (page 84) should be studied so that the sequence suggested is followed.

The elements of chemical pain-relief, via DLPA or germanium, plus anxiety reduction and a feeling of increasing control of the pain, will reduce the exhaustion factor and allow for a greater degree of energy. Use of drugs for pain relief should be considered only if these methods fail.

CHAPTER 29

Posture, musculoskeletal tension and fatigue

There exists an intimate relationship between states of anxiety, poor posture and body mechanics, and physical, muscular tension states. This can be measured electrically and in other ways, as well as being felt quite clearly by anyone trained to assess the physical state of the soft tissues of the body.

Professor H. Wolff, in his classic study of head pain in the late 1940s, stated (speaking of those with headaches): 'By far the largest group of patients was made up of those with marked contraction of the muscles of the neck. Such sustained contraction may be secondary to the noxious impulses (pain) arising from disease of any structure of the head: more common, however, are the sustained contractions associated with emotional strain, dissatisfaction, apprehension and anxiety' (*Headache and Other Head Pain*, OUP, 1948).

Should you wish to see just how much discomfort a tense muscle can produce, try clenching your fist, even lightly, and not releasing this for some minutes. The tension will become an ache, the ache will become a pain and ultimately it is doubtful whether you will be able to maintain the clenching action.

Try to imagine just what such a degree of contraction does when it is maintained, not for a few minutes, but for years, and you will begin to appreciate what happens to many people who live with permanent shortening of postural and other muscles due to a variety of causes. And the effect is not just of pain, with all its repercussions, but of a continual loss of energy. See section Pain and Fatigue (page 164).

Such a drain of energy leads inevitably to fatigue. Indeed, fatigue and pain are the main symptoms in conditions of chronic musculoskeletal dysfunction. Good posture is the state of balance which exists when the body parts are aligned so as to produce the least tension and strain on its component parts and supporting structures.

A balanced resting state, such as we might observe in a cat, or in the graceful carriage of someone with good posture, is unforgettable. Just as obvious is the slumped and ungainly posture of the person who is not so balanced. This latter individual will be using muscles in a manner which far exceeds the actual needs of the situation, producing increased strain and use of far more energy than is necessary.

Whether the causes of poor body mechanics lie in habits of use, occupational

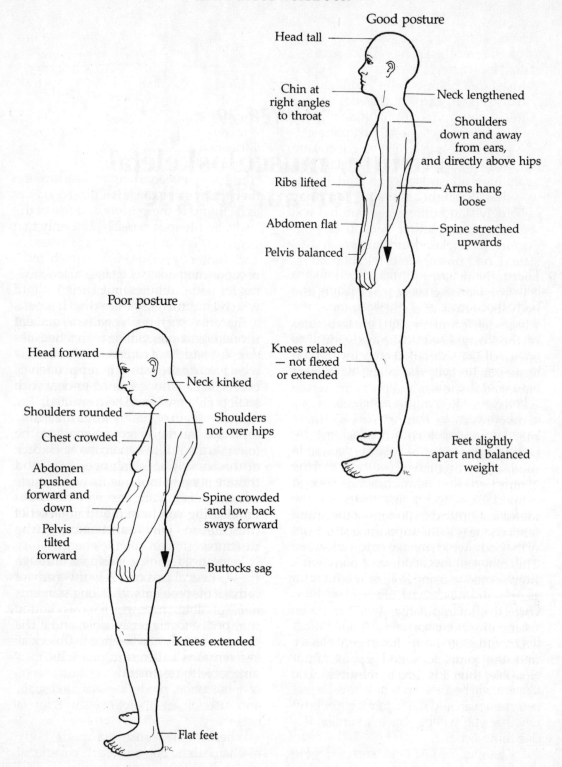

Good posture

Head tall ——

Chin at
right angles
to throat ——

—— Neck lengthened

Shoulders
down and away
from ears,
and directly above hips

Ribs lifted ——

—— Arms hang
loose

Abdomen flat ——

—— Spine stretched
upwards

Pelvis balanced ——

Knees relaxed
— not flexed
or extended ——

Feet slightly
—— apart and balanced
weight

Poor posture

Head forward ——

—— Neck kinked

Shoulders rounded ——

—— Shoulders
not over hips

Chest crowded ——

Abdomen
pushed
forward and
down ——

—— Spine crowded
and low back
sways forward

Pelvis
tilted
forward ——

—— Buttocks sag

—— Knees extended

—— Flat feet

demands, emotional tensions or inborn defects, is not at issue (they may all be involved in any one person). What matters is that, for whatever reason, you are using yourself in a manner which causes pain and discomfort, and which wastes energy.

To tell you if you are habitually using your body incorrectly, to 'stand up straight' is as meaningless as telling you, if you are rigid with anxiety and fear, to 'relax'. You could have no yardstick, no guideline as to what 'straight' means. You may obligingly stand differently, but that will represent just another version of poor posture, not a relaxed and balanced resting state. Good posture and relaxation both have to be relearned.

Before learning the correct use of the body, by means of a system such as the Alexander Technique, the tight structures of the body need to be softened and released. The shortened muscles and soft tissues may, over the years, have been subjected to stresses and pressures which will have created in them alterations of a semi-permanent nature. Among these may be some which are called 'trigger points' (myofascial triggers) which themselves become the cause of new contractions and pain in distant tissues.

Specialized techniques exist for the identification and treatment of these and other changes in the supporting structures of the body, which require expert attention. This may call for a course of body-work from someone using Rolfing methods, or deep neuromuscular treatment, as well as corrective manipulative work from an osteopath or chiropractor.

Once the soft tissues have been relaxed, and the joints loosened up as far as possible, then it is time to relearn how to use our 'primary machinery of life'. The Alexander Technique retrains us in that use. This is a method which requires persistence and a good teacher. The results are worth it because the saving in terms of pain lost and energy retained will be enormous.

If you have recurrent aches and pains of ill-defined origin, as well as a great degree of physical fatigue (with or without conscious emotional tensions and anxiety) then a part of the cause is almost certainly to be found in the posture and use of the body. Self-help is possible, but only to a degree. It is possible to use self-massage and various pressure and stretch techniques (methods such as acupressure, trigger-point self-treatment etc.) all of which lend themselves to this.

Systems such as yoga are equally invaluable in maintaining a stretched and supple body. For a comprehensive assessment and therapeutic approach a professional who is trained to deal with such problems should be consulted. The names of the major organizations representing these professions is to be found in the Addresses section at the back of the book. Contacting one or more of these will bring forth the names of those practitioners in your area who can assist in releasing you from the strait-jacket of muscular and joint restrictions, and who can thus restore in you the energy which is being lost almost continually through these physical tensions. A word of advice is that if the problems are of long-standing, some of the changes which have occurred may not be totally remediable, and it will almost certainly take a while to unlock all the tensions and restrictions which are amenable to treatment.

CHAPTER 30

Premenstrual Syndrome and fatigue

If symptoms appear in a cyclical fashion relating to the menstrual cycle then there is a strong likelihood that the two factors are connected. The array of symptoms reported to appear in many women in this fashion has led to a good deal of confusion.

One group of women in particular can be helped to overcome their PMT by an anti-Candida diet and programme (see page 110 for details of this). Medical studies have shown that if women have a history of vaginal candidiasis (thrush) as well as having PMT, then treating the yeast infection by systemic means (i.e. diet and supplements) eliminates the PMT as well as the Candida problem ('*Female Patient*', p 66, July 1987). The diet in this study was a low-sugar, low yeast one with additional Nystatin (an anti-yeast drug). This resulted in 10 of 15 women thus affected having complete or significant relief as compared with women receiving psychotherapy, vitamin B_6 and drugs.

Not all PMT sufferers are affected by fatigue, although it may be present as a symptom in all forms of PMT. It certainly is the major element in the symptoms of at least one of the major types (PMT-C, see below).

I shall, therefore, look comprehensively at the various types of PMT. These appeared to comprise a confusing tangle of symptoms until an eminent American practitioner, Dr Guy Abraham, categorized the symptoms of PMT into particular patterns, each of which requiring different approaches.

His categories are as follows:

Premenstrual tension type A (PMT-A)
The 'A' stands for anxiety. Major symptoms: Anxiety; irritability; nervous tension; mood swings; drowsiness; increased sensitivity to pain.

This form of PMT is thought to result from a high oestrogen/low progesterone level of hormones and is treated by the basic PMT diet (see the end of this section) and the addition of the specific nutrients discussed below.

High oestrogen levels lead to mood alterations. There is usually noted in PMT-A a deficiency of B-vitamins which require supplementation as well as a need for additional vitamin B_6 (pyridoxine) separate from the B-complex intake.

Flavonoids are accessory food factors often associated with vitamin C. These slow down the synthesis in the body of oestrogen and so can help when this is in excess as in Type A PMT. Quercitin is one flavonoid much recommended for this task.

The fact that progesterone is low in these people indicates that a strategy of high protein diet is needed, since this increases the functional ability of progesterone. This protein should ideally come mainly from vegetarian sources rather than animal ones, as it has been found that the flora inhabiting the bowel of people who eat a lot of meat manufactures (synthesizes) and maintains oestrogen at high levels, which is just what Type A PMT sufferers do not need.

It has been found that women with PMT-A are likely to be consumers of as much as three times the levels of refined sugar and five times the levels of dairy produce, compared with other PMT sufferers. This is thought, among other things, to interfere with levels of magnesium in the system (decreased absorption and increased elimination) leading to a need for magnesium supplementation. As mentioned above, pyridoxine is found to be needed for a variety of reasons, and zinc is found to enhance these beneficial effects.

PMT-A, therefore, needs all the supplements listed at the end of this section together with additional Quercitin in doses of 500mg twice daily. The diet should be low in sugar, high in vegetable sources of protein such as pulse/cereal combinations.

Premenstrual tension type C (PMT-C)

The 'C' stands for craving. Major symptoms: Increased appetite; craving for sweets and sugar rich food; headache; fatigue; dizziness and fainting spells; palpitation (heart pounding).

This form of PMT is thought to result from imbalances in the way the person handles sugars, with, in some instances, hypoglycaemia (low blood sugar) being a major factor (see page 144). It has been suggested that this may relate to a high salt intake as well as to possible magnesium deficiency, both of which affect the way insulin is produced and acts. A substance known as prostaglandin E (PGE) is found in some instances to be deficient in these women. This is produced more efficiently in the body when adequate levels of vitamin B_6 (pyridoxine), vitamin C, vitamin B_3 (niacin), magnesium and zinc are present. PGE is less efficiently produced when there is excessive presence of animal fats and processed vegetable oils in the diet. Alcohol and stress also inhibit PGE production.

A number of other metabolic peculiarities are noted in PMT-C which has led to the additional use of vitamin E and substances such as oil of evening primrose as a source of gamma-linoleic acid, both of which have been shown to reverse some of the negative patterns discussed above, often markedly reducing the symptoms of this form of PMT.

The strategy for PMT-C should, therefore, be similar to the hypoglycaemic pattern of high protein, high complex carbohydrate, low sugar, low alcohol, low caffeine, low salt, low saturated fat. There should, in addition to all the supplements listed at the end of the section be added 200IU per day of vitamin E and 1,000mg per day of oil of evening primrose in divided doses.

Premenstrual tension type D (PMT-D)

The 'D' stands for depression. Major symptoms: Depression; forgetfulness; crying; confusion; insomnia.

This form of PMT is the least common and relates to lowered levels of oestrogen produced by the ovaries during the luteal phase of the menstrual cycle, or other hormonal abnormalities of a cyclical nature. Stress is thought to be a major factor in its causation.

Another factor which is often noted in this form of PMT is lead (and other heavy metal) toxicity which influences oestrogen metabolism. (See also page 68 on toxicity.) A hair analysis should be conducted to prove presence or otherwise of heavy metal poisoning. A deficiency in magnesium is also a likelihood since this increases lead absorption and retention.

In addition to specific nutrients to remove heavy metals, as outlined on page 68, the general supplementation (and diet) as listed at the end of this section is suggested.

PMT-D sufferer may benefit from the use of specific amino acids which remove symptoms of depression, such as tryptophan and/or tyrosine. Advice from a nutritionally orientated practitioner is suggested, however, as there may be contraindications to this. Self-medication for depression is inadvisable.

Premenstrual tension type H (PMT-H)
The 'H' stands for hyperhydration (too much water). Major symptoms: Weight gain (largely through fluid retention); swelling of extremities (face, hands, ankles); breast tenderness; abdominal bloating.

If weight gain of more than 3lb is noted in the week prior to menstruation, together with some or all of the other symptoms (e.g. breast sensitivity, etc.) then PMT-H is a likely diagnosis. The fluid retention is thought to result from increased levels of the hormone aldosterone which results from either high stress levels, increased levels of oestrogen, or other biochemical peculiarities relating to adrenal gland and/or pituitary involvement.

Magnesium deficiency is noted when the adrenal gland is producing inappropriate levels of aldosterone, and this should be supplemented. Another factor in this condition is thought to be a high sugar diet which can increase salt retention, leading to fluid retention and swellings. Pyridoxine (vitamin B_6) deficiency may be another important element in the chain of events resulting in this pattern.

PMT and other conditions
As noted above Candidiasis may be a major element in some women's PMT problems. Hypoglycaemia often inter-relates, especially with PMT-C and sometimes with PMT-H. Hormonal imbalances, including over- or under-activity of the thyroid, are common associated factors. These other conditions need attention as outlined in the appropriate sections.

General dietary pattern for all PMT conditions
Limit or severely decrease intake of:

● **Refined carbohydrates (sugar-rich foods, white flour products, white rice etc.); concentrated carbohydrates such as dried fruits, fruit juices, honey.**

● **Fat rich foods especially milk, butter, cheese, etc., and meat containing high levels of fat such as beef, pork, and lamb.**

● **Meat which has been raised using oestrogen growth enhancers (this means most commercially produced poultry, pig meat and beef).**

● **Salt.**

● **Alcohol.**

● **Tobacco.**

● **Caffeine-containing foods and drinks such as coffee, chocolate, tea, cola.**

Increase:
● **Vegetarian protein intake such as pulse/cereal combinations, as well as fish and game.**

● **Rely less on meat and dairy produce for proteins.**

● **Increase high fibre plant foods, salads, vegetables, fruits and legumes.**

● **Especially valuable are the green leafy vegetables (avoid excessive amounts of the brassicas such as cabbage and cauliflower).**

General supplementation for All types of PMT

● One daily of a high dosage B-complex capsule/tablet containing not less than 25mg and not more than 50mg of each of the major B vitamins.

● 100mg daily vitamin B_6 (pyridoxine) with this doubled for the ten days prior to menstruation (200mg daily at this time in divided doses). Take B_6 away from the time B-complex is taken.

● 500mg daily of vitamin C.

● Vitamin E 200IU.

● Beta-carotene 25,000IU to 50,000IU daily.

● Magnesium in the form of magnesium aspartate, 500mg to 1,000mg daily in divided doses.

● Zinc in the form of zinc picolinate, 15mg to 30mg daily.

● Linseed oil (ensure that this is meant for human consumption) 1 to 2 tablespoonsful daily.

Additional supplements:
PMT-A: Quercitin, 500mg twice daily.
PMT-C: oil of evening primrose, 500mg twice daily.
PMT-D: Tyrosine or tryptophan under guidance.
Detoxification nutrients (oral chelation) — see page 68 — if lead toxicity noted.

NOTE: Oral contraceptives are undesirable for anyone with PMT.

References for PMT section
1 Abraham G., 'Nutritional factors in Etiology of PMT syndromes'. *J. Reproductive Medicine*. 28: 446-64. 1983.

2 *Textbook of Natural Medicine*. J. Pizzorno and M. Murray. JBCNM. Seattle. 1985.

CHAPTER 31

Thyroid problems and fatigue

An underactive thyroid can cause all or any of the following symptoms:

- **Fatigue and weakness.**
- **Extreme sensitivity to cold.**
- **Constipation.**
- **A decrease in appetite.**
- **Gain in weight.**
- **Dry, thinning hair.**
- **Dry skin.**
- **Slow reflexes.**
- **Mental confusion.**
- **Heavy menstruation.**
- **Aching muscles.**

These symptoms result from reduced levels of hormones produced by the thyroid, leading to energy depletion. One of the major reasons for this can be simple deficiency of iodine (excess iodine can also cause the thyroid to slow down production). However, it is necessary to evaluate the causes of the condition rather than simply treating the symptoms, since there may well be reasons other than iodine deficiency for the problem.

The fatigue which characterizes hypo-thyroidism is similar to that noted in anaemia, i.e. it is a constant factor. Whereas hypoglycaemia (low blood sugar) or myalgic encephalomyelitis (post viral fatigue syndrome) for example, as well as other causes of fatigue, often have a cyclical nature, anaemia and low thyroid are both almost constant in the degree of exhaustion experienced.

Feelings of coldness when others are warm; general ongoing fatigue; weight gain which does not appear to relate to increased eating; aches in muscles for no reason; thinning dry hair and dry skin; all these are indications of an underactive thyroid. This problem affects women more than men and is frequently noted to be a family problem. An underactive thyroid also leads to a depression in immune function (the defence system of the body).

The symptoms of hypothyroidism usually arise slowly so that there is often a tendency to miss the fact that anything is wrong until symptoms are quite severe. The same is true for overactive thyroid conditions. The condition may be diagnosed by blood tests, although this is far from definitive because it may be that, whilst blood levels of thyroid hormone are normal, some aspect of the metabolism of the body may be preventing these hormones from functioning normally.

Thus, the general symptoms as outlined above are a better guide to the nature of the problem.

Hypothyroidism is far more common than current blood tests indicate. In some studies less than half those assessed for thyroxine were accurately diagnosed by blood tests. An additional 'proof' can be ascertained by a simple temperature check which you can do for yourself, and which is described below. While this is not a totally accurate indication — some people with low body temperatures may be suffering from allergic conditions or adrenal dysfunction, for example — it is a useful indication which when taken together with the symptom picture is fairly reliable.

The part of the world where you live can easily be a factor in thyroid underfunction, since where soil levels of iodine are low there will be a generally high level of people with hypothyroid problems. The use of iodized salt can often be a simple solution to the problem of prevention in such areas.

When thyroid hormone is under-produced there will be a failure of beta carotene to be transformed into vitamin A. This leads to the dry, flaky, skin condition often seen in hypothyroid cases. Also, due to the accumulation of unconverted beta carotene, there is a tendency towards a yellowish tinge to the skin, most often noted on the palms of the hands and soles of the feet.

A common feature with marginal hypo-thyroidism is a lack of gastric secretions, most notably hydrochloric acid. Anyone with an underactive thyroid may well require supplemental thyroid hormone, which should be obtained from a medical practitioner. This can initially lead to a period of adjustment as the body gets used to the new sense of energy. There may for example be transient palpitations and a feeling of being jittery, which passes fairly soon.

An alternative to this is to use desiccated thyroid. This comprises thyroid tissue from animals, usually lamb's or calf's, which is freeze dried after being defatted. There is controversy about this since it is claimed by some to be unstable and also not to be of standard potency, as well as having other contraindications.

The argument on the other side is that use of this organic material is preferable to use of synthetic thyroxine, and that primarily, it works better in most cases. The fact that it is of variable potency seems to be unimportant in practice. The advantage of this method is that supplementation with glandular extracts of this sort is possible by simply purchasing the material from a health store or manufacturing company.

Before this is supplemented, however, iodine and/or the amino acid tyrosine should be supplemented as these are the raw material of thyroxine, the hormone, produced by the thyroid. The taking of professional advice on such supplement-ation is recommended. See description of tyrosine in sections on Deficiencies and Fatigue (page 52), and Proteins and Energy (page 47).

Barnes' axillary underarm basal temperature test

● **From a pharmacy obtain a body thermometer. Shake the thermometer to below 95°F/35°C and place this by the bed before retiring.**

● **Immediately upon waking, before getting out of bed, and before eating or drinking anything, place the thermo-meter under the armpit and leave it there for precisely ten minutes. During this time move as little as possible.**

● **After ten minutes read the tempera-ture, and record this as well as the date.**

● **Follow this procedure for three**

consecutive mornings. If you are a menstruating woman then this test should be carried out starting on the second day of your period. Anyone else can perform the test at any time of the month.

Interpretation of test results
The ideal temperature is between 97.8°F/36.55°C and 98.2°F/36.8°C. If your temperature is consistently below 97.8°F/36.55°C (find the average of the three days by adding the totals together and dividing by three) then you are probably hypothyroid.

This is especially so if all or some of the following are current: depression; difficulty in losing weight; dry skin; headaches; lethargy or fatigue; menstrual problems; recurrent infections; sensitivity to cold.

If your temperature is consistently above 98.2°F/36.8°C then you are probably hyperthyroid. This is especially so if all or some of the following are current: bulging (prominent) eyes; fast pulse rate; hyperactivity; difficulty in gaining weight; fatigue; insomnia; irritability; menstrual problems; nervousness.

UNDERACTIVE THYROID QUESTIONNAIRE

Answer the following with a 'YES' if this applies once a week or more (score 2); 'SOMETIMES' if twice a month or more, but not as much as once a week (score 1); 'NO' if less than twice monthly (score 0).

1 Does your weight increase very easily?
2 Is your appetite poor?
3 Do you get tired easily?
4 Do you get a ringing in the ears?
5 Do you feel sleepy during the day?
6 Is your skin thick, dry, scaly, etc.?
7 Are you very sensitive to the cold?
8 Do you suffer from constipation?
9 Is your hair coarse and falling out?
10 Are the outer thirds of your eyebrows thinning?
11 Is your pulse below 65 per minute?
12 Do you need to urinate frequently?

If the underarm temperature test (page 175) indicates underactive thyroid and you have a score of six or more, then you probably have an underactive thyroid.

In general, the nutrients needed to help normalize this include: iodine, and/or tyrosine, zinc, vitamin B-complex, calcium/magnesium, essential fatty acids.

OVERACTIVE THYROID QUESTIONNAIRE

Answer the following with a 'YES' if this applies once a week or more (score 2); 'SOMETIMES if twice a month or more but not as much as once a week (score 1); 'NO' if less than twice a month (score 0).

1 Have you a very big appetite?	
2 Are you disturbed by heat and/or do you enjoy cool or chilly weather?	
3 Do you blush very easily?	
4 Do you have night sweats?	
5 Are you conscious of an inner trembling sensation?	
6 When you are at rest does your heart race and/or seem to beat very strongly?	
7 Are you irritable and restless?	
8 Do your eyelids and/or face twitch?	
9 Is your skin frequently moist?	
10 Do you have sleep problems?	
11 Is it difficult for you to gain weight?	

If the underarm temperature test (page 175) indicates overactive thyroid and you have a score of five or more, then you probably have an overactive thyroid. In general the nutrients needed to help normalize this include: vitamin A, B-complex, calcium, potassium and probably iodine.

An over-active thyroid can cause all or any of the following symptoms:

● **General weakness and fatigue.**

● **Anxiety.**

● **Irritability.**

● **Insomnia.**

● **Profuse sweating/inability to cope with heat.**

● **Loss of weight, despite eating well.**

● **Palpitations.**

● **Cessation of menstruation.**

● **Breathlessness.**

● **Increased number of bowel movements.**

● **Exophthalmos (prominent eyes)**

● **Enlarged thyroid.**

In cases where weakness is a feature it is likely that the muscles of the hip region or the shoulders will be mainly affected, although all muscles may become involved.

The main feature of this condition is a speeding up of all metabolic processes, leading to increased demands on many aspects of the system. The condition usually arises in the person's 20s or 30s. The major condition which produces this is called Graves' disease, also known as thyrotoxicosis.

Diagnosis requires blood tests in order to assess thyroid hormone levels. An enlargement of the thyroid gland may be found, as well as prominence of one or both eyes together with extreme sensitivity to light. The causes of this condition are unknown at this time, although there is speculation that it involves an auto-immune reaction in which the body becomes sensitive to aspects of itself.

NOTE: Treatment of this condition requires expert medical attention. This may involve use of radioactive iodine or other drugs or even surgery which suppresses aspects of thyroid activity.

Many of the orthodox therapeutic measures mentioned result in subsequent low thyroid activity (hypothyroidism) and the need for permanent thyroid hormone supplementation. If you have a feeling of having permanently increased metabolic activity, a sense of being supercharged and unable to slow down, with all or any of the signs listed above, most notably an enlarged thyroid gland or prominence of the eyes (a fixed staring look), with or without fatigue, then chances are the thyroid is overactive. The condition demands additional nutrient supplement-ation and this should include a high dosage B-complex formulation and general multi-vitamin, multi-mineral supplements.

Treatment of hypothyroid and hyperthyroid conditions

Both forms of thyroid problem may relate to hypoglycaemia and/or allergic res-ponses. There is seldom anything simple about unravelling such conditions, which require patience and determination. Once the diagnosis is clear and the appropriate treatment instituted, self-help is vital in maintenance of the improved levels of well-being. In some instances detoxification, perhaps via supervised fasting, can be instrumental in normalizing thyroid function. In others, a dietary programme and supplementation can be helpful. For example, the major hormone produced by the thyroid, thyroxin, is derived from iodine and the amino acid tyrosine. Supplementation of these, in suitable conditions, can result in restoration of normal levels of thyroxin with dramatic relief of symptoms, including improved energy levels, weight reduction, etc. Levels of these substances (iodine and tyrosine) which should be prescribed, and whether the condition is suitable for such prescription, requires expert advice.

If possible a nutritionally orientated medical practitioner or a naturopathic practitioner should be consulted about suitable treatment for such conditions. Desiccated thyroid extract could be supplementated in dosages of 1 to 2 tablets of 150mg each after meals, instead of tyrosine/iodine.

CHAPTER 32

Young people and fatigue

Fatigue amongst the young is unusual and demands attention and appropriate action before it starts to interfere with normal development. Psychosocial factors are just as likely to be causes of fatigue in young people as physical causes. Such as:

● **Disharmony in the family, including divorce, bereavement, change of home and, therefore, loss of friends etc.**

● **Problems at school, with teachers or other students, or with workload, examinations etc.**

● **Drug usage, such as glue sniffing, alcohol, smoking, etc.**

Dealing with all such problems requires insight, time and love. There are certainly no pat answers, but a more involved degree or parenting, with emphasis on traditional values, would seem to offer hope, for in societies where the extended family is still in existence these problems are seen far less. Where the family structure has been lost, or where both parents are working due to economic pressures, social support and medical/counselling assistance should be sought.

As with all stress situations, though, a better degree of coping will be found if nutritional excellence prevails.

The work of researchers such as Alexander Schauss in the USA has shown just how much effect a combination of deficient diet, allergy and toxic load plays in producing violent behaviour in youngsters.

His research reported on in his book *Diet, Crime and Delinquency* (Parker House, 1981) indicates that if these elements are taken care of (i.e. sound diet and non-exposure to toxins, such as lead and mercury) many anti-social patterns disappear.

Among the major irritants he noted in violent behaviour of young offenders was milk sensitivity.

In a study in 1978 of chronic juvenile offenders the major variant between their diets and other juveniles who were regarded as moderate to severely disordered behaviourally, was found to be an average intake of milk which was twice as high (64 fl oz daily as against 30 fl oz daily). In double blind trials, removal of milk from the diet of severely hyperactive children has resulted in what is described as 'markedly positive' improvements in those children taken off milk.

Many other nutritional associations have been uncovered in similar research indicating that the factor of allergic reaction (so-called 'brain allergy') as well as excessive toxic heavy metal levels (lead, mercury and cadmium in the main) and nutritional deficiencies, all interact in many such youngsters.

These factors seem to be at least as important as the home environment and social situation in producing delinquent and behaviourally abnormal children. High sugar consumption is a strong feature of many problems of this sort as well.

Fatigue is considered by many to be a basic part of hyperactivity, with the inability to sit still, the violent behaviour and inability to concentrate all aspects of the chronic nervous fatigue related to a combination of high or low blood sugar, toxicity, allergy and deficiency.

Amongst the physical causes of fatigue in the young are infections such as:

● **Infectious mononucleosis. See Infections and Fatigue (page 149) and Post-viral Fatigue Syndrome (page 153).**

● **Tuberculosis. This is more likely in immigrant children.**

● **Urinary tract infection. See Infections and Fatigue (page 149).**

● **Tooth infection. See Infection and Fatigue (page 149).**

● **Myalgic encephalomyelitis (see page 153).**

Or other medical problems such as:

● **Anaemia. See Anaemia and Fatigue (page 108).**

● **Diabetes. See Diabetes and Fatigue (page 133).**

● **Rheumatoid arthritis.**

● **Muscular dystrophy.**

The latter conditions obviously fall outside the scope of self-treatment. However, in all such serious cases there may be operating elements of conditions discussed in the text, such as low blood sugar (Hypoglycaemia and Fatigue, page 144) or toxic accumulations (Toxicity and Fatigue, page 68) or nutrient deficiency (Deficiency and Fatigue, page 52) and especially allergy (Allergies and Fatigue, page 104). This latter factor should be seriously considered in cases of juvenile rheumatoid arthritis as should heavy metal toxicity and nutrient deficiency.

If the child has a history of antibiotic treatment for infections then there is a very good chance that their fatigue relates to Candida albicans overgrowth. This can affect children as much as adults.

If a child has recurrent infections of the nose, throat, etc.; seems to be developing less well than would be expected; displays signs of hyperactivity or lethargy, then suspect Candida, and assess and deal with this in accordance with the guidelines in the section Candida and Fatigue (page 110). A child who becomes lethargic or changes behaviour after immunization may well be reacting to it. High dosage (several grams daily) vitamin C for several days before and after any vaccination/immunization helps reduce the chances of this.

Whatever other elements are operating in childhood fatigue, nutrition is almost always a factor. Sugar in particular should be considered a culprit and eliminated from the diet as far as is possible. See the section on Hypoglycaemia and Fatigue (see page 144) and apply whatever is possible from that.

Strategies

In the young the single most important aspect of restoration of vitality lies in supplying adequate nutrition. The use of other elements such as relaxation and meditation may also be found extremely useful, as well as reducing TV time and encouraging fresh air and exercise. The foods most likely to be disturbing normal development, in the absence of other obvious conditions as outlined above, are dairy produce, grains and chemical food additives.

Malabsorption of nutrients from the bowel is frequently experienced when the bowel mucosa becomes irritated by milk or wheat. This seems to result from the too early weaning of children away from mother's milk to these foods, before the delicate digestive system is capable of handling them. This is especially true in families with a history of sensitivities to dairy or cereal products.

Use of the patterns of eating discussed in Allergies and Fatigue (see page 104) and occasional periods of supervised fasting or mono-diet (modified fasting) as outlined in Toxicity and Fatigue (see page 68) can help to restore the bowel's integrity. Malabsorption can mean that, although the diet appears adequate, and all the nutrients are getting to the bowel, they are just not being absorbed, leaving the child deficient, and therefore prone to fatigue. It can also mean that partially digested fragments of food are absorbed into the bloodstream leading to allergic type reactions, one of the major symptoms of which is fatigue.

Use of free form amino acids and acidophilus supplementation can assist in recovery along with elimination of those foods which are irritating the total organism of the child. Careful detective work may be called for as described in the section on Allergies and Fatigue (see page 104), although it is suggested that arbitrary abolition of refined sugar products, wheat products and dairy products, with attention to the wholefood dietary pattern spelled out in that section of the book, will restore health and energy to most children.

A relaxation of these restrictions may be made, following rotation patterns (see page 105) after normal health returns.

Further reading

Fatigue

Atkinson, Holly, MD, *Women and Fatigue*, Macmillan, London, 1985.

Krakowitz, Rob, MD *High Energy: How to Overcome Fatigue and Maintain Your Peak Vitality*, Ballantine, New York, 1986.

Norfolk, Donald, DO, *Farewell to Fatigue*, Pan, London, 1985.

Proto, Louis, *How to Beat Fatigue*, Century Arrow, London, 1986.

Health and nutrition

Ardell, Donald, *High Level Wellness*, Rodale, Emmaus, PA, 1977.

Ballantyne, Rudolph, MD, *Diet and Nutrition*, Himalayan Institute, Honesdale, Penn., 1978.

Bland, Jeffrey, Ph.D., *Your Personal Health Programme*, Thorsons, Wellingborough, 1983.

Brekhman, Izrail, *Man and Biologically Active Substances*, Pergamon Press, Oxford, 1980.

Chaitow, Leon, DO, *Stone Age Diet*, Macdonald Optima, London, 1987.

Cheraskin, Emanuel, MD, Ringsdorf, W., DMD, Clark, J., DDS., *Diet and Disease*, Keats, New Canaan, 1978.

Davies, Stephen, MD, Stewart, Alan, MD, *Nutritional Medicine*, Pan, 1987.

Kenton, Leslie, *Ageless Ageing*, Century Arrow, London, 1985.

Morgan, Brian, MD, Morgan, Roberta, *Brain Food*, Michael Joseph, London, 1986.

Pizzorno, Joseph, ND, Murray, Michael, ND, *Textbook of Natural Medicine*, JBCNM, Seattle, 1986.

Weiner, Michael, MD, *Maximum Immunity*, Gateway Books, Bath, 1986.

Werbach, Melvyn, MD, *Nutritional Influences on Illness*, Third Line Press, Tarzana, Ca, 1987.

Amino acids

Chaitow, Leon, DO, *Amino Acids in Therapy*, Thorsons, Wellingborough, 1985.

Erdmann, Robert, Ph.D., Merion Jones, *The Amino Revolution*, Century, London, 1987.
Wade, Carlson, *Amino Acids Book*, Pivot Original, Keats, New Canaan, 1985.

Stress
Benson, Herbert, MD, *The Relaxation Response*, Fountain, Glasgow, 1975.
Chaitow, Leon, DO, *Your Complete Stress Proofing Programme*, Thorsons, Wellingborough, 1985.
Madders, Jane, *Stress and Relaxation*, Martin Dunitz, London, 1980.

Mind and spirit
Peck, M. Scott, *The Road Less Travelled*, Rider, London, 1985.
Siegel, Bernie, MD, *Love, Medicine and Miracles*, Rider, London, 1986.
Stone, Hal, Ph.D., Winkelman, Sidra, Ph.D., *Embracing Ourselves*, DeVorss, Marina del Rey, 1985.

Allergy/toxicity
Coca, Arthur, MD, *The Pulse Test*, Lyle Stuart, New York, 1967.
Dickey, Lawrence, MD, *Clinical Ecology*, Thomas, Springfield, 1976.
Schauss, Alexander, MA, *Diet, Crime and Delinquency*, Parker House, Berkeley, 1981.

Exercise
Pritikin, Nathan, *The Pritikin Program for Diet and Exercise*, Bantam, New York, 1980.
Cooper, Kenneth, *Aerobics*, Bantam, New York, 1980.

Specific conditions
Budd, Martin, *Low Blood Sugar*, Thorsons, Wellingborough, 1987.
Chaitow, Leon, DO, *Candida Albicans: Could Yeast Be Your Problem?* Thorsons, Wellingborough, 1985.
Crook, William, MD, *The Yeast Connection*, Jackson, Tennessee, 1983.
Goodliffe, Colin, *How to Avoid Heart Disease*, Blandford Press, Poole, 1987.
Melzack, Ronald, MD, Wall, Patrick, MD, *The Challenge of Pain*, Penguin, 1982.
Ott, John, *Light, Radiation and You*, Devin Adair, Old Greenwich, 1982.
Passwater, Richard, Ph.D., *Supernutrition for Healthy Hearts*, Thorsons, Wellingborough, 1977.
Shreeve, Caroline, MD, *The Premenstrual Syndrome*, Thorsons, Wellingborough, 1983.
Sacks, Oliver, MD, *Migraine*, Pan, London, 1980.

Index

accident proneness, 10
achievement, 10
adaptogens, 11, 94-5, 98, 119
Addison's disease, 100
adenosine,
    diphosphate, 32
    triphosphate, 31
adolescence, 66
ADP, 32
adrenal
    blood pressure test, 103
    insufficiency, 101-3
aerobic
    exercise, 35
    principles, 21-3
age factors, 8, 10
ageing, 67
AIDS, 155-6, 157-8
air movement, 27
AL721, 157-9
alcohol consumption, 8, 10, 24-5, 127, 128
Alexander Technique, 169
allergic
    conditions, 9, 104-7
    house syndrome, 28-9
    reaction, 8
aluminium toxicity, 69
American Psychiatric Association, 122
amino acids, 48-9, 50-1, 64-66
    in adrenal insufficiency, 101
    and depression, 125-7
    in premenstrual tension, 172
anaemia, 8, 9, 108-9

angina, 117
antioxidants, 34, 35
antiviral strategy, 157-8
anxiety, 8, 167, 170
arthritis, 166
atherosclerosis, 117
Atkinson, M., 53
atmospheric pressure, 27
ATP, 31

Barne's axillary underarm basal temperature
    test, 175-6
Basu, Dr, 53
biotin, 58
Bland, J., 55
blood pressure, 103, 117
boredom, 8
bowel
    flora, 35
    health, 119
breathing techniques, 141-3
'burn out', 10

cadmium toxicity, 69
caffeine, 127, 128
calcium, 61, 71
cancer pain, 166
Candida albicans, 7, 8, 11-12, 71, 110-16
Candida albicans: Could Yeast be Your Problem?,
    116
carbohydrates, 36-41
cardiovascular disease, 8, 42, 117-18, 120
chelation, 71-2, 98, 118

Cheraskin, E., 54
children, 8
  calcium deficiency, 61
  causes of fatigue, 179-81
  iron deficiency, 61
  nutritional requirements, 66
  psychological problems, 179
cholesterol, 43-5, 46, 117
chromium 64, 134
circulatory deficiency, 120
citric acid cycle, 30
coenzyme Q_{10}, 33, 98
colds, 8
colitis, 8
concentration, 7, 89
constipation, 7
copper, 63

dental
  disease, 151-2
  fillings, 70
depersonalization, 10
depression, 8, 10, 122-31
  and blood sugar, 146
  emotions and the mind, 129-32
detoxification, 35, 68, 73-6, 98
  in chronic ill-health, 119
  cycle, 9
diabetes, 8, 42, 133-4
diarrhoea, 7
diary keeping, 15
diet, 8, 9
  in allergy, 104-7
  and *Candida albicans*, 113-14
  and energy, 35
  and obesity, 161-3
  palaeolithic man, 50
  in Post Viral Fatigue Syndrome, 157
  for premenstrual syndrome, 172
  in young people, 179-80
Diet, Crime and Delinquency, 179
Diet and Disease, 54
digestive complaints, 7
disc pain, 166
drugs, 12, 76-7

elderly people (*see* old age)
eleutherococcus, 11, 94
emotional exhaustion, 10
endocrine imbalance, 9 (*see also* hormones)
enemas, 73, 75-6

energy, 20
  and carbohydrates, 36-41
  cycles, 30
  enhancing factors, 159-60
  and fats, 42-6
  and nutritional deficiency, 52-67
  production, 31-3, 32-4
  and protein, 47-51
environment, 26
Epstein-Barr virus, 155
Erdmann, R., 101
essential fatty acids, 43, 44, 60
exercise, 8, 20-3
  and cardiovascular disease, 18
  and depression, 129
  meditation, 87-8
  relaxation, 85-7
  and stress, 84
  visualization, 92-3

fasting, 72-5
fats, 42-6, 117
fertility, 66
fever, 8
Finlay, S., 11, 151
flavonoids, 170
folic acid, 58, 109
free oxidizing radicals (FORs), 34
frustration, 8

gall bladder disease, 42
general adaptation syndrome (GAS), 95, 100
germanium, 11, 35, 64
Getting Well Again, 92
ginseng, 11, 94
glandular extracts, 96
glucose tolerance factor, 134
goitre, 63
gout, 42

haemorrhoids, 8
Hamlyn, E., 153
headache, 7, 135-7, 167
Headache and Other Head Pain, 167
health history, 10
Health and Human Services, Department of (USA), 7
heart, 117, (*see also* cardiovascular disease)

herbal medicine, 151, 159
High Energy, 62
hormones, 170, 174
house dust and allergies, 28-9
humidity, 27
hyperthyroidism, 178
hyperventilation, 138-43
hypoglycaemia, 9, 37, 138, 144-8, 171
hypothyroidism, 120, 174-5, 178
hysteria, 8

ill-health, chronic, 119-21
immune
   function, 8, 9
   system, 115-16
infections, 8, 149-52, 180
insomnia, 23
insulin, 37, 133, 145
intrauterine coil, 150-1
iodine, 63, 175, 176
ionization, 27-8
iron, 60-1, 63
   deficiency anaemia, 109
irritability, 8, 10

Jeffries, T., 153
joint ache, 7

alpha-ketoglurate, 31-2
kidney problems, 8
Krakovitz, R., 62

labour pain, 166
lactation, 67
lead toxicity, 68-9, 171
lifestyle, 21, 23-4, 98
   and depression, 129
light, full spectrum, 28
Light, Radiation and You, 28
liver disorder, 8
loneliness, 8, 120

magnesium, 171, 172
malignant disease, 8, 166
manganese, 61
meditation, 84, 88-92, 98
   exercises, 87-8
Melzack, R., 164
menopause, 67
menstruation
   irregular, 8

nutritional requirements, 66
   pain, 166
mercury toxicity, 69-71
migraine, 135-7
mitochondria, 32
muscular effort, 7
Myalgic Encephalomyelitis (*see* Post Viral
   Fatigue Syndrome)

nutrients for energy production, 31
nutrition, 9
   in cardiovascular disease, 118
   checklist, 18-19
   in chronic ill-health, 119
   of the elderly, 1, 120
   optimum, 98
   protein, 47
   recommended daily amount (RDA), 54-6
nutritional deficiency, 8, 19
   amino acids, 64-6
   and depression, 124-5
   and energy, 52-67
   trace elements, 60-4
   vitamins, 56-60

obesity, 8, 39, 161-3
   in cardiovascular disease, 118
   high fat diet, 42
old age, 8, 119-21
oral contraceptives, 127-8
oxidation-reduction, 33-4

pain, 164-6
   control, 119
   and posture, 167
pernicious anaemia, 109
physical factors, 7-9
pollen, 95
Post Viral Fatigue Syndrome, 10, 11, 153-9
   involvement of *Candida albicans*, 116
   mercury, 71
   symptoms, 12
posture, 167-9
potassium, 61-2
pregnancy, 66
premenstrual syndrome, 170-3
Pritikin, N., 42
productivity, 10
protein, 47-51
psychosocial factors, 7-9
pulse, 107

questionnaire, 15-17

relaxation, 84-7, 98
  autogenic exercises, 85-7
  progressive muscular, 85
  visualization exercises, 92-3
royal jelly, 94

Schauss, A., 179
schizophrenia, 8
Schorah, Dr, 53
seasonal effects, 26
selenium, 63
Selye, H., 95
Simonton, C., 92
sleep, 23
smoking, 118, 127, 128
sodium, 62
Somnamin, 23
strategies for overcoming fatigue, 98-9
stress, 8, 11, 78-95
  and adaptogens, 94-5
  and blood sugar, 145
  and cardiovascular disease, 118
  in chronic ill-health, 119
  identification, 81-4
  reaction questionnaire, 80-1
  reduction, 98
  response to, 79
sugar
  blood levels, 37-8, 117, 144-5
  and *Candida albicans*, 113
  fruit, 40
  intake reduction, 40-1

temperature, body, 175-6
temperature, environment, 26-7
tension, muscle, 167, 169
The Amino Revolution, 101
The Challenge of Pain, 165
The Mile High Staircase, 153

The Pritikin Program for Diet and Exercise, 42
thyroid disorders, 8, 49, 63, 174-8
tiredness, 10
tobacco (*see* smoking)
toxicity, 68
  heavy metal, 68-71, 172
tranquillizers, 76-7

urea cycle, 9

visualization, 98
  exercise, 92-3
  in pain relief, 166
vitamin
  A, 58-9
  B, 31, 56-8, 109, 170, 172
  C, 59, 61, 70, 98, 109, 150
  D, 61
  deficiency and depression, 124-5
  E, 59, 70, 171
  and energy, 35
  F, 60
  in glandular extracts, 96
  K, 59-60
  requirements, 52-6
  supplements in infections, 151
Vitamin C in Health and Disease, 53

Wall, P., 164
weakness, 12-13
weight loss, 8
Wolff, H., 167
Women and Fatigue, 53

yeasts, 110-1
Your Complete Stress-Proofing Programme, 92
Your Personal Health Programme, 55

zinc, 31, 62-3, 96